KT-474-874

ENCYCLOPEDIA OF
DINOSAURS
AND PREHISTORIC LIFE

ENCYCLOPEDIA OF
DINOSAURS
AND PREHISTORIC LIFE

Consulted by Steve Parker

Miles
KeLLy

First published in 2014 by Miles Kelly Publishing Ltd
Harding's Barn, Bardfield End Green, Thaxted, Essex, CM6 3PX, UK

Copyright © Miles Kelly Publishing Ltd 2014

2 4 6 8 10 9 7 5 3 1

Publishing Director Belinda Gallagher
Creative Director Jo Cowan
Editorial Director Rosie Neave
Senior Editor Claire Philip
Designers Helen Bracey, Joe Jones
Cover Design Jo Cowan, Rob Hale
Image Manager Liberty Newton
Indexer Jane Parker
Production Manager Elizabeth Collins
Reprographics Stephan Davis, Jennifer Cozens, Thom Allaway
Contributers Andrew Campbell, Dr Jim Flegg,
Rupert Matthews, Steve Parker

ISBN 978-1-78209-515-6

Printed in China

British Library Cataloguing-in-Publication Data
A catalogue record for this book is available from the British Library

Made with paper from a sustainable forest

www.mileskelly.net
info@mileskelly.net

Contents

Ancient life

Beginnings of life	12		Corals	30
Prehistoric timescale	14		Arthropods	32
Fossil formation	16		Trilobites	34
Earliest plants	18		Insects	36
Vascular plants	20		Starfish and sea urchins	38
Gymnosperms	22		Brachiopods	40
Angiosperms 1	24		Molluscs and graptolites	42
Angiosperms 2	26		Ammonites	44
The first invertebrates	28			

Age of fishes

Pikaia	48		Bony fish	58
Jawless fish	50		Dunkleosteus	60
Jawed fish	52		Leedsichthys	62
Sharks	54			
Megalodon	56			

Animals onto land

From fins to limbs	66		First reptiles	78
Breathing air	68		Eggs	80
Acanthostega	70		Skulls	82
Great amphibians	72		Synapsids	84
Eyrops	74		Dimetrodon	86
Frogs and salamanders	76		Crocodilians	88

Sarcosuchus	90	Nothosaurs	98
Turtles and tortoises	92	Plesiosaurs	100
Snakes	94	Ichthyosaurs	102
Placodonts	96	Mosasaurs	104

Reptiles in the air

Reptile gliders	108	Later pterosaurs	116
Xianglong	110	Guidraco	118
Rhamphorhynchoids	112	Giant pterosaurs	120
Darwinopterus	114		

Dinosaurs

Age of Dinosaurs	124	Carcharodontosaurus	154
Archosaurs	126	Mapusaurus	156
Inventing the dinosaur	128	Giganotosaurus	158
Ancestors	130	Spinosaurus	160
Earliest dinosaurs	132	Ornitholestes	162
Eodromaeus	134	Oviraptor	164
Coelophysis	136	Caudipteryx	166
Dilophosaurus	138	Smallest dinosaurs	168
Eustreptospondylus	140	Pack hunters	170
Sciurimimus	142	Raptors	172
Baryonyx	144	Deinonychus	174
Allosaurus	146	Utahraptor	176
Carnotaurus	148	Gigantoraptor	178
Yutyrannus	150	Feathered dinosaurs	180
Tyrannosaurus	152	Microraptor	182

Xiaotingia	184	Duckbills	242
Ostrich dinosaurs	186	Brachylophosaurus	244
Therizinosaurs	188	Latirhinus	246
Falcarius	190	Psittacosaurus	248
Beipiaosaurus	192	Ceratopsians	250
Herbivores	194	Protoceratops	252
Lesothosaurus and Fabrosaurus	196	Spinops	254
Prosauropods	198	Ajkaceratops	256
Plateosaurus	200	Xenoceratops	258
Massospondylus	202	Triceratops	260
Anchisaurus	204	Pachycephalosaurs	262
Biggest dinosaurs	206	Prenocephale	264
Sauropods	208	Estimating size	266
Brachiosaurus	210	Skin	268
Camarasaurus	212	Colours	270
Brontomerus	214	Armour	272
Diplodocus	216	Horns	274
Mamenchisaurus	218	Head crests	276
Stegosaurs	220	Teeth	278
Stegosaurus	222	Beaks	280
Tuojiangosaurus	224	Noses	282
Ankylosaurs	226	Eyes	284
Scelidosaurus	228	Brains	286
Nodosaurus	230	Stomach stones	288
Sauropelta	232	Sails	290
Heterodontosaurus	234	Hips	292
Pegomastax	236	Legs and posture	294
Fruitadens	238	Feet	296
Iguanodon	240	Claws	298

Tails	300	Africa	330
Male and female	302	Asia	332
Warm or cold blood?	304	Gobi Desert	334
Speed	306	China	336
Coprolites	308	Anchiornis	338
Footprints	310	Australia	340
Herds	312	Diamantinasaurus	342
Migration	314	North America	344
Hibernation	316	Dinosaur National Monument	346
Sounds	318	South America	348
Nests	320	Antarctic dinosaurs	350
Eggs	322	Dinosaur fossil hunters	352
Growth	324	Dinosaur names 1	354
Age and lifespan	326	Dinosaur names 2	356
Europe	328	Reconstructions	358

Birds

Birds and dinosaurs	362	Other flightless birds	372
Bird fossils	364	Water birds	374
Archaeopteryx	366	Land birds	376
Confuciusornis	368	Argentavis	378
Terror birds	370		

Age of mammals

Mammal fossils	382	Juramaia	388
Mammal offspring	384	Repenomamus	390
Early mammals	386	Fruitafossor	392

Marsupials	394	Perissodactyls	420
Australian mammals	396	Artiodactyls	422
South American mammals	398	Entelodonts	424
Megatherium	400	Bats	426
Creodonts	402	Elephant evolution	428
Carnivores	404	Woolly mammoth	430
Cats	406	Rhinoceroses	432
Smilodon	408	Paraceratherium	434
Dogs	410	Megacerops	436
Herbivores	412	The first horses	438
Rodents	414	Later horses	440
Ruminants	416	The first whales	442
Condylarths	418	Later whales	444

Humans

Early primates	448	Towards homo sapiens	474
Archicebus	450	Modern humans	476
Darwinius ('Ida')	452	Hobbit people	478
Apes	454	Denisovan and Red Deer people	480
Sahelanthropus	456	Brains and intelligence	482
Orrorin	458	Language	484
Ardipithecus	460	Tools	486
Australopithecus africanus	462	Hunting	488
Australopithecus afarensis	464	Rituals	490
Homo habilis	466	Cave art	492
Homo erectus	468		
Homo heidelbergensis	470	Index	496
Homo neanderthalensis	472	Acknowledgements	512

Beginnings of life

- **About 4600 mya**, like the rest of the Solar System, the Earth formed from swirling gas, dust and rocks in space.

- **Early Earth had violent storms**, volcanoes and meteorite bombardments as the mountains, valleys, seas and oceans formed.

- **Gradually conditions calmed down** and the early atmosphere of air came into being, although it was poisonous to life as we know it today.

- **The first signs of preserved life-forms** – fossils – date from about 3500 mya, but they are only tiny specks in the rocks.

- **Experts debate** whether the remains are from small soft-bodied organisms or if they can be explained by natural features of rock formation.

The first living things were probably simple single cells similar to today's bacteria and cyanobacteria (blue-green algae).

They would have appeared in the water, as hostile atmospheric conditions and bare rock prevented life from forming on land.

Those early life-forms, or organisms, probably gained energy from sunlight or from chemical sources in the sea.

Some idea of how they grew can be gained from stromatolites that still form today. They are stony structures in warm, shallow water made from small particles of rock cemented together by cyanobacteria and other microbes.

▼ *Early life may have looked like today's stromatolites – low-domed or flat-topped stony mounds that grow in shallow coastal waters. They are formed by microbes mixed with fragments of rock minerals.*

Prehistoric timescale

- **Earth's immense history is divided** into huge spans of time known as eras. These are drawn on a chart showing how long ago they occurred, in millions of years.

- **The main eras for living things** are Paleozoic or 'ancient life', Mesozoic or 'middle life', and Cenozoic or 'recent life'.

- **The eras are divided into periods**. For example the Mesozoic Era comprises the Triassic, Jurassic and Cretaceous Periods.

- **Each period is named after a feature** of the main rocks formed at that time. For example, the Jurassic Period is named after rocks from the Jura Mountains, part of the European Alps.

- **The last period**, the Quaternary, covers 2.6 million years ago to the present day. It includes the most recent group of ice ages, the last one being at its coldest just 21,000 years ago.

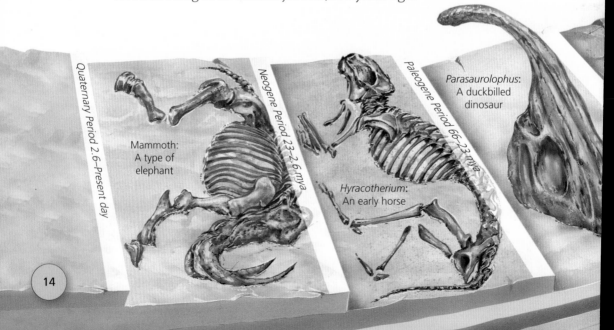

Quaternary Period 2.6–Present day

Mammoth:
A type of
elephant

Neogene Period 23–2.6 mya

Hyracotherium:
An early horse

Paleogene Period 66–23 mya

Parasaurolophus:
A duckbilled
dinosaur

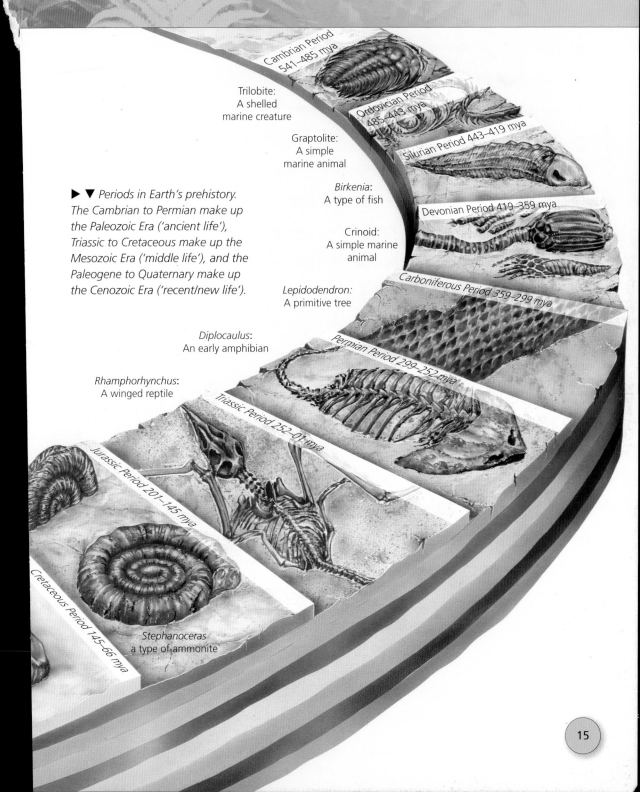

Cambrian Period
541–485 mya

Trilobite:
A shelled
marine creature

Ordovician Period
485–443 mya

Graptolite:
A simple
marine animal

Silurian Period 443–419 mya

Birkenia:
A type of fish

▶ ▼ *Periods in Earth's prehistory.
The Cambrian to Permian make up
the Paleozoic Era ('ancient life'),
Triassic to Cretaceous make up the
Mesozoic Era ('middle life'), and the
Paleogene to Quaternary make up
the Cenozoic Era ('recent/new life').*

Devonian Period 419–359 mya

Crinoid:
A simple marine
animal

Lepidodendron:
A primitive tree

Carboniferous Period 359–299 mya

Diplocaulus:
An early amphibian

Permian Period 299–252 mya

Rhamphorhynchus:
A winged reptile

Triassic Period 252–01 mya

Jurassic Period 201–145 mya

Cretaceous Period 145–66 mya

Stephanoceras
a type of ammonite

Fossil formation

Most of the information we know, or guess, about dinosaurs and other ancient life comes from fossils.

Fossils are the remains of once-living things that have been preserved in rocks and turned to stone, usually over millions of years.

Many kinds of living things from prehistoric times have left fossils, including mammals, birds, lizards, fish, insects as well as plants such as ferns and trees.

Using a dinosaur as an example of fossil formation, the flesh, guts and other soft parts of the dead body were probably eaten by scavengers, or rotted away, so these parts rarely formed fossils.

▼ *Fossil formation is a very long process, and extremely prone to chance and luck. Only a tiny fraction of dinosaurs that ever lived have left remains preserved by this process. Because of the way fossils are formed, dinosaurs that died in water or along banks and shores were most likely to become fossilized. It is extremely rare to find all the parts of a dinosaur arranged as they were in life.*

1 Dinosaur dies and its soft parts are scavenged or rot away

2 Sand, mud or other sediments cover the hard parts, such as the claws, teeth or bones

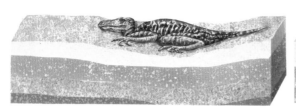

- **Fossils usually formed** when a dinosaur's remains were quickly covered by sediments such as sand, silt or mud, especially along the banks of a river or lake, or on the seashore.

DID YOU KNOW?

The hard parts of a dinosaur's body were the most likely parts to form fossils, especially teeth, bones, claws and horns.

- **The sand or other sediment** around a dinosaur's remains was gradually buried deeper by more sediment, squeezed under pressure, and cemented together into a solid mass of rock.

- **As the sediment turned** to rock, so did the dinosaur remains encased within it.

- **Information about dinosaurs** comes not only from fossils of their body parts, but also from 'trace' fossils. These were not actual parts of their bodies, but other items or signs of their presence.

- **Trace fossils** include egg shells, footprints, marks made by claws and teeth, and coprolites – fossilized dinosaur droppings.

3 More layers build up as the minerals in the bones and other hard parts turn to rock

4 Erosion (wearing away) of upper rock layers exposes the fossil, which is now solid stone

Earliest plants

- **Among the very first living things** on Earth were single-celled bacteria and cyanobacteria, also known as blue-green algae.

- **Blue-green algae emerged** as long ago as 3500 mya. They contain chlorophyll and were the first living organisms to photosynthesize (make energy from sunlight).

- **Photosynthesis** also produces oxygen. Over millions of years, the blue-green algae produced enough oxygen to enable more complex life forms to develop.

▲ *Lichens such as these are made up of an alga and a fungus. Early lichens – like modern-day ones – grew on rocks and, over time, eroded part of the rock and helped to form soil.*

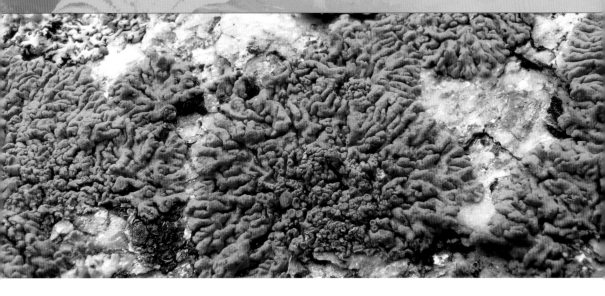

▲ Lichens can survive in many places where other plants would die, such as the Arctic, on mountaintops and in deserts. Some Arctic lichens are over 4000 years old.

True algae, which are usually regarded as plants, developed more than 1500 mya.

By about 550 mya, multi-celled plants had begun to appear, including simple seaweeds.

Algae and lichens were the first plants to appear on land.

Bryophytes (mosses and liverworts) emerged on land by around 400 mya. They are simple green seedless plants.

Unlike vascular plants, which emerged later, bryophytes cannot grow high above the ground because they do not have strengthened stems.

DID YOU KNOW?

Liverworts grew on mats of blue-green algae, which trapped nitrogen from the air. Liverworts used this nitrogen to grow.

Vascular plants

- **Vascular plants are more suited** to living on drier land than mosses and liverworts.

- **They have branching stems** with tube-like pipes (vascular bundles) that carry water and nutrients.

- **These stems and tubes** also mean the plants can stand tall. Early vascular plants had spores (reproductive cells, like seeds) – the taller the plant the more widely it can disperse its spores.

- **One of the first known** vascular plants was *Cooksonia*. It was about 5 cm tall, with a forked stem.

- **Scientists called palaeontologists** discovered fossil remains of *Cooksonia* in Wales. Palaeontologists study fossils of prehistoric plants and animals to see how they lived and evolved.

- **Rhynie in Scotland** is one site where lots of vascular plant fossils have been found.

- **The plants at Rhynie** would have grown on the sandy edges of pools in the Early Devonian Period (about 410 mya).

- **One plant fossil** found at Rhynie is *Aglaophyton*, which stood around 45 cm high.

- *Aglaophyton* had underground roots and tissues that supported the plant stem. It also had water-carrying tubes and stomata (tiny openings) that allowed air and water to pass through.

- **Land-living plants** were essential for providing conditions for animals to make the transition from the seas to land. They created soil, food and ground cover for shelter.

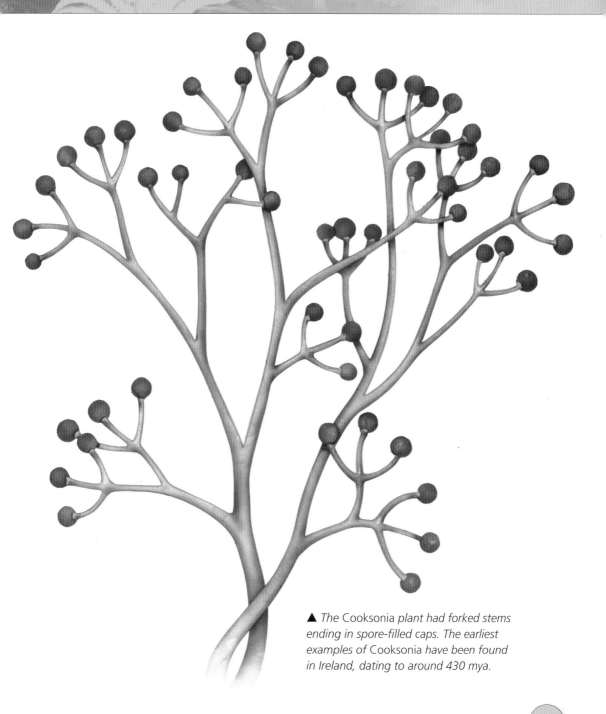

▲ *The* Cooksonia *plant had forked stems ending in spore-filled caps. The earliest examples of* Cooksonia *have been found in Ireland, dating to around 430 mya.*

Gymnosperms

- **Gymnosperms are plants** that produce exposed seeds on the surface of structures such as cones. The word gymnosperm comes from two Greek words: *gymnos*, meaning 'naked', and *sperma*, meaning 'seed'.

- **These plants** had appeared by 320 mya. They probably developed from early plants such as *Cooksonia*.

- **Gymnosperms** grew well in the damp, tropical forests of the Late Carboniferous Period (359–299 mya).

- **Varieties of gymnosperms** include conifers, cycads and seed-ferns.

- **Cycads are palm-like plants** with feathery tops. They were more common in prehistoric times than they are today.

▲ *Cycads have fern-like leaves growing in a circle around the end of the stem. New leaves sprout each year and last for several years.*

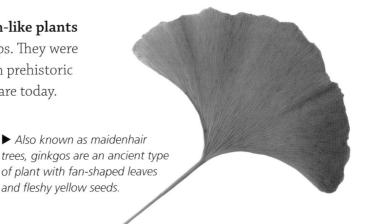

▶ *Also known as maidenhair trees, ginkgos are an ancient type of plant with fan-shaped leaves and fleshy yellow seeds.*

- **One type of cycad** is the maidenhair tree, *Ginkgo biloba*. It still grows in towns and cities, but is now very rare in the wild.

- **One extinct gymnosperm** is *Glossopteris*, which some palaeontologists believe was similar to the ancestors of later flowering plants.

- **Together with ferns** and horsetails (a type of herb), gymnosperms dominated landscapes during the Mesozoic Era (252–66 mya).

- **In the Jurassic Period** (201–145 mya), plant-eating dinosaurs ate their way through huge areas of coniferous forest.

- **Today, conifers are found** most often in cold or dry areas, to which they are well adapted.

▲ *Conifer trees have needle-like leaves and make their seeds in cones rather than in flowers.*

▶ *This* Araucaria, *or monkey puzzle tree, is a type of conifer that dates back to the Jurassic Period.*

23

Angiosperms 1

- **Angiosperms are flowering plants**. They produce seeds within an ovary, which is contained within a flower. The word comes from the Greek terms *angeion*, meaning 'vessel', and *sperma*, meaning 'seed'.

- **These plants** first appeared about 140 mya.

- **The earliest evidence** of flowering plants comes from the fossil remains of leaves and pollen grains.

- **Plant experts** used to think that magnolias were one of the first angiosperms, but they now think that an extinct plant called *Archaefructus* was older. It lived about 125 mya.

- **Fossil remains** of *Archaefructus* were discovered in northeast China in the mid to late 1990s.

- **By 100 mya**, angiosperms had developed into many dozens of families of flowering plants, most of which still survive today.

- **By 60 mya**, angiosperms had taken over from gymnosperms as the dominant plants on Earth.

- **The start of the Paleogene Period** (around 66 mya) saw a rise in temperatures that produced the right conditions for tropical rainforests.

- **It was in the rainforests** that angiosperms evolved into many different types of plants.

- **Angiosperms were successful** because they could grow very quickly, they had very extensive root systems to anchor them and take up water and nutrients, and they could grow in a greater range of environments than other plants, such as gymnosperms.

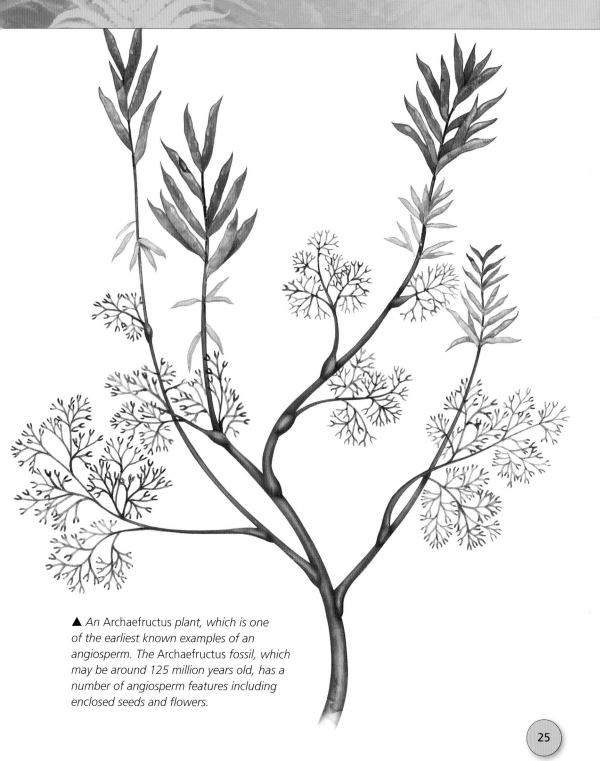

▲ An Archaefructus *plant, which is one of the earliest known examples of an angiosperm. The* Archaefructus *fossil, which may be around 125 million years old, has a number of angiosperm features including enclosed seeds and flowers.*

Angiosperms 2

- **Unusual and very old fossils** of what seems to be a small flowering plant were found in the 1990s in clay-based rocks in Southern England.

- **The fossils have been dated to about 130 mya**, the Early Cretaceous Period, around the time of *Archaefructus*.

- **They show a plant around 20–30 cm tall**, similar to today's ferns, with roots that suggested it lived in a watery environment such as a swamp.

- **At the end of the stems and leaves** are what appear to be small flowers, making this plant an angiosperm.

▲ *Today's water lilies have large and colourful flowers, but their basic structure is similar to fossil plants 120 million years old.*

- **The plant has been named *Bevhalstia*,** in honour of the British palaeontologist and science communicator Beverly Halstead.

- **The amborella, *Amborella trichopoda*,** is a living shrub or small tree with flowers thought to be similar to very early angiosperm flowers from the Cretaceous Period.

- **Amborellas live wild** only on the islands of New Caledonia, northwest of Australia.

- **The cream-coloured flowers are tiny,** only about 5 mm across, but have features that link them with ancient fossil flowers.

- ***Amborella* also has unusual tube-like vessels** in its roots, stems and twigs, which are much simpler than the vessels found in other flowering plants.

▶ *Studies of plant genes, as well as flower structure, show that* Amborella *is one of the earliest known angiosperms.*

The first invertebrates

- **An invertebrate is an animal** that does not have a spinal column. Invertebrates were the first animals to live on Earth, in the prehistoric seas.

- **The very first animal-like** organisms that fed on other organisms or organic matter were single-celled and sometimes called protists (protozoans).

- **Only prehistoric protists** with hard parts survive as fossils. The earliest fossils are more than 600 million years old.

- **One of the earliest known fossils** that could be a multi-celled animal is around 600 million years old. Called *Mawsonites*, it may have been a primitive jellyfish or worm – or the remains of a burrow or colony of microbes.

- **Some early invertebrate fossils** are from now-extinct groups of animals.

- **Some of these animals** had segmented bodies that looked a bit like quilts.

- **One such invertebrate** is *Spriggina*, named after geologist Reg Sprigg. In 1946, he discovered 550-million-year-old fossil remains near Ediacara in southern Australia.

- **Palaeontologists** have unearthed the fossils of many other invertebrates that resemble jellyfish from Ediacara.

Another famous invertebrate discovery was made by Roger Mason, an English schoolboy, in 1957. This was the fossil of *Charnia*, an animal that was similar to a living sea pen.

▼ Charnia *was a prehistoric animal that grew in feather-like colonies attached to the seabed, like living sea pens.* Charnia *fossils date to more than 500 mya.*

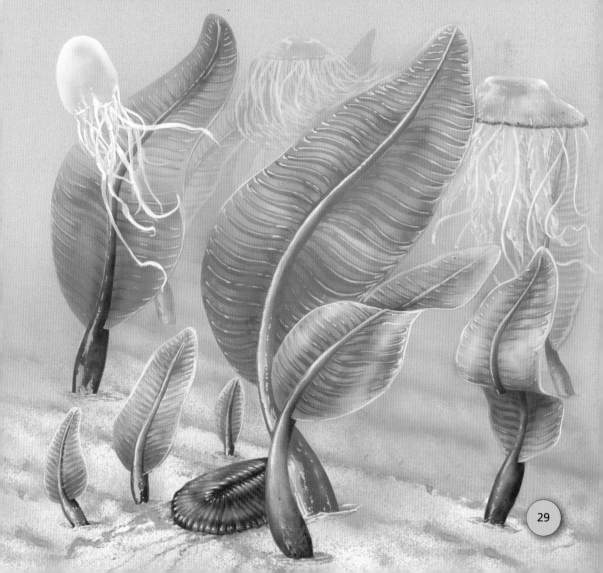

Corals

🐾 **Corals are the simplest living animals**. They have no brain, nerves, eyes or stomach.

🐾 **Despite being so simple**, corals are very common in seas and oceans around the world, from warm tropical shallows to deep cold, water.

🐾 **Most coral animals**, called polyps, look like tiny sea anemones, with a stalk topped by a ring of tentacles. They sting and catch tiny prey to pull into the opening at the top of the stalk.

▼ *One coral creature, or polyp, gives off branches that grow into more individuals.*

Coral colony begins to grow through 'budding'

Polyp begins to grow a stony cup

Young polyp attaches to a hard surface

🐾 **Most corals also form** hard cup-like structures around themselves, from stony minerals they take from sea water. Over thousands of years these 'skeletons' build up into amazingly shaped formations we call coral reefs.

🐾 **The rocky formations of ancient corals** have left many wonderful fossils, showing how these simple creatures lived in the seas millions of years ago.

- *Halysites* **was a type of tabulate coral**, whose rocky shapes look like layers and piles of six-sided bee honeycombs. It lived mainly during the Silurian Period, 443–419 mya.

- *Halysites* **is also called chain coral**, from the way its colony members grew next to each other – their fossils look like links in a chain.

- **Another tabulate coral was** *Syringopora*, which survived to the Carboniferous Period, over 300 mya. Tabulate corals are now all extinct.

- **Rugose corals are also now extinct**. Some lived alone rather than in groups and made horn-shaped living chambers, such as *Caninia*.

- **The modern group of corals**, scleractinians, appeared about 230 mya, in the Middle Triassic Period.

◄ *Corals live mainly in warm shallow seas, which were more common long ago.*

31

Arthropods

- **Arthropods form** the largest single group of animals. They include insects, crustaceans (crabs and lobsters), arachnids (spiders) and myriapods (millipedes) – any creature with a segmented body and jointed limbs.

- **Some of the earliest known remains** of arthropods come from the 505-million-year-old mudstone deposits of the Burgess Shale in Canada.

- *Marrella* **is one of the most common fossils** discovered at the Burgess Shale. It was about 2 cm long and had a head shield and two antennae.

- **Its body was divided** into segments, each of which had a jointed limb, probably for scurrying over the seabed.

- **At first**, palaeontologists thought *Marrella* was a trilobite, but they now regard it as an entirely different type of arthropod.

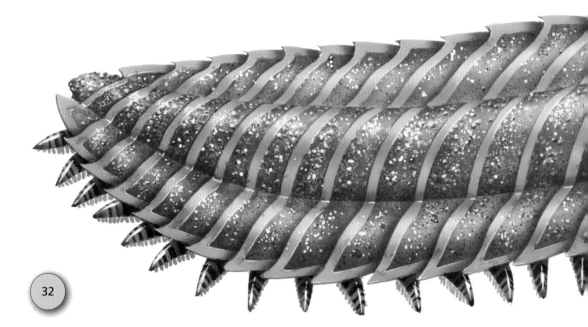

- **One of the first** – if not the first – groups of animals to emerge from the sea and colonize the land were arthropods, some time between 500 and 400 mya.

- **Arthropods were well suited** for living on land. Many had exoskeletons (outer skeletons) that prevented them from drying out. Their jointed limbs meant they could move over the ground.

- **Woodlice-like creatures** may have been among the first arthropods on land. They fed on rotting plant material, which they would have found on seashores.

- **The largest-ever land arthropod** was a millipede-like creature called *Arthropleura*, which was 1.8 m long.

- *Arthropleura* **lived on forest floors** during the Carboniferous Period (359–299 mya). Like woodlice, it ate rotting plants.

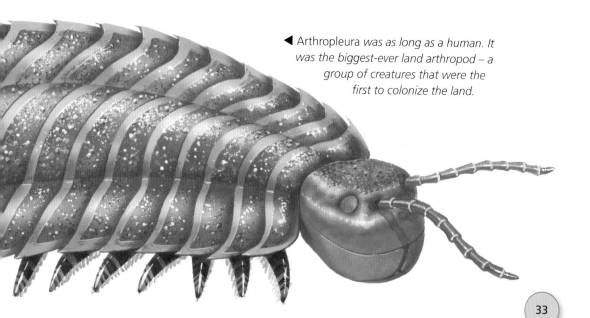

◀ Arthropleura *was as long as a human. It was the biggest-ever land arthropod – a group of creatures that were the first to colonize the land.*

Trilobites

Trilobites belonged to the invertebrate group called arthropods – animals with segmented bodies and hard outer skeletons.

The name trilobite means 'three lobes'. Trilobites' hard outer shells were divided into three parts.

The first trilobites appeared by about 520 mya. By 500 mya, they had developed into many different types.

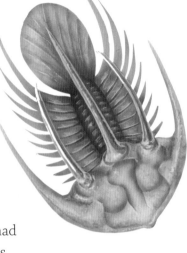

▲ Kolihapeltis, *from about 400 mya, had many long rear-pointing spines.*

These invertebrates had compound eyes, like insects' eyes, which could see in many different directions at once.

Some trilobites could roll up into a ball, like some woodlice do today. This was a useful means of protection.

Long, thin, jointed legs enabled trilobites to move quickly over the seabed or sediment covering it.

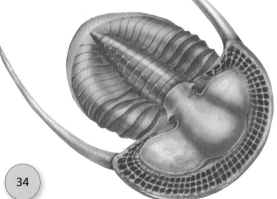

◀ Trinucleus *was hardly larger than a thumb but had two very long swept-back head spines.*

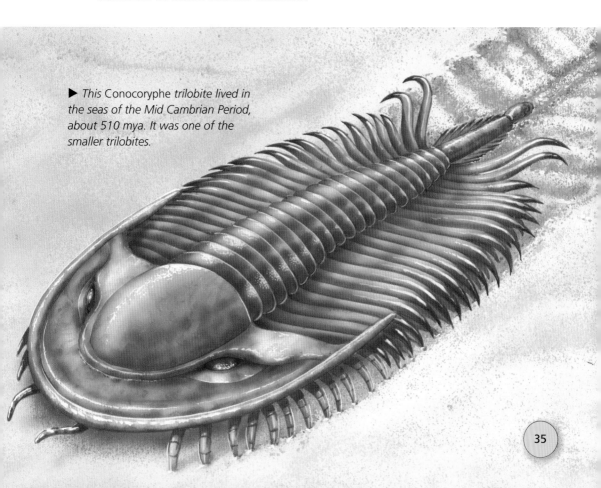

- **Trilobites moulted** by shedding their outer skeletons. Most trilobite fossils are the remains of these shed skeletons.

- **One of the largest known trilobites** was *Isotelus*, which grew more than 70 cm long.

- **Other trilobites** were much smaller, such as *Conocoryphe*, which was about 2–5 cm long.

- **Trilobites became extinct** around 250 mya – along with huge numbers of other marine animals.

▶ *This* Conocoryphe *trilobite lived in the seas of the Mid Cambrian Period, about 510 mya. It was one of the smaller trilobites.*

Insects

- **One of the oldest fossils** that is probably a true insect is named *Rhyniognatha*.

- **Its fossils are about 400 million years old** and were preserved in a formation of rocks called Rhynie chert, in Scotland.

- **As land habitats became more common** during the Devonian Period, 419–359 mya, many new kinds of insects started to appear.

- **These early insects included cockroaches**, the grasshopper and cricket group known as odonatans, and the first flying insects similar to today's mayflies and dragonflies.

- **The biggest-ever flying insect** was *Meganeuropsis*, a dragonfly-like griffinfly that lived in Late Carboniferous and Early Permian forests, around 300–290 mya.

- ***Meganeuropsis* lived in North America** and had wings spanning 70 cm, compared to the largest dragonflies today, at 20 cm.

- **The most numerous insects today**, beetles, probably appeared during the Early Permian Period, around 290 mya.

- **An amazing insect fossil** was found in China and named in 2008 as *Ororaphidia*.   .

- **It was a type of snakefly**, from the insect group Rhaphidioptera.

- ***Ororaphidia* was only 12 mm long** but the details of the fossil show many tiny parts such as the veins on its wings.

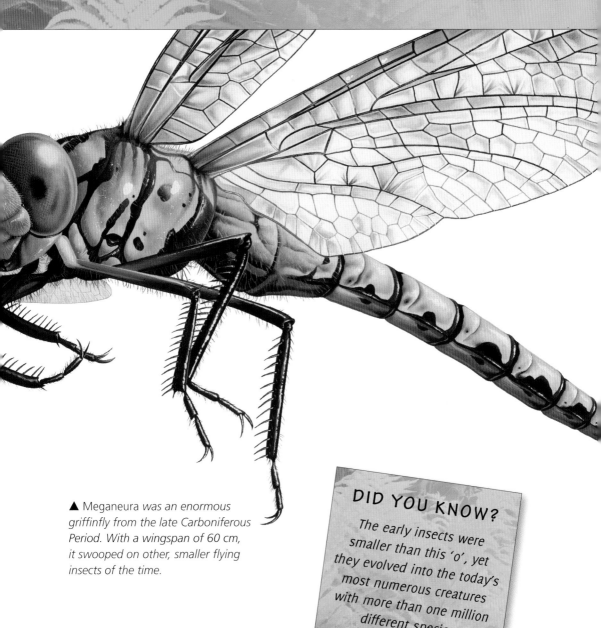

▲ Meganeura *was an enormous griffinfly from the late Carboniferous Period. With a wingspan of 60 cm, it swooped on other, smaller flying insects of the time.*

DID YOU KNOW?

The early insects were smaller than this 'o', yet they evolved into the today's most numerous creatures with more than one million different species.

Starfish and sea urchins

- **The animal group called echinoderms**, meaning 'spiny skins', includes starfish, brittlestars, sea urchins, sea cucumbers, and sea lilies and feather stars, or crinoids.

- **All echinoderms live in the sea** and have a radial or 'circular' body design.

- **Echinoderms have one of the longest fossil histories** of any large animal group, stretching back to the Early Cambrian Period more than 530 mya.

- **There are about 7000 kinds** of living echinoderms – but twice this number are known only from fossils.

▼ Fossil brittlestars from as long as 500 mya are very similar to today's versions, scavenging on the deep seafloor.

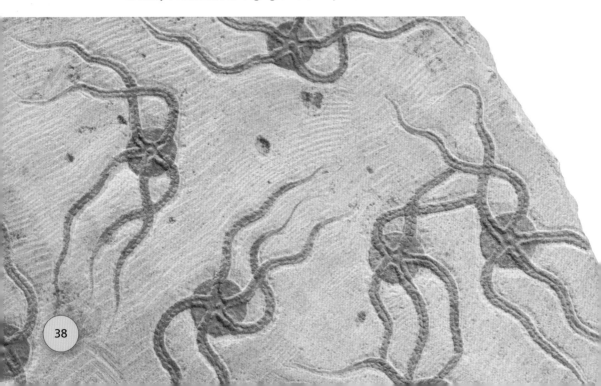

▲ Today's starfish are mostly predators, levering open shellfish with their powerful arms and dissolving the soft flesh inside.

A fossil find from 2012 in Morocco, North Africa, was *Helicocystis* – one of the first known echinoderms, from 520 mya.

The *Helicocystis* fossils show it had five grooves in a spiral shape around its body, which probably trapped small bits of food.

Many modern starfish and brittlestars have arms in multiples of five, linking *Helicocystis* to this group.

***Geocoma* was a brittlestar from Europe** that lived about 170 mya in the Middle Jurassic Period. Its fossils are very similar to living brittlestars.

***Pentacrinites* was a sea lily** that was widespread in the oceans from 220 to 40 mya, a huge time span of survival.

***Pentacrinites* remains** were so common in some rocks that they are known as 'penta beds'.

Brachiopods

Brachiopods are filter-feeding shellfish that were once hugely diverse and common in all seas and oceans, but are now much more limited.

More than 12,000 kinds of brachiopods are known from fossilized remains, compared to about 320 living species.

Brachiopods resemble mollusc shellfish such as mussels and clams, with a two-part shell, and each part is known as a valve.

However in a brachiopod the valves cover the top and bottom of the animal inside, while in molluscs, the valves are on the left and right sides.

Some brachiopods are known as lampshells, since the shell shape resembles that of an old oil lamp.

Brachiopods first evolved in the Cambrian Period, more than 500 mya, and dominated the seas of the Paleozoic Era.

One of the first known from fossils was *Aldanotreta*, which lived in what is now Siberia, 525 mya.

Brachiopods

◀ *Two brachiopods, lower left (upright with fleshy pink strips) thrive in this early reef scene, along with corals, sea urchins, anemones and other still-flourishing sea invertebrates.*

Many brachiopods died out in the greatest mass extinction, which occured at the end of the Permian Period, 252 mya, known as the 'Great Dying'.

The living brachiopod *Lingula* is very similar to its relatives from 450–400 mya.

Most living brachiopods are less than 5 cm long, while some fossil kinds were over 20 cm in length.

▼ The living brachiopod *Lingula* has a long fleshy stalk at its rear end that anchors it into the mud or sand of the seabed.

Molluscs and graptolites

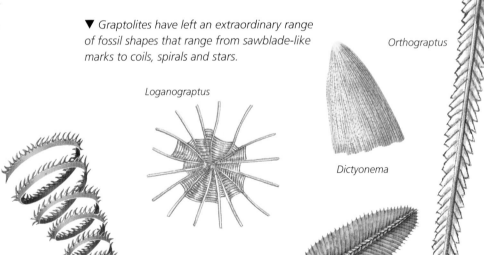

Modern molluscs include gastropods (slugs, snails and limpets), bivalves (clams, oysters, mussels and cockles) and cephalopods (octopuses, squids and cuttlefish).

Modern and prehistoric molluscs represent one of the most diverse animal groups ever to have lived.

The first molluscs were the size of a pinhead. They appeared early in the Cambrian Period, about 540 mya, or even before.

The first cephalopod molluscs emerged towards the end of the Cambrian Period, around 490 mya.

One early cephalopod was *Plectronoceras*, which had a horn-shaped shell divided into different chambers.

Gastropod molluscs (snails and slugs) were one of the first groups of animals to live on land.

▼ Graptolites have left an extraordinary range of fossil shapes that range from sawblade-like marks to coils, spirals and stars.

Loganograptus

Orthograptus

Dictyonema

Monograptus

Phyllograptus

▲ *Nautiloids such as* Orthoceratites *had a long shells and squid-like tentacles, shown here hunting on the seabed almost half a billion years ago.*

Snails and slugs are limited to where they can live on land as they require moist conditions.

Cephalopods are the most highly developed of all molluscs. Squids and octopuses evolved big brains, good eyesight, tentacles and beak-like jaws.

Graptolites are an extinct group of simple animals that lived in string-like communities. Graptolite means 'written stone' because the fossils of these creatures resemble scrawled handwriting.

Graptolites had tentacles that they may have used to sieve food particles from the water or the seabed.

Ammonites

- **Ammonites belong to** the cephalopod group of molluscs. They were once widespread in the oceans, but they died out at the end of the Cretaceous Period (about 66 mya).

- **The number of ammonite fossils** that have been found shows how plentiful these animals once were.

- **Ammonites were predators** and scavengers. They had very good vision, long seizing tentacles and powerful mouths.

- **Their mouths consisted** of sharp beaks, perhaps venom glands, and a tooth-covered tongue.

- **Ammonites had multi-chambered shells** that contained gas and worked like flotation tanks, keeping the creatures afloat.

- *Stephanoceras* **was an ammonite** with a spiral, disc-shaped shell, 20 cm across. It was very common in the seas of the Mesozoic Era.

- **A living relative** of ammonites is *Nautilus*, a cephalopod that lives near the seabed and feeds on small creatures and carrion.

Chambers

▶ A rock containing an ammonite fossil, clearly displaying the shell's division into different chambers. The innermost chamber was the home of a newborn ammonite. As it grew, it built a bigger chamber and moved into it. When it outgrew that chamber it built another one, and so on, to form a spiral-patterned shell.

People once thought that ammonite fossils were the fossils of curled-up snakes.

Builders have traditionally set ammonite fossils into the walls of buildings for decoration.

▼ *An ammonite swims through the sea in search of food. The animal swam backwards, with its tentacles trailing behind.*

Ages of fishes

Pikaia

- **A small, worm-like creature** called *Pikaia* is thought to be similar to the ancestors of backboned animals.

- **Its fossil remains** were found in the 505-million-year-old mudstone deposits of the Burgess Shale in Canada.

- *Pikaia* **may have been** an early chordate, a group of animals with a stiff supporting rod, called a notochord, along their back. All vertebrates belong to this group, as well as marine animals called tunicates and acraniates.

- *Pikaia* **was 5 cm long** with what could be a notochord (stiffening rod) running along its body – a kind of primitive spine that gave its body flexibility.

- **The notochord** also allowed the animal's simple muscles to work against it, and the body organs to hang from it.

- *Pikaia* **was very similar** to *Branchiostoma*, a small, transparent modern-day creature that lives in sand at the bottom of the sea.

- **As it lacked a bony skeleton**, paired fins and jaws, *Pikaia* was not really a fish.

- *Pikaia* **was a more complex creature** than many other animals found in the Burgess Shale. It suggests that other complex creatures must have lived before it, from which it evolved.

- **The head of *Pikaia*** was very primitive with a pair of tentacles, a mouth and a simple brain (a swelling of the nerve cord) for processing information.

- ***Pikaia* swam** in a zigzag fashion, similar to a sea snake.

▼ Pikaia *looked a little like an eel with tail fins. The stiff rod that ran along its body developed into the backbone in later animals.*

Jawless fish

The first fish probably appeared during the Late Cambrian Period, about 500 mya.

These fish had permanently gaping mouths – as they had no jaws they could not open and close their mouths.

Early fish were called agnathans, which means 'jawless'.

▼ *Early jawless fish such as* Hemicyclaspis *could swim much farther and quicker than most invertebrates. This meant they could more easily search for and move to new feeding areas.*

- **Agnathans ate** by sieving plankton through their simple mouth opening, also perhaps scooping up small items such as algae, tiny animals and rotting flesh on the seabed.

- **Among the oldest** complete agnathan fossils are *Arandaspis*, which comes from Australia and was found in 1959, and *Sacabambaspis*, which comes from Bolivia and other countries in South America, the fossils of which were discovered in the 1980s.

- *Hemicyclaspis* was another agnathan. It was a flat fish with a broad head shield and a long tail.

- **Later jawless fish** had more streamlined, rounder bodies and eyes at the front of their heads. This suggests they were not restricted to the seabed.

- **Most jawless fish** died out by the end of the Devonian Period (around 360 mya).

- **Living agnathans** include lampreys and hagfish, which have soft bodies and look like eels. Like their ancient relatives, they do not have jaws.

▶ *The hagfish is a scavenger and parasite, even burrowing into a living host to eat it from the inside.*

Jawed fish

- **The first jawed fish probably** emerged during the Silurian Period (443–419 mya).

- **An early group of jawed fish** were acanthodians, from the Greek word *akantha*, meaning 'thorn' or 'spine'.

- **Jaws and teeth** gave acanthodians a huge advantage over jawless fish – they could eat a greater variety of food and defend themselves more effectively.

- **Jaws and teeth allowed** acanthodians to become predators.

- **Acanthodians' jaws** evolved from structures called gill arches in the pharynx (throat), the tube from the mouth to the stomach.

- **Gill arches are bony rods** and muscles that support the gills, the breathing organs of a fish.

- **As acanthodians developed jaws**, they also developed teeth.

- **The earliest fish teeth** were cone-like shapes along the jaw, made out of bone and coated with hard enamel.

- **The teeth** of early acanthodians varied greatly. In some species they were sharp and spiky, in others they were like blades, while in others they resembled flat plates.

DID YOU KNOW?

Another difference between jawed and jawless fish was that jawed fish had a pair of nostrils, while jawless fish only had one.

▲ Climatius, *a type of acanthodian or jawed fish, lived around 400 mya. Another name for acanthodians is 'spiny sharks' – although they were not sharks, many had spines on the edges of their fins.*

Sharks

- **The earliest known shark fossils** are scales from rock layers of the late Silurian Period, about 420 mya.

- **Sharks belong to the group** known as cartilaginous fish, which also includes rays and skates. Their skeletons are made from cartilage, not bone.

- *Cladoselache* **was a prehistoric shark**, which could grow up to 2 m long.

- *Cladoselache* **appears** to have been quite similar to a modern shark – it had a streamlined body, a pair of dorsal (back) fins and triangular-shaped pectoral (front side) fins.

- **Early sharks hunted squid**, small fish and crustaceans.

- *Stethacanthus* was a prehistoric shark that looked nothing like a modern one. It had an anvil-shaped head projection covered in teeth.

> **DID YOU KNOW?**
>
> Prehistoric sharks' jaws were fixed to the side of their skull, while modern sharks' jaws hang beneath their braincase, which gives them a more powerful bite.

▶ This modern blue shark is a fast swimmer and a fierce hunter. The main features of sharks – from their tightly packed, needle-sharp teeth to their streamlined shape – have changed little over 400 million years.

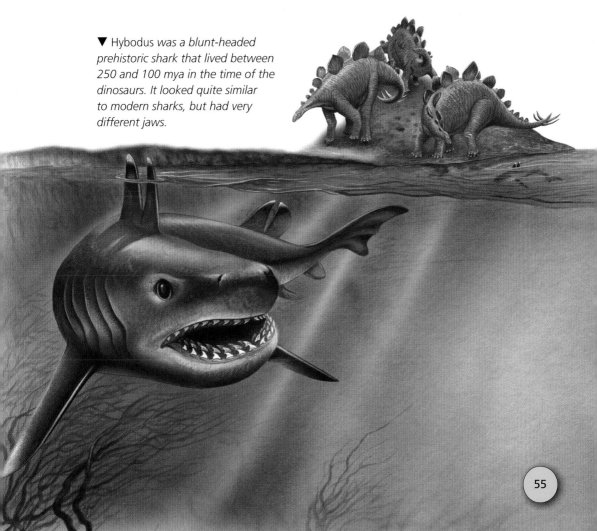

- *Stethacanthus* **lived** in the Carboniferous Period (359–299 mya).

- **Sharks are at the top** of the food chain in modern seas, but this was not the case during the Devonian Period.

- **Other Devonian fish** were much larger than sharks. For example, *Dunkleosteus* grew to be up to 3.7 m long and would have been able to snap up any contemporary shark in a flash.

▼ Hybodus *was a blunt-headed prehistoric shark that lived between 250 and 100 mya in the time of the dinosaurs. It looked quite similar to modern sharks, but had very different jaws.*

Megalodon

- **The giant shark _Megalodon_**, _Carcharodon megalodon_, was one of the greatest-ever predators to roam the ocean.

- **This enormous hunter was similar** to the great white shark of today, but over three times as long and perhaps 20 times heavier.

- **Also known as 'big tooth'**, _Megalodon_ is estimated to have been up to 18 m long and weighed over 40 tonnes.

- **Shark skeletons are made of cartilage (gristle)** rather than bone, which fossilizes less well.

- **So the main fossils of _Megalodon_** are its teeth, from which experts estimate the size of the whole animal.

- **Its jaws were more than 2 m across** and could have easily swallowed a human, even several at once.

- **Luckily _Megalodon_ died out about 2 mya**, having swum in all the world's oceans for more than 25 million years.

- **A top or apex predator**, _Megalodon_ was able to attack and eat almost any other creature in the sea, even other big sharks.

- **To avoid injury**, it probably hunted medium-sized whales and fish.

▶ Megalodon _might have attacked a whale by biting or ripping off its bony flippers, thereby weakening the animal due to blood loss, then moving in to bite off huge chunks of flesh._

DID YOU KNOW?

Why such a massive predator should die out is unclear. Perhaps Megalodon suffered competition from killer whales and was affected by ocean cooling.

Bony fish

- **Bony fish have internal skeletons** and external scales made of bone.

- **Fossil evidence shows** they first appeared during the Late Silurian Period, around 420 mya.

- **Bony fish evolved** into the most abundant and varied fish in the seas.

- **There are two types** of bony fish – ray-finned fish and lobe-finned fish.

- **There were plenty** of prehistoric lobe-finned fish, but only a few species survive today. They belong to one of two groups – lungfish or coelacanths.

- **Amphibians** – and ultimately reptiles and mammals – evolved from lobe-finned fish.

- **Ray-finned fish** were so-called because of the bony rays that supported their fins. Most early ray-finned fish were small, ranging in size from about 5–20 cm long.

- *Rhadinichthys* **and** *Cheirolepis* were two early ray-finned fish. They were small predators equipped with good swimming ability and snapping jaws.

- **Around 250 mya**, ray-finned fish lost many of the bony rays from their fins. The fins became more flexible and the fish became better swimmers.

- **New types of ray-finned fish**, called teleosts, also developed more symmetrical tails and thinner scales.

▼ *This modern-day coelacanth is a direct descendant of the lobe-finned bony fish that lived 350 mya. Coelacanths were thought to be extinct until a fisherman caught one off the coast of South Africa in 1938.*

Dunkleosteus

- **The now-extinct fish group** known as placoderms lived during the Silurian and Devonian Periods, 443 to 359 mya.

- **The name placoderm** means 'plated skin' and these fish had large shields of bone over the head and front of the body for protection.

- **The biggest placoderm** was *Dunkleosteus*, from around 370 mya, the Late Devonian.

- **Its fossils come from North America**, Europe and North Africa.

- *Dunkleosteus* **was 10 m** or more in length and weighed up to 5 tonnes.

- **It did not have teeth**, but curved plates or blades of bone that formed a sharp edge for biting and slicing.

- **The estimated closing force** of these 'blades' was greater than almost any other living or fossil creature, including *Tyrannosaurus*.

- *Dunkleosteus* **was named in 1956** after fossil expert David Dunkle of Cleveland, USA.

- **A very similar giant placoderm** called *Dinichthys* is known from few fossils and may be the same as *Dunkleosteus*.

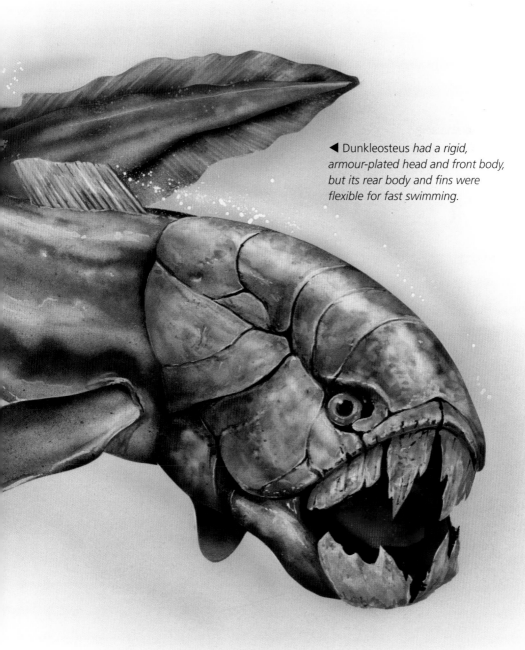

◀ Dunkleosteus *had a rigid, armour-plated head and front body, but its rear body and fins were flexible for fast swimming.*

Leedsichthys

- **The biggest-ever fish** known was *Leedsichthys*.

- **However it was not a hunter** – it filtered small plankton from the water, like the largest fish today, the whale shark.

- **Fossils of *Leedsichthys*** are fragmentary since its skeleton was mostly cartilage (gristle), which does not preserves as well as bone.

- **Recent estimates** put its length at 16–17 m, and its weight at more than 20 tonnes.

- **This fish was named 'Leeds' fish'** in 1889 in honour of fossil collector Alfred Leeds, who found its remains in 1886 in England.

- **Since then**, more fossils have been found in France, Germany, and perhaps Chile in South America.

- ***Leedsichthys* cruised the oceans** at the end of the Jurassic Period, 150 mya.

- **It had large pectoral (front side) fins**, but small or absent pelvic (rear side) fins, and a tall tail fin.

- **The probable lifespan** of *Leedsichthys* was 40–50 years.

DID YOU KNOW?

It's calculated that at one year of age, *Leedsichthys* was already larger than a human, at 2 m in length.

▶ Leedsichthys *had an enormous mouth through which water passed, containing floating morsels of food such as baby fish, shrimps and squid.*

Animals onto land

From fins to limbs

- **The first land-dwelling**, backboned animals were called tetrapods. They needed legs to hold up their bodies so they could move around in search of water and food.

- **Tetrapods evolved** from lobe-finned fish, which had all the right body parts to develop arms and legs.

- **The fossil skeleton** of the lobe-finned fish *Eusthenopteron* shows that the organization of bones in its front and rear fins was similar to the arrangement of limbs in tetrapods.

- *Eusthenopteron* **lived in** shallow waters. It could use its fins as primitive legs and move over land if the waters dried out.

- **Recent research suggests** that another lobe-finned fish, *Panderichthys*, could use its fins more effectively as limbs than *Eusthenopteron*. According to scientists, *Panderichthys* was more like a tetrapod than a fish.

- **The front fins** in lobe-finned fish connected to a shoulder girdle, while the rear fins connected to a hip girdle. These girdles connected to the backbone.

- **These hip and shoulder** connections meant that the limbs of future tetrapods were connected to a skeleton, which prevented the limbs from pressing against the inside of the body and damaging it.

- **The shoulder girdle** of lobe-finned fish also connected to their heads. Tetrapods, however, developed heads that were separated from their shoulders and joined instead by a neck.

- **Necks were a great advantage** to land-living animals. They could use them to bend down, to reach up, and to turn around to see in other directions.

▲ Eusthenopteron *using its fins to move out of the water.* Eusthenopteron, *which means 'good strong fin', was once thought to be the closest ancestor to tetrapods. However palaeontologists have recently discovered other fish, such as* Kenichthys, Tiktaalik, Gogonasus *and* Panderichthys, *that may have been even closer relatives.*

Breathing air

- **Fish breathe oxygen** in water through their gills. When a fish is out of the water, these gills collapse.

- **For creatures to adapt** to living on land, they had to develop air-breathing lungs.

- **Tetrapods were not the first creatures** to develop lungs – this step was taken by lobe-finned fish.

- **Lungfish are lobe-fins** that still exist today. They live in hot places and when rivers dry out, they bury themselves in mud and breathe through lungs.

- **Early tetrapods**, such as *Ichthyostega* and *Acanthostega*, had gills and lungs, suggesting they could breathe in both air and water.

- **Later tetrapods breathed** through gills when they were first born, but, like modern frogs and newts, their gills became smaller as they got older and were replaced by lungs.

- **Modern amphibians** also take in oxygen through their skin, which is soft and moist.

- **Early tetrapods** had tougher skin, so were unable to breathe through it.

- **Breathing through skin** limits an animal's size, which is why modern amphibians are much smaller than many of their prehistoric ancestors.

DID YOU KNOW?

Animals could only evolve to live on land due to plants producing oxygen over millions of years, which became part of Earth's atmosphere.

68

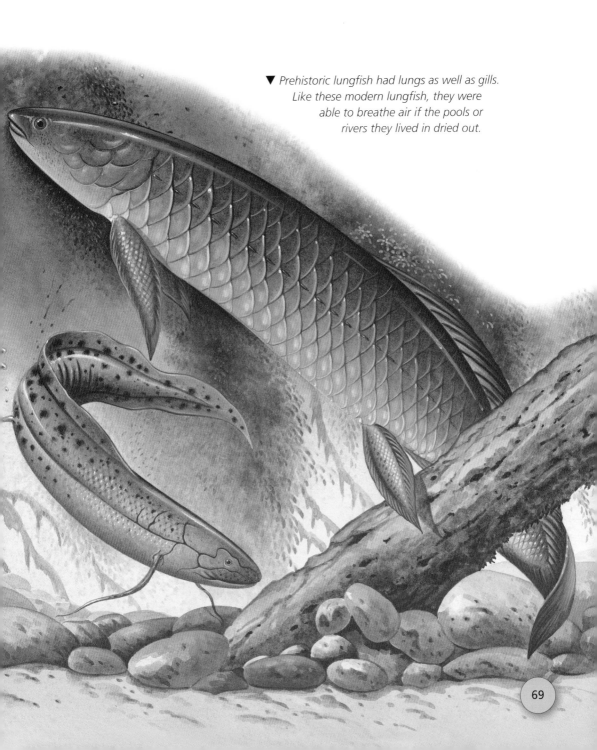

▼ *Prehistoric lungfish had lungs as well as gills.
Like these modern lungfish, they were
able to breathe air if the pools or
rivers they lived in dried out.*

Acanthostega

▲ Acanthostega *may have evolved from lobe-finned fish similar to* Eusthenopteron *and* Panderichthys. *It shared a number of features with these fish, including a similar set of gills and lungs, as well as a tail fin and braincase.*

- *Acanthostega* **was an early tetrapod**. It had a fish-like body, which suggests it spent most of its life in water.

- **Fossil remains** of *Acanthostega* were found in rock strata dating from the Late Devonian Period (around 365 mya).

DID YOU KNOW?
Acanthostega had fish-like gills for breathing water as well as lungs for breathing air.

- *Acanthostega*'s **body** was about one metre long.

- **This tetrapod had** a wide tail that would have been useful for swimming but inconvenient for moving on land.

- *Acanthostega*'s **legs** were well-developed, with eight toes on the front feet and perhaps seven on the rear ones.

- **The number of toes** on its feet surprised palaeontologists – they had previously thought all tetrapods had five toes.

- **The legs and toes** would have helped *Acanthostega* give its body a thrusting motion when it swam. They would also aid movement through plants at the bottom of rivers and lakes in search of prey.

- *Acanthostega* **had a flattened skull** and its eye sockets were placed close together on the top of its head.

- **A complete but jumbled-up** *Acanthostega* fossil was discovered in hard rock in Greenland. Palaeontologists had to work very carefully to prise the fossil from the rock.

Great amphibians

- **The Carboniferous** and Early Permian Periods, from around 350–270 mya, are sometimes called the 'Age of Amphibians'.

- **At this time** the main large land animals were amphibian tetrapods, which evolved to become plant-eaters and carnivores.

- **Some of these amphibians** looked similar to later creatures such as crocodiles.

- **From the Middle Permian Period** the reptiles began to take over as the dominant land animals, and the tetrapod amphibians were restricted to more specialized habitats.

- **One of the strangest was** *Diplocaulus*, which had a wide, curved head shaped like a boomerang.

- *Diplocaulus* **was about one metre long** and lived during the Late Permian Period in North America and North Africa.

- **One of the last great amphibians** was *Koolasuchus*, which lived about 120 mya in the Early Cretaceous Period.

- **Its fossils come from the state of Victoria**, Australia. Other fossils found with them suggest a cool climate with plenty of streams and rivers.

- *Koolasuchus* **was similar** to crocodiles and very large, up to 5 m long and weighing half a tonne.

▶ *The strange head of* Diplocaulus *may have worked like a hydrofoil or 'water-wing' to give front-end lift while swimming forwards.*

Eyrops

- **One of the toughest-looking** amphibian tetrapods was *Eyrops*, whose name means 'long face'.

- *Eryops* **lived in the Early Permian Period** some 295 mya, and was one of the biggest animals on land at that time.

- **Fossils of** *Eryops* have been found in various sites across North America, especially the southwest.

- **In particular the thick, heavy skull** bones have left many well-preserved fossils.

- *Eryops* **looked like** a combination of salamander and crocodile, and grew to about 2 m long and 100 kg in weight.

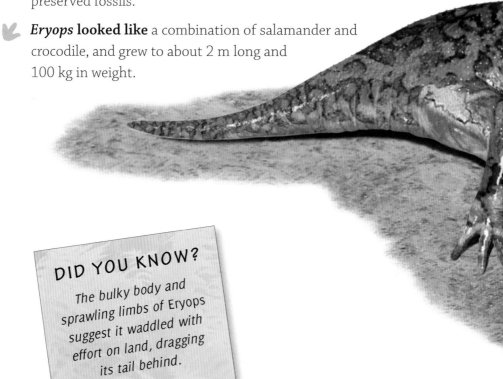

DID YOU KNOW?

The bulky body and sprawling limbs of Eryops suggest it waddled with effort on land, dragging its tail behind.

- **Eyes towards the top of its head** suggest *Eryops* lay on a river or lake bed, looking upwards for prey swimming past.

- **It would then lunge up** and bite the victim with its huge gaping mouth, armed with many sharp teeth.

- **In water it was probably** a powerful swimmer but not very speedy, due to its relatively short tail.

▼ *The skull of* Eryops *was relatively huge, more than 60 cm long, and the jaws were able to swallow large prey whole.*

75

Frogs and salamanders

- **Modern amphibians**, such as frogs, toads, salamanders and newts, all belong to the group called the lissamphibians.

- **Lissamphibians evolved later** than the early tetrapods, probably during the Late Permian Period (260 mya).

- *Triadobatrachus* **lived** in the Early Triassic Period in Madagascar, was 10 cm long and had a frog-like skull.

- **Compared to earlier amphibians**, *Triadobatrachus* had a shortened back with fewer spinal bones and a shortened tail.

- **Evolution did not stop** with *Triadobatrachus* – modern frogs have even fewer spinal bones and no tail.

- *Triadobatrachus'* **hind legs** were roughly the same size as its front legs. Again, this is different to modern frogs, which have long hind legs for hopping.

- **The first known salamanders** lived in the Middle Jurassic Period (174–163 mya) in China, Mongolia and Kazakhstan. They were about 20 cm long with a broad skull.

DID YOU KNOW?

Andrias scheuchzeri was a salamander from the Miocene Epoch (23–5 mya). It was named after the Swiss scientist Johannes Scheuchzer, who discovered it in 1726.

More modern-looking frog and salamander fossils have been discovered in Messel, Germany. They date from the Early Eocene Epoch (around 50 mya).

Some Messel frog fossils have their legs bent as if they were in mid-hop. There are even tadpole fossils from Messel.

▼ Triadobatrachus *was one of the earliest known frogs. Frogs and salamanders may be descendants of a group of amphibious temnospondyls known as dissorophids.*

First reptiles

- **Reptiles evolved** from amphibians during the Carboniferous Period (359–299 mya).

- **Unlike amphibians**, which usually live near and lay their eggs in water, reptiles are much more adapted for living on land.

- **Compared to amphibians**, reptiles had better limbs for walking, a more effective circulatory system for moving blood around their bodies, and bigger brains.

- **They also had more powerful** jaw muscles than amphibians and would have been better predators. Early reptiles ate millipedes, spiders and insects.

- **One of the earliest reptiles** was *Hylonomus,* a small creature that lived in the Late Carboniferous Period, 315–310 mya.

- *Hylonomus* **lived in forests** on the edges of lakes and rivers. Fossil remains of this reptile have been found inside the stumps of clubmoss trees.

- **Another early reptile** was *Paleothyris*. Like *Hylonomus*, it was about 20 cm long and had a smaller head than amphibians.

- **One animal that may represent** a staging post between reptiles and amphibians is *Westlothiana lizziae*, which was discovered in Scotland in the 1980s.

- *Westlothiana lizziae* lived in the Early Carboniferous Period (about 335 mya).

▲ Hylonomus, *meaning 'forest dweller', was one of the earliest reptiles. Fossil hunters discovered its remains in fossilized tree stumps at Joggins in Nova Scotia, Canada.*

At first, palaeontologists thought that *Westlothiana lizziae* was the oldest reptile. However, its backbone, head and legs more closely resemble those of an amphibian.

79

Eggs

Reptile eggs were a major evolutionary advance over amphibian eggs.

Early amphibians, like modern ones, laid their eggs in water. This is because their eggs were covered in jelly (like modern frogspawn) and would dry out on land.

Reptiles evolved eggs that were covered by a protective shell. This meant they could lay them on land and they would not dry out.

▲ Frogs lay their eggs in water in jelly-like clumps called spawn.

▲ A female snake protecting her eggs. Eggs laid on land are easier to protect than those laid in water.

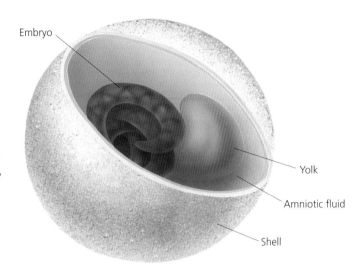

Embryo

Yolk

Amniotic fluid

Shell

▶ *Reptiles broke the link between reproduction and water by laying hard-shelled eggs on land. This snake shell contains the developing young (embryo), a food store (yolk) and a protective liquid (amniotic fluid).*

One advantage of shelled eggs was that reptiles did not have to return to water to lay them.

Another advantage was that reptiles could hide their eggs on land. Eggs laid in water are easy pickings for hungry animals.

Reptile embryos complete all their growth phases inside eggs. When they hatch they look like miniature adults.s

In contrast, baby amphibians hatch out of their eggs as larvae, such as tadpoles. They live in water and breathe through gills before they develop lungs and can live on land.

Reptile shells are hard and protect the growing embryos. The eggs also provide the embryos with food while they develop.

During the evolution from amphibians to reptiles, some tetrapods laid jelly-covered eggs on land.

A number of today's amphibians lay jelly-covered eggs on land, including some tropical frogs and mountain salamanders.

Skulls

- **The jaws of reptiles** are another feature that shows the evolutionary progression from amphibians.

- **Amphibian jaws** are designed to snap but not to bite together tightly.

- **In contrast**, reptiles had more jaw muscles and could press their jaws together more firmly. This meant they could break insect body casings and chew through tough plant stems.

- **By the Late Carboniferous Period** (about 300 mya), reptiles developed openings in their skulls behind the eye socket. These openings allowed room for more jaw muscles.

- **Four types of reptile skull** developed. Each belonged to a different type of reptile.

- **Anapsids had no openings** in their skull other than the eye sockets. Turtles and tortoises are anapsids.

- **Euryapsids had one opening** high up on either side of the skull. Sea reptiles such as ichthyosaurs and plesiosaurs were euryapsids, but this group has no surviving relatives.

- **Synapsids had one opening** low down on either side of the skull. Mammal-like reptiles and mammals are descended from this group.

- **Diapsids had two openings** on each side of the skull. Dinosaurs and pterosaurs were diapsids – so too are crocodiles, lizards, snakes and birds.

> **DID YOU KNOW?**
>
> Plants developed tough stems and leaves, spines and poisons to protect themselves from hungry reptiles.

▼ Varanosaurus *was a one metre-long synapsid* reptile that lived in North America in the Permian Period, about 280–260 mya. There are important similarities between the skulls of synapsid reptiles and mammals.

Synapsids

- **Synapsids were tetrapods** that had one opening on each side of the lower skull behind the eye socket, onto which their jaw muscles attached.

- **They appeared** in the Late Carboniferous Period (about 310 mya), and became the dominant land animals in the Permian Period (299–252 mya).

- **Synapsids are the ancestors** of mammals, which explains why they are sometimes described as 'mammal-like reptiles'.

- **The first synapsids** are called pelycosaurs. They were large, heavy-bodied animals that walked a bit like modern-day crocodiles.

- **The fierce meat-eater** *Dimetrodon* and the plant-eating *Edaphosaurus* – both of which had long, fan-like spines on their backs – were pelycosaurs.

- **Later synapsids** are called therapsids. The earliest therapsids had bigger skulls and jaws than pelycosaurs, as well as longer legs and shorter tails.

- **Later therapsids** are divided into two subgroups – dicynodonts and cynodonts. Dicynodont means 'two dog teeth' – cynodont means 'dog tooth'.

- **Dicynodonts were herbivores**. Most had round, hippopotamus-shaped bodies, and beaks that they used to cut plant stems.

- **Cynodonts were carnivores**. They used different teeth in their mouth for different tasks – for stabbing, nipping and chewing.

- **Some cynodonts** had whiskers and may even have been warm-blooded, like mammals.

▼ Diictodon *was a small mammal-like reptile that lived about 255 mya. A plant-eater and a burrower,* Diictodon *was an advanced form of a synapsid known as a dicynodont.*

Dimetrodon

- **Although dinosaur-like in appearance**, *Dimetrodon* was not a dinosaur – although it is often classed as a reptile.

- *Dimetrodon* **lived** in the Early–Middle Permian Period, 290–270 mya, and was one of the largest land animals of that time.

- **It is known from plentiful fossils** in the Permian 'Red Beds' of Texas, USA, which are mainly reddish sandstone.

- *Dimetrodon* **grew to 3 m long** and was a fierce predator with a large mouth lined with sharp teeth.

- **One of the strangest features** of *Dimetrodon* was its tall back sail, probably of skin and muscle.

- **The back sail extended** to a height of 2 m and would have had a very large surface area.

- **It was held up by** tall, thin rods of bone extending from the backbones or vertebrae, called neural spines.

- **The sail may have helped** *Dimetrodon* to warm up quickly by absorbing the sun's heat early in the morning as the reptile stood side-on to the rays.

- **It may also have had** colours and patterns, to scare enemies or attract mates for breeding.

▲ Dimetrodon *belonged to the pelycosaur subgroup of synapsids. Although dinosaur-like, it lived 40 million years before dinosaurs appeared.*

Crocodilians

The broad group
containing living
and extinct crocodiles,
Crocodylomorpha, appeared
in the Late Permian Period, about
260–255 mya.

The first true crocodiles appeared during
the Late Triassic Period (220–201 mya). They were
called protosuchians and lived in pools and rivers.

As its name suggests, *Protosuchus* was a protosuchian. It had
a short skull and sharp teeth, and would have looked quite like a
modern crocodile.

Other early crocodiles, such as *Terrestrisuchus*, looked less like
modern crocodiles.

Terrestrisuchus **had a short body** and long legs. Its name means
'land crocodile' because palaeontologists think it may have been
more at home on land than in water.

The next group of crocodilians to evolve were the
mesoeucrocodylians, which lived in the sea.

Metriorhynchus was a marine mesoeucrocodylian. It had flippers
instead of limbs and very sharp teeth for stabbing fish. It lived in
the Late Jurassic Period (around 160 mya).

🐾 **The subgroup called eusuchians** includes all modern crocodiles, alligators, gharials and caimans.

🐾 *Deinosuchus*, **from 80–75 mya**, was thought to be the largest-ever crocodile at 11 m in length, until a recent discovery of more *Sarcosuchus* fossils.

▼ *Fossils of* Protosuchus, *meaning 'first crocodile', have been discovered in Arizona, dating to around 200 mya. Although* Protosuchus *was similar to living crocodiles in many ways, its legs were much longer.*

DID YOU KNOW?

Modern crocodiles are living fossils. They look similar to the crocodiles that were alive 100 mya.

Sarcosuchus

- **The biggest-ever known crocodile** lived about 112 mya during the Early Cretaceous Period.

- **Its name *Sarcosuchus*** means 'flesh crocodile' and it would have been a massively powerful predator.

- ***Sarcosuchus* was about 12 m long**, which is twice the length of today's biggest reptile, the saltwater crocodile.

- **It was very bulky** and weighed close to 8 tonnes, more than five times heavier than the saltwater crocodile.

- **The skull was 1.8 m long**, and the jaws had more than 120 teeth, some as long as 17 cm.

- **The lifespan of *Sarcosuchus*** is estimated at more than 60 years.

- ***Sarcosuchus* fossils** have been found in North Africa in the Sahara desert.

- **Deserts may seem a strange habitat** for crocodiles, but at the time the Sahara had many rivers, swamps and lowlands.

- ***Sarcosuchus* would have preyed** on large dinosaurs that also lived in the area.

- **It probably attacked them** in the manner of today's crocodiles, seizing them as they came to the riverbank to drink.

▼ Sarcosuchus *would have preyed on iguanodon-like dinosaurs that thrived in the woods and swamps once covering the Sahara.*

Turtles and tortoises

▲ Proganochelys, *an early relation of modern turtles and tortoises, had a 60-cm-long shell, but it was unable to pull its head or legs inside.*

- **Turtles and tortoises** both have shells that cover and protect their bodies. They belong to a group of reptiles called chelonians.

- **Chelonian shells** evolved from belly ribs that grew outside of the body.

- **The earliest chelonian fossils** come from the Mid Triassic Period (220 mya). They have been found in Germany and Thailand.

- **One very early chelonian** was *Proganochelys*.

- *Proganochelys* **had a well-developed**, heavily-armoured shell, but palaeontologists think that it could not pull its head, legs or tail inside it.

- **The ability to pull the head**, legs and tail inside the shell is important for turtles and tortoises because it provides them with maximum protection.

DID YOU KNOW?

Turtles and tortoises evolved a toothless beak for slicing flesh or plants.

The protective shells of turtles and tortoises may have helped them survive at the end of the Cretaceous Period, 66 mya, when so many other reptiles became extinct.

Tortoises have bigger shells than turtles. This is because they are very slow-moving land creatures – unlike the swimming turtles – and need more protection.

A huge number and variety of turtle fossils have been discovered at Riversleigh in Australia, dating from the Miocene Epoch (23–5 mya).

▼ Archelon *fossils show that, at 4 m long, it was similar to, but much bigger than, modern leatherback turtles. Its front limbs were thinner and longer than its hind ones and were more useful in the water.*

93

Snakes

- **Snakes probably first appeared** 120–110 mya. *Dinilysia*, found in Argentina and from the Late Cretaceous Period, lived about 80 mya.

- **There are earlier** snake-like fossils, but palaeontologists generally think these were snake-like lizards and not true snakes.

- **The ancestors of snakes were lizards**. Palaeontologists think it would have been a varanid lizard, of which the modern monitor lizard is an example.

- **Snakes are an evolutionary triumph**. They are one of the few land-living animals to survive and flourish without limbs.

- **Compared to other reptiles**, snake fossils are rare. This is because snake bones are delicate and do not fossilize well.

- **Snakes evolved** into a huge variety of types from the Paleogene Period (66–23 mya). Today, there are more than 3400 snake species living in nearly every type of habitat.

- **The 50 million-year-old fossils** from Messel, Germany, include the well-preserved remains of a 2-m-long early python called *Palaeopython*.

- **Early snakes killed their prey** by squeezing it to death. Modern boas and pythons also use this method to kill.

- **Poisonous snakes**, such as vipers, adders and cobras, did not evolve until the Miocene Epoch (23–5 mya).

  ▶ Titanoboa *was the biggest known snake, up to 14 m long and weighing perhaps 1.2 tonnes. It lived in tropical forests around 60 mya in Colombia, South America, and may have hunted in water like today's bulkiest snake, the anaconda.*

DID YOU KNOW?

Snakes are one of the few reptiles groups that had their main evolutionary development after the time of the dinosaurs.

Placodonts

- **After adapting so well** to life on land, some groups of reptiles evolved into water-dwelling creatures.

- **Placodonts were early aquatic** (water-living) reptiles. They lived during the Triassic Period (about 252–201 mya).

- **The name placodont** means 'plate tooth'. These reptiles had large cheek teeth that worked like crushing plates.

- **Placodonts appeared** at about the same time as another group of aquatic reptiles called nothosaurs.

- **They had shorter**, sturdier bodies than the nothosaurs but, like them, they did not survive as a group for long.

- *Placodus* **was a placodont**. It had a stocky body, stumpy limbs and webbed toes for paddling. It may have had a fin on its tail.

- *Placodus* **probably used** its wide, flat teeth, which pointed outwards from its mouth, to prise shellfish off rocks or the seabed.

- *Psephoderma* was a turtle-like placodont. Its body was covered by a bony shell, which was in turn covered by hard horny plates.

- *Psephoderma* **also had** a horny beak, like a turtle's, and paddle-shaped limbs.

- *Henodus* **was another** turtle-like placodont. It also had a beak, which it probably used to grab molluscs from the seabed.

▶ Placodus *grew up to 2 m long and probably used its sticking-out front teeth to scrape up molluscs from the seabed. Its plate-like side teeth would then make short work of crunching the molluscs.*

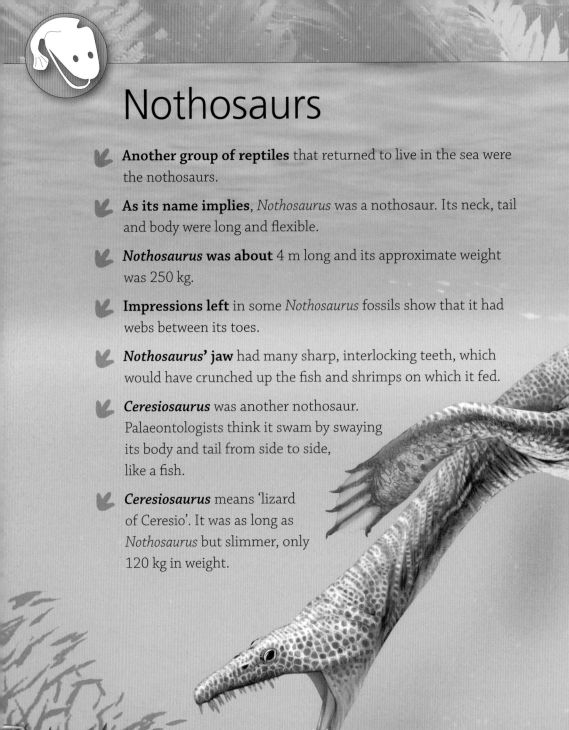

Nothosaurs

🐾 **Another group of reptiles** that returned to live in the sea were the nothosaurs.

🐾 **As its name implies**, *Nothosaurus* was a nothosaur. Its neck, tail and body were long and flexible.

🐾 *Nothosaurus* **was about** 4 m long and its approximate weight was 250 kg.

🐾 **Impressions left** in some *Nothosaurus* fossils show that it had webs between its toes.

🐾 *Nothosaurus'* **jaw** had many sharp, interlocking teeth, which would have crunched up the fish and shrimps on which it fed.

🐾 *Ceresiosaurus* was another nothosaur. Palaeontologists think it swam by swaying its body and tail from side to side, like a fish.

🐾 *Ceresiosaurus* means 'lizard of Ceresio'. It was as long as *Nothosaurus* but slimmer, only 120 kg in weight.

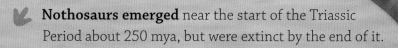

Nothosaurs emerged near the start of the Triassic Period about 250 mya, but were extinct by the end of it.

The place left by the extinct nothosaurs was taken by the plesiosaurs – another group of marine reptiles that were better adapted to life in the seas.

DID YOU KNOW?

Nothosaurus had nostrils on the top of its snout, which suggests that it came to the water's surface to breathe, like crocodiles.

▲ Nothosaurus *was an aquatic reptile that could use its webbed feet to move over land. The long-necked nothosaurs were probably the ancestors of plesiosaurs, many of which also had long necks.*

99

Plesiosaurs

🐾 **Plesiosaurs were marine reptiles** that were plentiful from the Late Triassic to the Late Cretaceous Periods (210–66 mya).

🐾 **They were better suited** to a marine lifestyle than nothosaurs or placodonts. Their limbs were fully-developed paddles, which propelled their short bodies quickly through the water.

🐾 **Many plesiosaurs** had a long, bendy neck. They had small heads with strong jaws and sharp teeth.

🐾 **These marine reptiles** had a diet that included fish, squid and probably pterosaurs (flying reptiles), which flew above the water in search of food.

🐾 **The first *Plesiosaurus* fossil** was discovered at Lyme Regis on the south coast of England by Mary Anning in the early 19th century. The fossil, which is in the Natural History Museum, London, is 2.3 m long.

🐾 ***Plesiosaurus* was not** a fast swimmer. It used its flipper-like limbs to move through the water but it had a weak tail that could not propel it forward very powerfully.

🐾 ***Elasmosaurus***, the longest plesiosaur, lived late in the Cretaceous Period, about 80 mya. It grew up to 14 m long and weighed up to 3 tonnes.

DID YOU KNOW?

The huge pliosaur Liopleurodon grew 10–12 m long and was one of the biggest sea animals of its time.

● **One group of plesiosaurs** were known as pliosaurs. They had much shorter necks and much larger heads, with huge jaws and enormous teeth.

● **Research suggests** that plesiosaurs may have caught their prey with quick, darting head movements.

▲ *Long-necked Elasmosaurus was one of the last of the plesiosaurs. It lived in a shallow sea that covered much of North America about 80 mya.*

Ichthyosaurs

- **Ichthyosaurs looked similar** to sharks, which are fish, and to later dolphins, which are mammals. When one type of animal comes to look like another, scientists call it convergent evolution.

- **Unlike plesiosaurs**, which relied on their paddles to propel them forwards, ichthyosaurs swayed their tails from side to side like fish.

- **Hundreds of complete skeletons** of the ichthyosaur *Ichthyosaurus* have been discovered. This reptile could grow up to 2 m long and weighed 90 kg.

- ***Ichthyosaurus* had very large ear bones**. It may have been able to pick up underwater vibrations caused by prey.

- **Some fossilized skeletons** of *Ichthyosaurus* and other ichthyosaurs were found with embryos inside. This shows that ichthyosaurs gave birth to live young, as opposed to laying eggs.

- **One of the largest ichthyosaurs** was *Shastasaurus*, which was over 20 m long and weighed perhaps 25 tonnes.

- **Ichthyosaurs were plentiful** in the Triassic and Jurassic Periods (252–145 mya), but became rarer in the Late Jurassic and Cretaceous Periods, dying out 66 mya.

- **Ichthyosaur means** 'fish lizard'.

- **Fossil hunters have found** ichthyosaur remains all over the world – in North and South America, Europe, Russia, India and Australia.

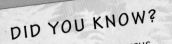

▼ *Fossil marine reptiles such as* Ichthyosaurus *created a sensation in the early 19th century, before dinosaurs were discovered. Ichthyosaurs had long, slim jaws to snap up fish and squid.*

Mosasaurs

- **Another group of large sea reptiles** was the mosasaurs. They appeared from about 140 mya at the time when ichthyosaurs were becoming less common.

- **Mosasaurs were diapsid reptiles** – a group that included dinosaurs and pterosaurs. Most other large sea reptiles belonged to another group – the euryapsids.

- **Unlike other** giant prehistoric sea reptiles, mosasaurs have living relatives. These include monitor lizards, such as the Komodo dragon.

- **The best known mosasaur** is *Mosasaurus*, which could grow up to 16 m long and 20 tonnes in weight.

- **The huge jaws of *Mosasaurus*** were lined with cone-shaped teeth, each of which had different cutting and crushing edges. They were the most advanced teeth of any marine reptile.

- **So distinctive** are *Mosasaurus* teeth that palaeontologists have identified its tooth marks on the fossils of other animals, in particular the giant turtle *Allopleuron*.

- **The jaws of a *Mosasaurus*** were discovered in a limestone mine in Maastricht, in the Netherlands, in the 1770s. The fossil disappeared in 1795 when the French invaded Maastricht, but later turned up in Paris.

- **At first, scientists thought** the jaws belonged either to a prehistoric whale or a crocodile, until they decided they were a giant lizard's.

▼ Mosasaurus *was a fast swimmer. It had an enormous tail and paddle-shaped limbs, which it probably used as rudders.*

Mosasaurus **means** 'lizard from the River Meuse' because it was discovered in Maastricht in the Netherlands, through which the River Meuse flows.

In 1998, more than 200 years after the discovery of the first *Mosasaurus* fossil, palaeontologists discovered the remains of another *Mosasaurus* in the same location – the St Pietersburg quarry in Maastricht.

Reptiles in the air

Reptile gliders

- **Only four groups of animals** have developed true powered, sustained, controlled flight – insects, pterosaurs, birds and bats.

- **But many kinds of animals** can swoop or glide in an effective way, although they cannot stay airborne for long.

- **The living lizard Draco** is called the 'flying dragon' although it glides rather than truly flies.

- **Some prehistoric reptiles** could glide and swoop in a similar way, including *Kuehneosaurus* and *Icarosaurus*.

- *Kuehneosaurus* **lived** in what is now England during the Late Triassic Period, some 210 mya.

- **It had bony ribs** sticking out from the sides of its body, which probably held out flaps of skin to work as a parachute.

- *Kuehneosaurus* **was about 70 cm long** and each 'wing' was up to 15 cm wide.

- *Icarosaurus* **was a similar** lizard-like reptile, but not a true lizard, from about 230 mya in North America.

- *Icarosaurus* **had much wider wings** in proportion to its smaller body, with a total length of 30 cm and wingspan of 25 cm.

- **Both of these gliders** probably leapt from trees to avoid enemies, landing some distance away.

▶ Kuehneosaurus *was slim and lightweight, with long legs to run and cushion its landing. It could probably change direction in the air and land on a tree trunk or branch as well as the ground.*

Xianglong

- **In prehistoric times** the reptile group contained several kinds of gliding, swooping members.

- **The only true lizard** that could do this was *Xianglong*, which translates as 'flying lizard' from Chinese.

- ***Xianglong* was an ancient relation** of the iguana group of lizards that still thrives today.

- **It was small**, about 15–25 cm long, with over half of its length made up by its tail – which it may have used to steer in the air.

- ***Xianglong*'s 'wings'** were flaps of skin on either side of its body, each held out by eight long, bony ribs.

- **Its total wingspan** was about 11 cm.

- ***Xianglong* lived some 125 mya** in the Chinese province of Liaoning, where many amazing detailed fossils have been unearthed.

- **Long, curved claws** show that it probably lived in trees, and jumped to glide away if menaced by predators.

- ***Xianglong* fossils are so detailed**, they even show impressions or 'prints' of the skin on its gliding wings.

DID YOU KNOW?

Calculations and computer models show that, given a suitable tall tree from which to take off, Xianglong may have glided up to 50 m.

▼ Fossil bones of Xianglong *suggest it may have grown to 25 cm in length with a wingspan of up to 20 cm.*

Rhamphorhynchoids

- **The earliest pterosaurs** (flying reptiles) were the rhamphorhynchoids. They first appeared in the Mid–Late Triassic Period (around 230–220 mya).

- **Rhamphorhynchoids had long tails** that ended in a diamond-shaped vane, like a rudder. Their tails gave them stability in flight, which meant they could soar and swoop effectively.

- **One of the first rhamphorhynchoids** – and first flying vertebrates – was *Peteinosaurus*.

- **Well-preserved fossils** of *Peteinosaurus* have been found near Cene, Bergamo in Italy.

- **They reveal** *Peteinosaurus'* sharp, cone-like teeth and suggest it ate insects that it caught in the air.

- **In contrast**, another early rhamphorhynchoid, *Eudimorphodon*, had fangs at the front of its mouth and smaller spiked ones behind. This suggests that it ate fish.

- *Dimorphodon* was a later rhamphorhynchoid from the Early Jurassic Period (201–174 mya). It had a huge head that looked a bit like a puffin's.

- *Rhamphorhynchus* was one of the later rhamphorhynchoids, appearing in the Late Jurassic Period (about 160 mya).

▼ Dimorphodon *had a wingspan of about 1.5 m and a body length of 1 m. Palaeontologists think that it lived and hunted along seashores and rivers.*

DID YOU KNOW?

Fossil hunters have found Rhamphorhynchus fossils alongside those of the early bird Archaeopteryx in Solnhofen, Germany.

Darwinopterus

- **Darwinopterus is a relatively** recent pterosaur discovery from China. It was named 'Darwin's wing' in 2010 after famous naturalist Charles Darwin (1809–1882).

- **Darwinopterus dates towards** the end of the Jurassic Period, about 160 mya.

- **Its fossils were found** in northwest China, along with those of many other animals and plants, showing the habitat at the time.

- **Darwinopterus shows** in-between features of the two main groups of pterosaurs, the rhamphorhynchoids and the pterodactyls.

- **Its long, trailing tail** probably acted as a stabilizer and rudder to steer in mid air.

- **However, it also had teeth**, skull and backbones similar to the later, more advanced pterodactyls. Rhamphorhynchoids also had this feature.

- **Darwinopterus even had signs** of a bony head crest, another pterodactyl feature.

- **In this respect** Darwinopterus is regarded as a possible 'missing link', or transitional form, between the two groups.

- **Darwinopterus was about one metre** long in total, with the skull taking up 20 cm.

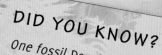

DID YOU KNOW?

One fossil Darwinopterus was found with a preserved egg, which probably had a shell like soft card or parchment, like many other reptiles.

◀ Darwinopterus, *shown here swooping on feathered dinosaur Anchiornis, had the beginnings of a bony crest on its upper snout.*

Later pterosaurs

- **Pterodactyls are a later group** of pterosaurs (flying reptiles) than the rhamphorhynchoids.

- **They lived in the Late Jurassic** through to the Late Cretaceous Periods (about 160–66 mya).

- **Although pterodactyls** lacked the long, stabilizing tail of rhamphorhynchoids, they were probably more effective fliers and able to make quicker turns in the air.

- **These later pterosaurs** were also much lighter than rhamphorhynchoids because their bones were hollow.

- **The pterodactyl *Pterodactylus*** and the rhamphorhynchoid *Rhamphorhynchus* were roughly the same size, but *Pterodactylus* weighed between 1–5 kg, while *Rhamphorhynchus* was heavier at about 10 kg.

- **Some of the largest pterodactyls**, such as *Pteranodon*, appeared in the Late Cretaceous Period and had wingspans of over 5 m.

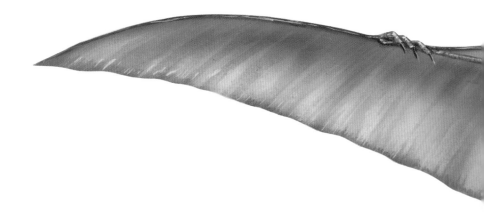

- **Unlike earlier flying reptiles**, *Pteranodon* had no teeth. Instead, it used its long, thin beak to scoop up fish.

- **At the bottom** of its mouth *Pteranodon* had a pelican-like pouch – it probably used this to store fish before swallowing them.

- ***Pteranodon* weighed** over 20 kg. This was heavier than earlier pterodactyls and suggests it was probably a glider rather than an active flyer.

- **A long crest** on *Pteranodon's* head may have worked as a rudder during flight.

◀ *The largest type of* Pteranodon *had a wingspan of more than 6 m. It lived about 88–80 million years ago, feeding on fish that lived in the shallow seas that then covered much of North America.*

Guidraco

- *Guidraco* **was named in 2012** from fossils found in northeast China, in Liaoning Province.

- **This pterodactyl-like pterosaur** lived around 120 mya during the Early Cretaceous Period.

- *Guidraco* **had a mouth full** of extraordinary long, fang-like teeth which were different in shape along the jaws.

- **The foremost teeth** were longest and stuck out forwards.

- **The next few teeth were also long** and curved back, like a snake's fangs.

- **The teeth then become smaller** towards the back of the mouth and the jaw joint.

- *Guidraco* **had a very large wingspan** of over 4 m, more than any bird today.

- **It also had a tall crest** on top of its head.

- **The name** *Guidraco* means 'bad spirit' or 'malicious spectre'.

▶ Guidraco *had teeth ideal for grabbing slippery fish and squid, and a long flexible neck so its head could dart to and fro.*

DID YOU KNOW?

Guidraco probably caught fish by swooping down to the water's surface and snapping its mouth closed to form a 'basket' with the teeth.

Giant pterosaurs

- **The largest flying animals** that ever lived were the great pterosaurs from the end of the Cretaceous Period, around 80–66 mya.

- **One of the largest was** *Quetzalcoatlus*, named in honour of the feathered serpent god from mythical times in Southern North America and Central America.

- *Quetzalcoatlus* **is estimated** to have a wingspan of at least 10 m, and perhaps more than 12 m.

- **Previous wingspan estimates went to 20 m** or more, but these have been reduced as more fossils have been uncovered.

- *Quetzalcoatlus* **dates** from the very end of the Cretaceous Period, about 72–66 mya.

- **Its fossils come from North America**, but because pterosaurs had such light, fragile bones, the fossils are scarce and fragmentary.

- **Studies of the wings and legs** of *Quetzalcoatlus* now suggest it stalked across the land on all fours, pecking at small victims with its enormously long, toothless beak.

- **Another giant pterosaur** was *Hatzegopteryx*, from Transylvania, Romania.

- **Its remains are also very scarce** but they may show even bigger wings spanning more than 13 m.

▶ Quetzalcoatlus *could probably soar and glide long distances to reach suitable feeding areas, then return to its sheltered roost at night.*

DID YOU KNOW?

Quetzalcoatlus was once thought to swoop down like a vast vulture to feed on the carcasses of dead dinosaurs and other big animals.

121

Dinosaurs

Age of Dinosaurs

🦖 **The Age of Dinosaurs** corresponds to the time period that geologists call the Mesozoic Era, from about 252–66 mya.

🦖 **The Mesozoic Era** is divided into three shorter time spans – the Triassic, Jurassic and Cretaceous Periods.

🦖 **In the Triassic Period**, 252–201 mya, the dinosaurs began to evolve.

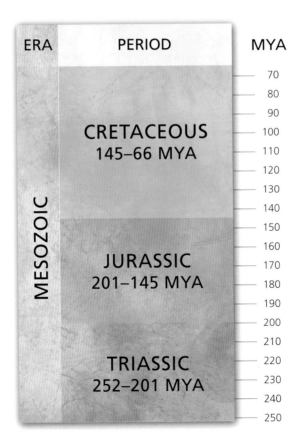

ERA	PERIOD	MYA
		70
		80
		90
	CRETACEOUS 145–66 MYA	100
		110
		120
		130
MESOZOIC		140
		150
		160
	JURASSIC 201–145 MYA	170
		180
		190
		200
		210
	TRIASSIC 252–201 MYA	220
		230
		240
		250

◀ Dinosaurs ruled the land for 185 million years – longer than any other animal group.

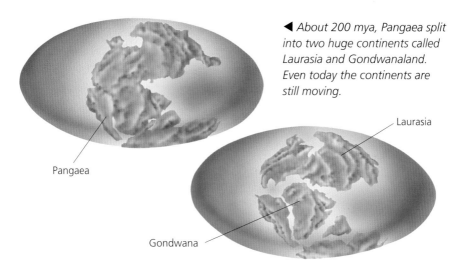

◀ About 200 mya, Pangaea split into two huge continents called Laurasia and Gondwanaland. Even today the continents are still moving.

Laurasia

Pangaea

Gondwana

During the Jurassic Period – about 201–145 mya – many dinosaurs reached their greatest size.

The Cretaceous Period is when dinosaurs were at their most varied – about 145–66 mya.

All through the Mesozoic Era, and before and since, the major landmasses gradually moved across the globe in a process known as continental drift.

In the Triassic Period, all the continents were joined as one supercontinent – Pangaea.

In the Jurassic Period, Pangaea separated into two huge landmasses – Laurasia in the north and Gondwana in the south.

In the Cretaceous Period, Laurasia and Gondwana split, and the continents began to take the positions we know now.

The joining and separating of the continents affected which kinds of dinosaurs lived where.

Archosaurs

- **Archosaurs were a large group** of reptiles that included the dinosaurs as one of their subgroups.

- **Other archosaur subgroups** included flying pterosaurs, crocodiles, and birds – since birds evolved from dinosaurs.

- **Pseudosuchians are living crocodilians** as were the lesser-known reptile group, the ornithosuchians, which were closely related to them but are now all extinct.

- **A dinosaur-like ornithosuchian** was *Ornithosuchus*, which gave its name to this group.

- **Four-metre-long** *Ornithosuchus* could stand almost upright and was probably a powerful predator.

- ***Ornithosuchus* fossils** have been found in Scotland.

▼ Ornithosuchus *had a mix of features, both non-dinosaur (hips and back plates) and dinosaur (legs and skull).*

Features in *Ornithosuchus'* backbone, hips and feet indicate that it was not quite a dinosaur, but still an archosaur.

Some experts classify *Archosaurus* from the Permian Period as one of the first archosaurs, while others disagree.

◀ *Crocodilians, like this hatchling, are living members of the great archosaur group of reptiles.*

127

Inventing the dinosaur

When fossils of dinosaurs were first studied by scientists in the 1820s, they were thought to be from huge lizards, rhinoceroses or even whales.

The first dinosaur to be officially named in 1824 was *Megalosaurus*, by Englishman William Buckland.

Fossils of dinosaurs were found and studied in 1822 by Gideon Mantell, a doctor in Sussex, southern England.

In 1825, Mantell named the creature *Iguanodon*, because its teeth were very similar in shape to, but larger than, the teeth of the iguana lizard.

In the late 1830s, British scientist Richard Owen realized that some fossils did not belong to lizards, but to an as yet unnamed group of reptiles.

In 1841–42, Richard Owen invented a new name for the group of giant prehistoric reptiles – Dinosauria.

The name 'dinosaur' means 'terrible lizard/reptile'.

Life-sized models of several dinosaurs were made by British sculptor Waterhouse Hawkins in 1852–54.

Hawkins' models were displayed at the Crystal Palace Exhibition in London, and caused a public sensation.

▼ Megalosaurus *was the first dinosaur to be given an official scientific name, even though the term 'dinosaur' had not yet been invented.*

DID YOU KNOW?

The three main dinosaurs of the newly named Dinosauria in the 1840s were Iguanodon, meat-eater Megalosaurus and the nodosaur Hylaeosaurus.

Ancestors

- **Experts have many opinions** about which group (or groups) of reptiles were the ancestors of the dinosaurs.

- **Very early dinosaurs** walked and ran on their strong back limbs, so their ancestors probably did the same.

- **One group name** for the dinosaurs' ancestors was the thecodonts, or 'socket-toothed', but this is no longer regarded as a true scientific grouping.

- **However there are several kinds** of small, slim, bipedal (walking on back legs), sharp-toothed reptiles that could show what the dinosaurs' ancestors looked like.

- *Largerperton*, 70 cm long, lived about 240 mya in Argentina, South America.

- *Marasuchus* was a similar creature but even smaller, less than 50 cm in length, also from Argentina.

- *Lagosuchus* was another small predator about 30 cm long from the same area, although it may have been the same as *Marasuchus*.

- *Euparkeria* from South Africa dates from 235 mya, but its rear legs were not as well developed.

DID YOU KNOW?
The earliest known dinosaurs came from South America, so their ancestors probably did, too.

▶ Euparkeria, or 'Parker's good animal', was named in 1913. It was about 60 cm in total length, slim and agile, and resembled the creatures from which dinosaurs probably evolved.

Earliest dinosaurs

- **The first dinosaurs** had appeared about 230 mya, in the Middle Triassic Period.

- **These dinosaurs** were small-to-medium meat-eaters with sharp teeth and claws. They ran quickly on their two longer, stronger back legs.

- **Fossils of *Herrerasaurus*** date from 230 mya and were found near San Juan in Argentina, South America.

- ***Herrerasaurus* was about** 3–5 m in total length, and probably weighed some 200–250 kg.

- **Perhaps slightly earlier**, about 231 mya, and in the same place as *Herrerasaurus*, there lived a similar-shaped dinosaur named *Eoraptor*, which was only 1–1.5 m long and weighed 10 kg.

- **The name *Eoraptor*** means 'dawn plunderer' or 'early thief'.

- ***Staurikosaurus*** was a meat-eater similar to *Herrerasaurus*. It is known to have lived around 225 mya, in present-day Brazil, South America.

DID YOU KNOW?

Eoraptor and Herrerasaurus hunted small animals such as lizards, insects and lizard-like reptiles.

Procompsognathus **was another** early meat-eater. It lived 210 mya in the Late Triassic Period in Germany.

Pisanosaurus **lived in Argentina** in the Late Triassic Period, and was only one metre long. It may have been a plant-eater.

▼ *The very early meat-eater* Herrerasaurus *dates to about 230 mya. The discovery of an almost complete skeleton in 1988 allowed a good reconstruction.*

133

Eodromaeus

- **Eodromaeus was another** of several small, bipedal (walking on two legs) dinosaurs from early in their time.

- **Its fossils were discovered** in Argentina in 1996, and at first they were thought to be from the similar *Eoraptor*.

- **More studies showed** they were a different dinosaur, which was named *Eodromaeus*, meaning 'dawn runner', in 2011.

- **Eodromaeus lived** about 230 mya during the early part of the Late Triassic Period, making it one of the earliest known dinosaurs.

- **It was quite small**, with a nose-tail length of 1.2 m. It was slim too, weighing 4–6 kg.

- **Its rear legs were much larger**, longer and stronger than the front ones, which were more like arms.

- **This body build indicates** a fast, nimble creature that could dart and zigzag away from bigger predators.

DID YOU KNOW?

Eodromaeus and similar fossils were found in Ischigualasto Park's Valle de la Luna, 'Valley of the Moon', named from its strange, stark, unearthly rock formations.

▲ The skull of *Eodromaeus* has widely gaping jaws, with the jaw joint at the rear, and small sharp teeth suited to eating bugs and worms.

The top speed of *Eodromaeus* is estimated at anywhere between 25 and 40 km/h.

Like *Eoraptor*, *Eodromaeus* probably snapped up small bugs, worms and little reptiles.

Coelophysis

- *Coelophysis* **was a small, agile dinosaur** that lived early in the Age of Dinosaurs, about 220–200 mya.

- **A huge collection** of *Coelophysis* fossils was found in the 1940s, at a place called Ghost Ranch, New Mexico, USA.

- **Hundreds of *Coelophysis*** were preserved together at Ghost Ranch – possibly a herd that drowned in a flood.

- *Coelophysis* **was almost 3 m** in total length. Its slim, lightweight build meant that it probably weighed only 15–25 kg.

- *Coelophysis* **belonged** to the group of mostly meat-eating dinosaurs known as theropods. It probably ate small animals such as insects, worms and lizards.

- **Long, powerful back legs** allowed *Coelophysis* to run fast.

- **The front limbs** were like arms, each with a hand bearing three large, strong, sharp-clawed fingers to grab prey, and one small, non-functional finger.

The bird-like skull was filled with small, sharp teeth.

Coelophysis means 'hollow form'. It was so-named because some of its bones were hollow, like the bones of birds, making it lightly built.

▲ Coelophysis *would have stood almost waist-high to a person as it darted about on its long back legs.*

Dilophosaurus

- *Dilophosaurus* **was** a large meat-eating theropod dinosaur that lived about 195–190 mya.

- **Fossils of** *Dilophosaurus* were found in Arizona, USA, and possibly other parts of the USA.

- **The fossils in Arizona** were discovered by Jesse Williams, a Navajo Native American, in 1942.

- **Studying the fossils** proved very difficult, and the dinosaur was not given its official name until 1970.

- *Dilophosaurus* **measured** about 6–7 m from its nose to the end of its very long tail.

- **The name** *Dilophosaurus* means 'two ridged reptile', from the two thin, rounded, bony crests on its head, each shaped like half a dinner plate.

- **The crests were too thin** and fragile to be used as weapons for head-butting.

- **Brightly coloured skin** may have covered the head crests, as a visual display to rivals or enemies.

▼ Dilophosaurus *is one of the first big, powerful, predatory dinosaurs known from fossil evidence.*

DID YOU KNOW?
Dilophosaurus probably weighed over 500 kg – as much as the biggest polar bears today.

Eustreptospondylus

- **Eustreptospondylus was a large meat-eater** that lived in present-day Oxfordshire and Buckinghamshire, in England. It lived about 165–160 mya.

- **In the 1870s**, a fairly complete skeleton of a young *Eustreptospondylus* was found near Oxford, but was named as *Megalosaurus*, the only other big meat-eater known from the region.

- **In 1964**, British fossil expert Alick Walker showed that the Oxford dinosaur was not *Megalosaurus*, and gave it a new name, *Eustreptospondylus*.

- **A full-grown *Eustreptospondylus*** measured about 6 m in length and is estimated to have weighed over 400 kg, although the Oxford specimen was only part-grown.

- **In its enormous mouth**, *Eustreptospondylus* had a great number of small, sharp teeth.

- ***Eustreptospondylus*** may have hunted sauropods such as *Cetiosaurus* and stegosaurs, two groups of dinosaurs that roamed the region at the time.

DID YOU KNOW?

Eustreptospondylus means 'well-curved backbone'. This is due to the arrangement of its spine as seen in its fossils.

▼ *The fossils of* Eustreptospondylus *were found with those of sea creatures, suggesting it may have hunted along the seashore. This medium-sized theropod weighed about the same as two very large lions.*

Sciurimimus

- **The name *Sciurimimus*** means 'squirrel mimic' and was given to this dinosaur in 2012.

- **The name comes from the tail** of this dinosaur, which has filament-like or fibre-like feathers along its length – reminiscent of a squirrel's bushy tail.

- **Only one fossil of *Sciurimimus*** is known to date, from Bavaria, southwest Southern Germany.

- **The fossil is in fine-grained limestone** dated to the Late Jurassic Period, some 150 mya.

- **The fossilized remains** are very detailed, showing up fine features such as the tail feathers.

- **Details of the bones** show that this specimen of *Sciurimimus* was a juvenile, not yet fully grown.

- **The nose-tail length** of the *Sciurimimus* fossil is 70 cm, but the dinosaur could have been over one metre long when adult.

- ***Sciurimimus* had small sharp teeth** and probably preyed on small creatures such as insects.

- **Although *Sciurimimus* had feathers**, it was not related to the main groups of bird-like feathered dinosaurs – showing that feather-like coverings evolved in widely separate kinds of dinosaurs.

▼ *The fast-moving, agile dinosaur* Sciurimimus *lived at about the same time, and in the same region, as the early bird* Archaeopteryx.

Baryonyx

- ***Baryonyx* was a large meat-eating dinosaur** that lived about 130 mya.

- **The first fossil find** of *Baryonyx* was its huge thumb claw, discovered in Surrey, England, in 1983.

- **The total length** of *Baryonyx* was 9–10 m.

- ***Baryonyx* had a slim build** and a long, narrow tail, and probably weighed less than 2 tonnes.

The **snout was unusual** for a meat-eating dinosaur because it was very long and narrow – similar to today's slim-snouted crocodiles.

The **teeth were long** and slim, especially at the front of the mouth.

The **general similarities** between *Baryonyx* and a crocodile suggest that *Baryonyx* may have been a fish-eater.

It may have lurked in swamps or close to rivers, darting its head forward on its long, flexible neck to snatch fish.

The **massive thumb claw**, which measured 35 cm in length, may have been used to hook fish or amphibians from the water.

The **dinosaur was named** after this outsized feature – the name *Baryonyx* means 'heavy claw'.

◀ *Fossils of* Baryonyx *were found with the remains of fish scales, suggesting this dinosaur was a semi-aquatic fish catcher.*

Allosaurus

- **A big meat-eater**, *Allosaurus* was almost the same size as *Tyrannosaurus*. It lived about 155–150 mya, during the Late Jurassic Period.

- *Allosaurus* **was up to 11–12 m** in total length and its weight is variously estimated between 1.5 and 4 tonnes.

- **The head** was almost one metre in length, but its skull was light, with large gaps, or 'windows', that would have been covered by muscle and skin.

- **Not only could** *Allosaurus* open its jaws in a huge gape, it could also flex them so that the whole mouth became wider, for an even bigger bite.

- **Most** *Allosaurus* **fossils** come from the states in the American Midwest, especially Utah, Colorado and Wyoming.

- *Allosaurus* **may have hunted** giant sauropod dinosaurs such as *Diplodocus*, *Camarasaurus* and *Brachiosaurus*.

- **Fossils similar to** *Allosaurus* were identified in Europe and Africa, and a smaller 'dwarf' version was found in Australia.

DID YOU KNOW?

The remains of 60 Allosaurus were found in the Cleveland-Lloyd Dinosaur Quarry, Utah, USA.

▲ Allosaurus *almost rivalled*
Tyrannosaurus *in size, but lived*
90 million years earlier.

Carnotaurus

- **The big, powerful, meat-eating** *Carnotaurus* belongs to the theropod dinosaur group. It lived about 75–70 mya.

- *Carnotaurus* **fossils** come mainly from the Chubut region of Argentina, South America.

- **A medium-sized dinosaur,** *Carnotaurus* was about 8–9 m in total length and weighed over one tonne.

- **The skull was relatively tall** from top to bottom and short from front to back, compared to other meat-eaters such as *Allosaurus* and *Tyrannosaurus*. This gave *Carnotaurus* a snub-snouted appearance.

- **The name** *Carnotaurus* means 'meat-eating bull', referring partly to its bull-like face.

- *Carnotaurus* **had** two cone-shaped bony crests, or 'horns', one above each eye.

- **Rows of extra-large scales**, like small lumps, ran along *Carnotaurus* from head to tail.

- **Like** *Tyrannosaurus*, *Carnotaurus* had small front limbs that could not reach its mouth and may have had no use.

- *Carnotaurus* **probably ate** plant-eating dinosaurs such as *Chubutisaurus*, although its teeth and jaws were not especially big or strong.

▼ *The first, and so far only, fossil remains of Carnotaurus were discovered in 1984 and the dinosaur was named in 1985. It had small pebble-like scales embedded in its skin.*

Yutyrannus

🐾 **Named in 2012**, *Yutyrannus* or 'feathered tyrant' is a large predator dinosaur in the same group as the great *Tyrannosaurus*.

🐾 **However, it lived** almost 60 million years earlier than *Tyrannosaurus*, about 125 mya, in what is now northwest China.

🐾 *Yutyrannus* **was almost 9 m long** and could have weighed more than 1.5 tonnes.

🐾 **It is the biggest dinosaur** so far that has feathers preserved with its fossil bones and teeth.

🐾 **The feathers were slim**, flexible filaments, some more than 15 cm long.

🐾 **Different specimens** of *Yutyrannus* have feathers on different parts of the body, so taking them all together, the filaments could have covered most of the dinosaur.

🐾 **The skull of the largest** *Yutyrannus* specimen is almost one metre long.

It also has a small 'horn' above each eye, like several other tyrannosaur-group dinosaurs.

Like its relatives, *Yutyrannus* was a powerful predator with a huge mouth and many sharp teeth.

◀ Yutyrannus *lived in a region that was quite cool 125 mya, so its hair-like or plume-like feathers may have helped to control its body temperature.*

Tyrannosaurus

- **Tyrannosaurus is not only** one of the most famous dinosaurs, it is also one about which a great deal is known. Several discoveries have revealed fossilized bones, teeth and whole skeletons.

- **Tyrannosaurus lived** at the end of the Age of Dinosaurs, about 68–66 mya. It was 12 m long and weighed 7 tonnes.

- **Its full name** is *Tyrannosaurus rex*, which means 'king of the tyrant reptiles'.

- **The head** was 1.2 m long and had more than 50 dagger-like teeth, some longer than 15 cm.

- **Tyrannosaurus fossils** have been found at many sites in North America, including Alberta and Saskatchewan in Canada, and Colorado, Wyoming, Montana and New Mexico in the USA.

- **The arms and hands** of *Tyrannosaurus* were so small that they could not pass food to its mouth, and may have had no use at all.

- **Recent fossil finds** of a group of *Tyrannosaurus* include youngsters, suggesting that they may have lived as families in small herds or packs.

- **Tyrannosaurus may have been** an active hunter, pounding along with long strides after its fleeing prey, or it may have been a skulking scavenger that ambushed old and sickly victims.

- **Until the 1990s**, *Tyrannosaurus* was known as the biggest meat-eating dinosaur, and the biggest meat-eating animal ever to walk the Earth, but its size record was broken by *Giganotosaurus* and then *Spinosaurus*.

▼ *Tyrannosaurus' massive, powerful rear legs contrasted greatly with its puny front limbs or 'arms'. As it ran, its thick-based tail balanced its horizontal body and the head, which was held low. The rear feet were enormous, each set of three toes supporting some 3–4 tonnes.*

Carcharodontosaurus

- **Carcharodontosaurus** was one of the biggest meat-eating dinosaurs and land predators ever, rivalling *Tyrannosaurus* and similar types.

- **Some of its fossils** are very detailed, with the cavity inside the skull showing the shape of the dinosaur's brain, including the parts dealing with sight and smell.

- **Carcharodontosaurus'** teeth were about 20 cm long and triangular in shape.

- **The whole dinosaur** was about 13 m in total length and very powerfully built, with a weight of perhaps 10 tonnes.

- **Putting together** several specimen finds shows the skull was up to 1.7 m long.

- **Carcharodontosaurus lived** in North Africa about 100–95 mya, when the region had rivers, lakes, swamps and forests.

- **Its first fossils were dug up** in 1925, but more, larger specimens unearthed in the 1990s showed its true size.

- **Carcharodontosaurus belonged** to the group known as Carnosauria, which used to include all kinds of big meat-eaters but has recently been restricted to just a few kinds.

A cousin of *Carcharodontosaurus* may have been *Allosaurus* from North America, which lived about 50 million years before and was almost as large.

DID YOU KNOW?

Carcharodontosaurus was named 'ragged tooth reptile' after the great white shark, Carcharodon carcharias, due to similar jagged serrations along the tooth edges.

◀ Carcharodontosaurus *was not the largest predator of its time and place, since the even greater* Spinosaurus *roamed the same region some 100 mya.*

155

Mapusaurus

- *Mapusaurus* **is in the top ten** of giant meat-eating dinosaurs.

- **Fossils from parts** of several individuals were excavated from 1997 at Cañadón del Gato, Neuquén Province, Argentina.

- **The rocks containing** *Mapusaurus* fossils are around 95 million years old.

- **More than 170 bones** and parts of bones have been recovered, from up to nine different individuals of different sizes.

- **The main fossils suggest** *Mapusaurus* was at least 10 m long, and clues from larger bone fragments could make the length 13 m and weight over 8 tonnes.

- *Mapusaurus* **was probably related** to another great predator, *Giganotosaurus*, from the same area and a similar time span.

- **Close inspection of the fossils** showed that some individuals had been injured, with their bones mending, while other bones revealed signs of being infected.

- **The science of studying injuries** and diseases in prehistoric animals and plants is known as paleoepidemiology.

- **Finding remains of so many individuals** together could indicate *Mapusaurus*, whose name means 'earth lizard', lived and perhaps even hunted in groups.

▲ Mapusaurus *lived in a region that was generally dry, but with seasonal flood streams that probably attracted large prey to drink at waterholes.*

Giganotosaurus

- **In 1994** there was great news that remains of a meat-eating dinosaur even bigger than *Tyrannosaurus* had been found in Patagonia, in the south of Argentina.

- **The new find** was named as *Giganotosaurus*, 'giant southern lizard'.

- **The length of *Giganotosaurus*** was estimated at up to 13 m, and the weight between 8 and 10 tonnes.

- **The skull was at first said to be** 1.8 m in length, although this was then reduced to 1.6 m. It is still one of the most massive skulls of any dinosaur.

- **The remains of *Giganotosaurus*** were first noticed by Rubén Carolini, a local vehicle mechanic who went fossil-hunting in his spare time.

- **Its full name is *Giganotosaurus carolinii***, in honour of its discoverer.

- **Carolini went on to become** Director of the Villa El Chocón Municipal Museum, which celebrates his enormous find.

- **The main *Giganotosaurus* find** was an exceptional specimen, almost three-quarters complete.

- ***Giganotosaurus* lived** around 100–95 mya.

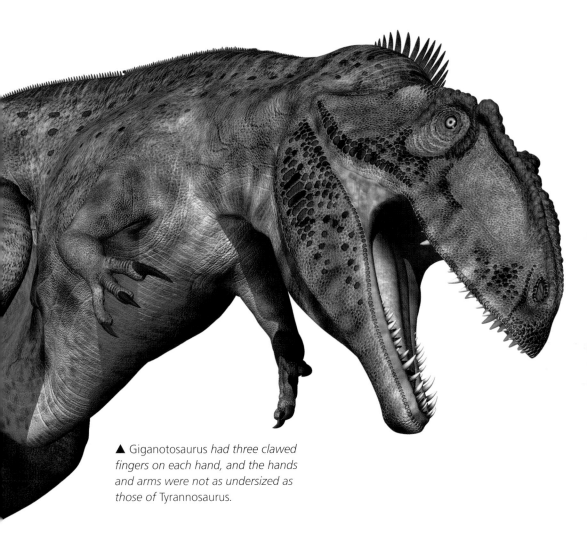

▲ Giganotosaurus *had three clawed
fingers on each hand, and the hands
and arms were not as undersized as
those of* Tyrannosaurus.

 Not far away, the fossils of the colossal plant-eater
Argentinosaurus were located, which lived around the same time –
perhaps a victim of *Giganotosaurus*?

159

Spinosaurus

- **No other meat-eating dinosaur**, or any other land-based carnivore, found so far is as big as *Spinosaurus*.

- **This immense predator** has been known for over 100 years, but new finds in the 1990s and 2000s showed that it was the new record-holder.

- **The original *Spinosaurus* fossils** came from Egypt in 1912. They were named in 1915 by German palaeontologist Ernst von Stromer.

- **However those fossils**, kept in Munich Museum, Germany, were destroyed in 1944 by a World Ward II bombing raid. In 1996, 1998, 2000, 2002 and 2005, more fossils in North Africa were uncovered and identified as *Spinosaurus*.

- **This giant was probably** more than 14 m long and weighed over 9 tonnes, perhaps 15.

- **It had tall rods** of bone along its back called neural spines, that probably held up a sail-like area of skin, or perhaps a hump of flesh.

- ***Spinosaurus* and other finds** led to a new group of huge hunting dinosaurs being identified, the spinosaurs, which also included *Giganotosaurus*, *Carcharodontosaurus*, *Baryonyx*, *Oxalaia* and *Suchomimus*.

▶ *The skull and jaws of* Spinosaurus *were long and low, similar in shape to a crocodile and alligator and also to the medium-sized dinosaur* Baryonyx.

Ornitholestes

- *Ornitholestes* was a smallish meat-eater from the theropod dinosaur group.

- The name *Ornitholestes* means 'bird robber' – experts who studied its fossils in the early 1900s imagined it chasing and killing the earliest birds.

- The home of *Ornitholestes* was actually in present-day Wyoming in the USA – a continent away from the earliest birds in Europe.

- Only one specimen of *Ornitholestes* has been found. Parts of a hand at another site have been assigned to a different dinosaur.

- *Ornitholestes* was about 2 m long from nose to tail and probably weighed about 12–15 kg.

- The teeth were small and well-spaced, but also slim and sharp, well suited to grabbing small animals for food.

DID YOU KNOW?

According to some experts, Ornitholestes may have had a slight ridge or crest on its nose. Other experts disagree.

Ornitholestes *had very strong arms* and hands with powerful fingers and long claws – ideal for grabbing baby dinosaurs newly hatched from their eggs.

▼ Ornitholestes *relied on speed and its good senses of sight and smell for survival.*

163

Oviraptor

- *Oviraptor* **was an unusual meat-eater** from the theropod dinosaur group. It lived during the Late Cretaceous Period, about 75 mya.

- **Its fossils were found** in the Omnogov region of the Gobi Desert in Central Asia.

- **From beak to tail**, *Oviraptor* was about 2 m long.

- **It was named 'egg thief'** because its fossils were found lying among the broken eggs of what was thought to be the dinosaur *Protoceratops*. In fact they were probably the eggs of *Oviraptor* itself, the adult brooding or protecting them.

- *Oviraptor* **had no teeth**. Instead, it had a strong, curved beak, like that of a parrot or eagle.

- **On its forehead**, *Oviraptor* had a tall, rounded piece of bone, like a crest or helmet, sticking up in front of its eyes.

- *Oviraptor's* **head crest** resembled that of today's flightless bird, the cassowary.

- *Oviraptor* **may have eaten eggs**, or cracked open shellfish with its powerful beak.

DID YOU KNOW?

Oviraptor had two bony spikes inside its mouth that it may have used to crack eggs when it closed its jaws.

◄ Oviraptor's *unusual features included its parrot-like beak. It may have been covered in filament-like feathers.*

Caudipteryx

- **The discovery of *Caudipteryx* fossils** in 1997 in Liaoning Province, China, increased the debate about the relationship between dinosaurs and birds.

- **The detailed fossils show** *Caudipteryx* was not much larger than a chicken and had a very bird-like shape and proportions.

- **They also revealed feathers** like a modern bird's, each with a shaft or quill and side vanes, on its front limbs and tail.

- **Some of these feathers** were up to 20 cm long.

- **There were also simple**, fluffy feathers on the body of *Caudipteryx*.

- **The fossils of *Caudipteryx*** come from 125 mya during the Early Cretaceous Period.

- **There are several views** about the grouping of *Caudipteryx*. Some experts say is was a small meat-eating dinosaur in the same group as *Oviraptor*, related to the raptors.

- **Another opinion** is that it is a dinosaur-like bird, rather than a bird-like dinosaur.

- **The front limbs and build** of *Caudipteryx* meant it could not fly.

- ***Caudipteryx* could have come from** a group of birds that evolved flight, of which some kinds became flightless again.

▲ Caudipteryx, 'tail feather', was about one metre long and weighed 5–8 kg. At the end of the tail the long quilled feathers spread out like a fan.

Smallest dinosaurs

▶ *About half of the length of* Compsognathus *was its tail.*

🦶 **One of the smallest** dinosaurs was *Compsognathus*, which lived during the Late Jurassic Period, 155–150 mya.

🦶 **Its fossils** come from Europe, especially southern Germany and southeastern France.

🦶 *Compsognathus* **was probably** just over one metre in length and may have weighed less than 3 kg.

🦶 **It had small, sharp, curved teeth** and it probably darted through the undergrowth after insects, spiders, worms and similar small prey.

🦶 **Discovered in 2004** in China, *Mei* was just 50 cm long. It is not only one of the smallest dinosaurs ever found, it also has the shortest dinosaur name of just three letters.

🦶 *Mei* **was fossilized** in a bird-like position with its head bent to one side under its front limb or 'arm', just like a bird tucks its head under its wing when asleep.

► *The tiny dinosaur* Mei. *Its full name,* Mei long, *means 'soundly sleeping dragon'.*

The smallest fossil dinosaur specimens found to date are of *Mussaurus*, which means 'mouse reptile'. The fossils were of babies, just 20 cm long, newly hatched from eggs. The babies would have grown into adults measuring 3 m in length.

Two other small dinosaurs were the 60-cm-long *Caenagnathasia* and the 40-cm-long *Parvicursor*.

Pack hunters

- **Dinosaurs were reptiles**, but no reptiles today hunt in packs in which members co-operate with each other.

- **Certain types of crocodiles** and alligators come together to feed where prey is abundant, but they do not co-ordinate their attacks.

- **Fossil evidence suggests** that several kinds of meat-eating dinosaurs hunted in groups or packs.

- **Sometimes the fossils** of several individuals of the same type of dinosaur have been found in one place, suggesting the dinosaurs were pack animals.

- **The fossil bones** of some plant-eating dinosaurs have been found with many tooth marks on them, apparently made by different-sized predators, which may have hunted in packs.

- *Tyrannosaurus* may have been a pack hunter.

- **At several North American sites**, the remains of several *Deinonychus* were found near the fossils of a much larger plant-eater named *Tenontosaurus*.

- **One *Deinonychus*** probably would not have attacked a full-grown *Tenontosaurus*, but a group of three or four might have.

▼ *Small predatory dinosaurs such as* Troodon *may have gathered in groups to chase prey or scavenge.*

Raptors

🐾 **'Raptors' is a nickname for** the dromaeosaur group. It is variously said to mean 'plunderer', 'thief' or 'hunter' (birds of prey are also called raptors).

🐾 **Dromaeosaurs were** medium- to large-sized, powerful, agile, meat-eating dinosaurs that lived mainly about 110–66 mya.

🐾 **Most dromaeosaurs** were 1.5–3 m from nose to tail, weighed 20–60 kg, and stood 1–2 m tall.

🐾 ***Velociraptor* lived** 75–70 mya, in what is now the barren scrub and desert of Mongolia in Central Asia.

🐾 **Like other raptors**, *Velociraptor* probably ran fast and could leap great distances on its powerful back legs.

🐾 **The dromaeosaurs** are named after the 1.8-m-long *Dromaeosaurus* from North America – one of the least known of the group, from very few fossil finds.

DID YOU KNOW?
On each second toe, a dromaeosaur had a large, curved claw that it could swing in an arc to slash through its victim's flesh.

The most-studied raptor is probably *Deinonychus*.

The large mouths of dromaeosaurs opened wide and were equipped with many small, sharp, curved teeth.

◀ Velociraptor, *the 'speedy thief', was a typical dromaeosaur. Fossils of it were found in Central Asia. Most raptors probably had feathers, although for some there is no direct fossil evidence.*

Deinonychus

- *Deinonychus* **is one of** the best known raptors.

- **It thrived** in the Middle Cretaceous Period, about 115–105 mya.

- **Fossils of** *Deinonychus* come from the American Midwest, mainly from Montana and Wyoming.

- *Deinonychus* **was about 3–3.5 m** long from nose to tail and weighed 60–70 kg, about the same as an adult human.

- **When remains of** *Deinonychus* were dug up and studied in the 1960s, they exploded the myth that dinosaurs were slow, small-brained and stupid.

- **Powerful, speedy and agile**, *Deinonychus* may have hunted in packs, like today's lions and wolves.

- **It had large hands** with three powerful fingers, each tipped with a dangerous sharp claw.

- *Deinonychus* **also had** the massive, scythe-like claw, typical of the raptor group, on each second toe.

- **The tail was stiff** and could not be swished.

- *Deinonychus* **and other similar dromaeosaurs**, such as *Velociraptor*, were the basis for the cunning and terrifying raptors of the *Jurassic Park* films.

▶ *There is no direct fossil evidence for feathers in Deinonychus, but remains of many other raptor-type dinosaurs show feathers of various kinds, not for flight, but perhaps for insulation or display.*

Utahraptor

- **The finding of *Utahraptor*** fossils dates back to 1975 near Moab, Utah, USA, but these cause little excitement.

- **More fossils** from the early 1990s were added to the discovery and dated to about 130–125 million years ago, the Early Cretaceous Period.

- **By 1993** enough remains had been identified to name this new medium-sized meat-eater *Utahraptor*.

- **It was one of the biggest members** of the raptor or dromaeosaur group, far larger than *Velociraptor* and *Deinonychus*.

- ***Utahraptor* measured** about 7 m long and weighed up to 420 kg.

- **Like other raptors**, it was fast and powerful, with a fearsome curved claw on each foot.

- **One of these claws** was more than 22 cm long. It could swing on its flexible toe in a slashing or slicing movement to wound prey.

- **Preserved feathers** have not been found with *Utahraptor* remains, but since many of its close relatives had them, it may have possessed feathers, too.

The full name is *Utahraptor ostrommaysorum*, partly in honour of the US palaeontologist John Ostrom whose work on *Deinonychus* did so much to change people's opinions of dinosaurs.

▲ *The main fossils of Utahraptor were excavated following the discovery of its huge foot claw in a quarry in Utah, USA.*

Gigantoraptor

- *Gigantoraptor* **was certainly very large**, but it was not a member of the raptor or dromaeosaur group of fast meat-eating dinosaurs.

- **Instead it belonged** to the very bird-like group called oviraptors, named after the much smaller *Oviraptor*.

- *Gigantoraptor* **has been compared** to a massive chicken, standing more than 3 m tall, with a length of 7–8 m and a weight of 1.5 tonnes.

- **It had toothless jaws** that in life were probably covered by a big, strong beak.

- **The legs of** *Gigantoraptor* were long and strong for fast running, and the toes ended in big claws.

- **From its size and skull**, *Gigantoraptor* was probably a herbivore, pecking at plant matter. Or it had a wider diet including bugs, eggs and small animals, being an omnivore.

- *Gigantoraptor* **lived about 70 mya**, near the very end of the Age of Dinosaurs.

DID YOU KNOW?

Signs of fossil eggs from the area where Gigantoraptor was found (Mongolia) suggest it may have laid eggs more than 45 cm long.

▲ Gigantoraptor *fossils were found in 2007 and officially named two years later. This dinosaur may have been an omnivore, pecking up all kinds of food like an outsized modern ostrich.*

Feathered dinosaurs

- **Fossils found** since the mid-1990s show that some dinosaurs may have been covered with feathers or fur.

- *Sinosauropteryx* **was a small**, one-metre-long meat-eater that lived 125–120 mya in China.

- **Fossils of** *Sinosauropteryx* show that parts of its body were covered not with the usual reptile scales, but with feathers instead.

- **The overall shape** of *Sinosauropteryx* shows that, despite being feathered, it could not fly.

- **The feathers may have been** for camouflage, for visual display, or to keep it warm – suggesting it was warm-blooded.

- **Fossils of** *Avimimus* come from China and Mongolia, and date from about 75–70 mya.

- **The fossil arm bones** have small ridges that are the same size and shape as the ridges on birds' wing bones, where feathers attach.

- **The 1.5-m-long** *Avimimus* had a mouth shaped like a bird's beak for pecking at food.

- **Most scientists today** believe that birds are descended from a group of small meat-eating dinosaurs called maniraptorans, such as *Troodon*.

If this is so, the modern way of classifying or grouping animals, called cladistics, means that birds are a subgroup of dinosaurs, not a separate group. That in turn means that dinosaurs are alive today – in the form of birds.

▲ Avimimus *may have evolved feathers for warmth, keeping cool, camouflage, display, to shield its eggs on the nest – or a combination of all these.*

Microraptor

- **Microraptor is one of the smallest** and most feathered dinosaurs ever found.

- **It probably weighed** less than one kilogram and was only 80–90 cm long.

- **Its fossils are 125–120 million years old** and come from the Liaoning area of northeast China.

- **Finds so far** are of more than 250 specimens, making *Microraptor* one of the most common creatures at that time.

- *Microraptor* **was probably** a raptor, in the dromaeosaur group.

- **It was also 'four-winged'** – it had feathers on its arms and legs.

- **These feathers were up to 20 cm long** on the arms, 15 cm on the legs, and well designed for flight.

- **There were also simpler**, plume-like feathers on the tail.

- **It is not clear** whether *Microraptor* was an extremely good glider, swooping down skilfully from trees, or whether it could truly fly in a controlled, sustained way, like a bird.

- **The feathers meant** *Microraptor* would have had problems walking and running on the ground, so it probably lived in trees.

▼ Microraptor *was the first known 'four-winged dinosaur', receiving its official name in 2000.*

DID YOU KNOW?

Detailed fossil remains of several Microraptor contain tiny bones and other parts from mammals, birds, lizards and even fish, many smaller than thumb-sized, which were probably their last meals.

183

Xiaotingia

- 🦖 ***Xiaotingia* was a tiny, bird-like dinosaur** (probably) belonging to the dromaeosaur or raptor group.

- 🦖 **It is one of the earlier feathered dinosaurs**, dating from about 160–150 mya, towards the end of the Jurassic Period – before the time of the famed bird *Archaeopteryx*.

- 🦖 **Fossils of *Xiaotingia*** were found in Liaoning, China and named in 2011.

- 🦖 **The remains consist** of most of one skeleton, although missing parts of the pelvis, one leg and most of the tail bones, but with feather impressions present.

- 🦖 **In life**, *Xiaotingia* was around 60 cm long and weighed some 2 kg, and probably ate small bugs, insects and worms.

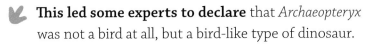

- 🦖 **Some features of *Xiaotingia*** are very similar to those of *Archaeopteryx*, including the feathers, claws on its arms – or wings – and teeth in its jaws.

- 🦖 **This led some experts to declare** that *Archaeopteryx* was not a bird at all, but a bird-like type of dinosaur.

- **Other experts suggested** *Xiaotingia* was not a dinosaur but a bird, and since it lived before *Archaeopteryx*, *Xiaotingia* should take its place as the earliest bird known from fossils.

- **Such debates demonstrate** how similar dromaeosaur dinosaurs and early birds were, and may cause us to revise our definitions of what is a bird in the future.

▲ Xiaotingia, *named in honour of Chinese fossil expert Zheng Xiaoting, was probably capable of a certain amount of controlled flight, but was not as agile as today's birds.*

Ostrich dinosaurs

- **'Ostrich dinosaurs'** is the common name of the ornithomimosaurs, because of their resemblance to today's largest bird – the flightless ostrich.

- **These dinosaurs** were tall and slim, with two long, powerful back legs for running fast.

- **The front limbs** were like strong arms, with grasping fingers tipped by sharp claws.

- **The eyes were large** and set high on the head.

- **The toothless mouth** was similar to the long, slim beak of a bird.

- **Ostrich dinosaurs** lived towards the end of the Cretaceous Period, about 100–66 mya, in North America and Asia.

- **Fossils of the ostrich dinosaur** *Struthiomimus* from Alberta, Canada, suggest it was almost 4 m in total length and stood about 2 m tall – the same height as a modern ostrich.

- **The ostrich dinosaur** *Gallimimus* was almost 8 m long and stood nearly 3 m high.

- **Ostrich dinosaurs** probably ate seeds, fruits and other plant material, as well as small animals such as worms and lizards, which they may have grasped with their powerful clawed hands.

- **Other ostrich dinosaurs** included *Dromiceiomimus*, at 3–4 m long, and the slightly bigger *Ornithomimus*.

▼ Ornithomimus *could reach speeds of perhaps 80 km/h when running. It had strong muscles in its hips and legs, enabling it to take long, quick strides.*

DID YOU KNOW?

Huge fossils of front limbs found in 1965, and named Deinocheirus, indicate a massive ostrich dinosaur 10 metres long, 4 metres high and weighing up to 5 tonnes. No other remains have been discovered.

187

Therizinosaurs

- **For years**, finds of huge fossil claws puzzled experts as to which creatures they came from.

- **In the mid 1990s** more finds made the picture clearer. They came from a previously unknown group of dinosaurs, related to meat-eaters, but plant-eaters themselves.

- **The new group was named in 1997** as the therizinosaurs, 'scythe lizards' or 'reaper lizards', after their massively long claws.

- **Another name used less often** is segnosaurs, 'slow lizards'.

- **Therizinosaurs belonged** to the dinosaur group known as theropods, in which all the other kinds were meat-eaters, from tiny raptors to giants like *Tyrannosaurus* and *Spinosaurus*.

- **But the skulls and teeth** of therizinosaurs show they were probably plant-eaters.

- **Most therizinosaurs stood** on their back legs, had wide hips, feathers and were large. Some were enormous – *Therizinosaurus* itself stood 5 m tall, was 10 m long, and weighed 5 tonnes.

- **Most therizinosaur fossils** come from the Middle and Late Cretaceous Period, 130–66 mya, and are found in East Asia, with some from North America.

- *Alaxasaurus* **was one of** the smaller therizinosaurs, about 2.2 m tall and 3.5 m long.

- **Its discovery in the 1990s** helped to establish the group, and show it was a subgroup of the theropods, whose close relatives were the raptors and oviraptors – themselves very bird-like.

▼ *Therizinosaurus was one of the last of its group, surviving about 70 mya in what is now Mongolia, Central Asia. Its first fossils, giant claws, were found in the 1940s but remained a mystery for almost half a century.*

189

Falcarius

- *Falcarius* **was a therizinosaur** that lived in what is now Utah, USA, around 125 mya.

- **It is one of the earliest known** therizinosaurs, or 'scythe lizards', and shows how the group evolved from other kinds of theropods.

- **Thousands of fossil specimens** from hundreds of individuals, of various sizes and ages, have been recovered, making this dinosaur very well known.

- *Falcarius* **was up to 4 m long** and 1.2 m tall, and weighed about 100 kg.

- **Some of the smallest**, youngest individuals were only 50 cm long.

- *Falcarius* **had leaf-shaped teeth** in its upper jaw, similar to those of plant-eating dinosaurs such as sauropods.

- **Some of its teeth** in the front of the lower jaw were more spike-shaped, perhaps showing *Falcarius* could also catch small animals like insects and little reptiles.

- **Like other therizinosaurs**, *Falcarius* had hugely elongated claws on each hand.

- *Falcarius* **fossils** were first noticed in 1999, and it was officially described and named in 2005.

- **No feathers have been found** preserved with *Falcarius* bones and teeth, showing that perhaps they had not yet evolved in its group.

◀ Falcarius, 'sickle slicer', had the typical therizinosaur claws on its hands, measuring 10–14 cm in length.

191

Beipiaosaurus

- *Beipiaosaurus* **was an early therizinosaur** from about 125 mya, the Middle Cretaceous Period, in China.

- **The dinosaur is named 'Beipiao lizard'** after the city near to the place of its discovery.

- **Fossils of** *Beipiaosaurus* were first uncovered in 1996 by a local farmer, Li Yinxian.

- **Three years later** the dinosaur was officially named, helping to give more details about the strange group called therizinosaurs.

- *Beipiaosaurus* **was about** 2–2.5 m long and probably weighed 80–90 kg.

- **Like other later therizinosaurs**, *Beipiaosaurus* had a body covering of feathers.

- **In fact it had two kinds of feathers**. One layer was similar to down, with small bendy fibres or filaments sticking out of a single short shaft.

- **The second layer was longer**, thicker feathers, each just one fibre or filament, up to 150 mm long and 3–4 mm wide.

- **The beak-like mouth** of *Beipiaosaurus*, with teeth only towards the back of the jaws, was suited to plucking, cutting and shredding plant food.

DID YOU KNOW?

The full name Beipiaosaurus inexpectus shows how this dinosaur had several features that were not expected to occur in the same animal.

▲ As well as their enormous hand claws, therizinosaurs like
Beipiaosaurus also had sharp curved foot claws that they
probably used for digging and self defence.

Herbivores

Hundreds of kinds of dinosaurs were herbivores, or plant-eaters. As time passed, the plants available for them to eat evolved, and new dinosaurs became adapted to them.

Early in the Age of Dinosaurs, during the Triassic Period, the main plants for dinosaurs to eat were conifer trees, ginkgoes, cycads and the smaller seed ferns, ferns, horsetails and club mosses.

A few cycads are still found today. They resemble palm trees, with umbrella-like crowns of long green fronds on top of tall, unbranched, trunk-like stems.

DID YOU KNOW?
To maintain their huge bodies, sauropods probably had to eat for 20 hours a day.

In the Triassic Period, only prosauropod dinosaurs were big enough or had necks long enough to reach tall cycad fronds or ginkgo leaves.

In the Jurassic Period, tall conifers such as redwoods and araucarias or 'monkey puzzle' trees became common.

The huge, long-necked sauropods of the Jurassic Period may have been able to reach high into tall conifer trees to rake off their needles.

In the Middle Cretaceous Period, a new type of plant food appeared – the flowering plants.

By the end of the Cretaceous Period there were many flowering trees and shrubs, such as magnolias, maples and walnuts.

These new plants meant that many new kinds of animals, including new herbivorous dinosaurs, evolved to eat them.

▼ *During the warm, damp Jurassic Period, plants grew in most areas, covering land that previously had been barren. Massive plant-eaters such as* Barosaurus *thrived on the fronds, needles and leaves of towering tree ferns, ginkgoes and conifers.*

Barosaurus was 26 m long and weighed 25–30 tonnes

Lesothosaurus and Fabrosaurus

There has been much confusion between two very small plant-eating dinosaurs, *Lesothosaurus* and *Fabrosaurus*.

Their fossils come from South Africa and date back to the Early Jurassic Period, 200–190 mya.

***Fabrosaurus* was named** in 1964 from just one fossil specimen of three teeth set in part of a jawbone.

Comparing this specimen with similar fossils from other regions, these indicated a dinosaur plant-eater about one metre long.

***Lesothosaurus* received its name** in 1978. Its more plentiful fossils showed a similar one-metre plant-eater to *Fabrosaurus*.

Slim and lightly built, *Lesothosaurus* was only one metre long from nose to tail-tip and would have stood knee-high to an adult human being.

Its long, slim back legs and long toes indicate that *Lesothosaurus* was a fast runner.

Teeth and other fossils of *Lesothosaurus* show that it probably ate low-growing plants such as ferns.

The rear teeth were set inwards slightly from the sides of its skull, suggesting fleshy cheek pouches for storing or chewing food.

It is possible that *Lesothosaurus* and *Fabrosaurus* were the same type of dinosaur. If so, all the fossils should receive the name given first – *Fabrosaurus*.

But the remains of *Fabrosaurus* are so limited, some experts say that it should not even exist as an official name.

***Lesothosaurus* may be** a very early type of ornithischian or 'bird-hipped' dinosaur, perhaps on the way to becoming an ornithpod like *Iguanodon* – or a stegosaur or ankylosaur.

▼ Lesothosaurus *may have stood on hind legs to spot danger, much like the mammals called meerkats in the region today.*

197

Prosauropods

- **The first big dinosaurs** were the prosauropods, also called plateosaurids. Most lived between 230 and 180 mya.

- **They were plant-eaters**, with small heads, long necks and tails, wide bodies and four sturdy limbs.

- **One of the first prosauropods** was *Plateosaurus*, which lived in Europe between about 215 and 205 mya.

- *Plateosaurus* **walked on all fours**, but may have reared up on its back legs to reach leaves. It was up to 9 m long, and weighed as much as 3 tonnes.

- **Another prosauropod** was *Riojasaurus*. Its fossils are about 220–215 million years old, and come from Argentina.

- *Riojasaurus* **was 10 m long** and weighed about 2 tonnes.

- **Over 20 fossil skeletons** of the prosauropod *Sellosaurus* have been found in Europe, dating from 215–210 mya.

DID YOU KNOW?

A similar and close relative to Riojasaurus was Melanorosaurus from Africa – South America and Africa were once joined together as part of Gondwana, 200 mya.

- *Lufengosaurus* **was an early Jurassic prosauropod** from China, measuring up to 9 m in length. It was the first complete dinosaur skeleton to be restored in that country.

- **The sauropods followed** the prosauropods and were even bigger, but had the same basic body shape, with long necks and tails.

▼ Riojasaurus *was South America's first big dinosaur.*

Plateosaurus

- **The name *Plateosaurus*** means 'flat reptile', and the first kinds appeared around 215 mya.

- **Groups of *Plateosaurus*** have been found at various European sites, totalling more than 100 individuals.

- *Plateosaurus* **had jagged teeth** for chewing plants.

- **Its flexible, clawed fingers** may have been used to pull branches of food to its mouth.

- *Plateosaurus* **could bend** its fingers 'backwards', allowing it to walk on its hands and fingers, in the same posture as its feet and toes.

- **The thumbs** had large, sharp claws, perhaps used to jab and stab enemies.

- **Fossil experts once thought** that *Plateosaurus* dragged its tail as it walked.

- **Experts today think** that *Plateosaurus* carried its tail off the ground to balance its head, neck and the front part of its body.

- *Plateosaurus* **was one of the earliest dinosaurs** to be officially named, in 1837, even before the term 'dinosaur' had been invented.

▼ Plateosaurus *may have
been able to reach leaves
2–3 m above the ground.*

Massospondylus

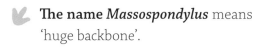

- *Massospondylus* **was a medium-sized** plant-eater belonging to the group known as the prosauropods.

- **Africa and perhaps North America** were home to *Massospondylus*, about 200–185 mya.

- **In total**, *Massospondylus* was about 4.5 m long, with almost half of this length being its tail.

- **The rear legs** of *Massospondylus* were bigger and stronger than its front legs, so it may have reared up to reach food high up.

- **The name** *Massospondylus* means 'huge backbone'.

- **Fossils of over 80** *Massospondylus* have been found, making it one of the best-studied dinosaurs.

- *Massospondylus* **had a tiny head** compared to its body, so it must have spent hours each day gathering enough food to survive.

The **front teeth** of *Massospondylus* were large and strong with ridged edges.

The **cheek teeth** were too small and weak to chew large amounts of food, so perhaps food was mashed in the dinosaur's stomach.

In the 1980s, some scientists suggested that *Massospondylus* was a meat-eater, partly due to its ridged front teeth, but this idea is now outdated.

▼ Massospondylus *probably spent most of its time eating to fuel its bulky body.*

DID YOU KNOW?

Massospondylus was named in 1854 by the anatomist and palaeontologist Richard Owen, who had invented the term 'dinosaur' about 12 years earlier. He thought at first the fossils came from three different reptiles.

Anchisaurus

- *Anchisaurus* **was** an early sauropod-like dinosaur.

- **Although officially named** as a dinosaur in 1885, *Anchisaurus* had in fact been discovered over 70 years earlier.

- *Anchisaurus* **was very small** and slim compared to other sauropods, with a body about the size of a large dog.

- **Fossils of** *Anchisaurus* date from the Early Jurassic Period, 200–190 mya.

- **The remains of** *Anchisaurus* were found in Connecticut and Massachusetts, eastern USA, and in southern Africa.

- **With its small, serrated teeth**, *Anchisaurus* probably bit off the soft leaves of low-growing plants.

- **To reach leaves** on higher branches, *Anchisaurus* may have been able to rear up on its back legs.

- *Anchisaurus* **had a large**, curved claw on each thumb.

- **The thumb claws** may have been used as hooks to pull leafy branches towards the mouth, or as weapons for lashing out at enemies and inflicting wounds.

DID YOU KNOW?

Remains of Anchisaurus or a similar plant-eater were the first fossils of a dinosaur to be discovered in North America in 1818.

▶ Anchisaurus *was about 2.2 m long. Its name means 'near lizard'.*

Biggest dinosaurs

- **Dinosaurs can be measured** by length and height, but 'biggest' usually means heaviest or bulkiest.

- **The sauropod dinosaurs** of the Late Jurassic and Early–Mid Cretaceous Periods were the biggest animals to walk on Earth, as far as we know.

- **However, today's whales**, and maybe the huge sea reptiles (pliosaurs) of the Dinosaur Age, rival them in size.

- **For any dinosaur**, enough fossils must be found for scientists to be sure it is a distinct type before they can give it a scientific name. They must also be able to estimate its size. With some giant dinosaurs, not enough fossils have been found.

- **Remains of *Supersaurus*** found in Colorado, USA, suggest a dinosaur similar to *Diplodocus*, but perhaps even longer, at 35 m.

- ***Diplodocus hallorum* fossils** found in 1991 in the USA may belong to a 35-m-long sauropod.

- ***Ultrasaurus* fossils** found in South Korea suggest a dinosaur similar to *Brachiosaurus*, but smaller. However these fossils are fragmentary and some experts disagree with their naming.

- ***Argentinosaurus***, from South America, is known from a few fossils, mainly backbones, found in the early 1990s. It may have weighed up to 100 tonnes.

▶ Seismosaurus *was named in 1991, but further studies in the 2000s show it was probably one of the species of* Diplodocus, *now known as* Diplodocus hallorum *or* Diplodocus longus.

Long neck for
reaching high
leaves

Sauropods

- **Sauropods were the biggest dinosaurs** of all. They lived mainly during the Jurassic Period, around 201–145 mya.

- **These huge plant-eaters** had tiny heads, very long necks and tails, huge, bulging bodies and massive legs, similar to those of an elephant, but much bigger.

- **Sauropods included** the well known *Mamenchisaurus*, *Cetiosaurus*, *Diplodocus*, *Brachiosaurus* and *Apatosaurus*.

- *Rebbachisaurus* **fossils** were found in Morocco, Tunisia and Algeria. It lived 100 mya.

- *Cetiosaurus* **was about** 15 m long and weighed 10–20 tonnes.

- **The first fossils** of *Cetiosaurus* were found in Oxfordshire, England, in the 1830s. It was the first sauropod to be given an official name, in 1841 – the year before the term 'dinosaur' was invented.

- *Cetiosaurus*, or 'whale reptile', was so-named because British fossil expert Richard Owen thought that its giant backbones came from a prehistoric whale.

DID YOU KNOW?

The name 'sauropod' means 'lizard/reptile foot'. It was given in 1878 by US fossil-hunter and dinosaur expert Othniel Charles Marsh, after the discovery of the famous Diplodocus.

▼ *Sauropods such as* Apatosaurus *could perhaps browse for food in tree tops.*

Brachiosaurus

- *Brachiosaurus* **lived about 155–150 mya** and its fossils have been found at several sites in North America. Fossils of a similar dinosaur from Africa, previously thought to have been *Brachiosaurus*, have been renamed *Giraffatitan*.

- **At 25 m in length** from nose to tail, *Brachiosaurus* was not one of the longest dinosaurs, but it was one of the heaviest. Its weight has been estimated between 20 and 50 tonnes.

- *Brachiosaurus* **fossils** were first found in 1900 and the dinosaur was named the year after.

- **The name *Brachiosaurus*** means 'arm reptile' – it was so-named because of its massive front legs.

- **With its huge front legs** and long neck, *Brachiosaurus* could perhaps reach food more than 13 m from the ground.

Its teeth were small and chisel-shaped for snipping leaves from trees. The nostrils were positioned high on its head.

◀ Brachiosaurus *had similar body proportions to a giraffe, but was more than twice as tall and 50 times heavier.*

Camarasaurus

- *Camarasaurus* **was a giant plant-eating sauropod** that lived during the Late Jurassic Period, about 155–150 mya.

- **It is one of the best known** of all big dinosaurs, because so many almost-complete fossil skeletons have been found.

- **Famous American fossil hunter** Edward Drinker Cope gave *Camarasaurus* its name in 1877.

- **The name means** 'chambered reptile', because its backbones, or vertebrae, had large, scoop-shaped spaces in them, making them lighter.

- *Camarasaurus* **was up to 21 m long** and had a very bulky, powerful body and legs.

North America was home to *Camarasaurus*, with similar fossils from Europe and Africa given different names.

A large, short-snouted head, similar to that of *Brachiosaurus*, characterized *Camarasaurus*.

A fossil skeleton of a young *Camarasaurus* was uncovered in the 1920s, and had nearly every bone in its body lying in the correct position, as they were when the dinosaur was alive – an amazingly rare find.

◀ Compared to other sauropods, Camarasaurus *had a short neck and tail.*

DID YOU KNOW?
Detailed fossil studies show that one Camarasaurus replaced its teeth every 8–9 weeks, and another reached adulthood at 20 years of age and died aged 26.

Brontomerus

- **Brontomerus is a recently named sauropod** dinosaur whose fossils come from a quarry in Utah, USA.

- **The fossils are from** about 100 mya, towards the end of the Early Cretaceous Period, or the Middle Cretaceous.

▼ *The pelvic (hip) bones and femur (thigh bone) of* Brontomerus *had large surfaces to anchor bulky, powerful muscles.*

- **The fossil fragments indicate** a medium-sized sauropod about 14 m long, weighing 5–6 tonnes, and similar in looks to the much better-known *Camarasaurus*.

- **The name *Brontomerus* means** 'thunder thigh' and refers to the very unusual, large hip bones, which would have anchored hugely powerful hip and thigh muscles for the rear legs.

- **Another 'bronto' was *Brontosaurus*,** 'thunder lizard', which used to be a very famous dinosaur name.

- **It was given in 1897** by fossil-hunter Othniel Charles Marsh to fossils of a large sauropod from the Midwest of the USA.

- **Two years before**, Marsh had named another similar sauropod, about 23 m long and weighing 20 tonnes, as *Apatosaurus*.

- **Later studies of these fossils** showed that those named *Brontosaurus* were in fact the same kind of dinosaur as *Apatosaurus*.

So the first specimens known as *Brontosaurus* were renamed *Apatosaurus*, and *Brontosaurus* was dropped from the official list of dinosaur names.

▼ *The muscle marks on the fossil limb bones of* Brontomerus *show that it could probably kick very hard with its rear legs.*

215

Diplodocus

A huge plant-eating sauropod, *Diplodocus* lived during the Late Jurassic Period, about 155–145 mya.

The first discovery of *Diplodocus* fossils was in 1877, near Canyon City, Colorado, USA.

The main fossils were found in the USA, in Colorado, Utah and Wyoming.

At an incredible 27 m or more in length, *Diplodocus* is one of the longest dinosaurs known. Some species may have reached 33 m.

- *Diplodocus* **probably** swung its tiny head on its enormous neck to reach fronds and foliage in the trees.

- **Its teeth were slim rods** that formed a comb-like fringe around the front of its mouth.

- *Diplodocus* **may have used** its teeth to strip leaves from twigs and swallow them without chewing.

- **Its nostrils** were once thought to be positioned almost above its eyes. Recent evidence shows they were probably lower down, halfway between the eyes and snout tip.

▼ Diplodocus *was long but light for a sauropod, weighing about 10–25 tonnes.*

Mamenchisaurus

- **A massive plant-eating dinosaur**, *Mamenchisaurus* was similar in appearance to *Diplodocus*.

- **It lived during** the late Jurassic Period, from 160–145 mya.

- **This huge dinosaur** measured about 30 m from nose to tail. Its weight has been estimated at 20–35 tonnes.

- **At up to 15 m**, *Mamenchisaurus* had one of the longest necks of any dinosaur. The neck had up to 19 vertebrae, or neckbones – more than almost any other dinosaur.

- **The remains of *Mamenchisaurus*** were found in China and the dinosaur is named after the place where its fossils were discovered – Mamen Stream.

- **Other sauropod dinosaurs** found in the same region include *Euhelopus* and *Omeisaurus*.

- *Mamenchisaurus* **may have stretched** out its neck to crop leaves, or – less likely – may have lived in swamps and eaten water plants.

▼ *The joints between the fossil bones of* Mamenchisaurus' *neck show that it was not very flexible.*

DID YOU KNOW?

The species Mamenchisaurus constructus was first named in 1954. Since then another five or six possible species have been identified – although some experts say the remains represent only two or three species.

Stegosaurs

- **Plant-eating dinosaurs** that mostly lived around 160–140 mya, stegosaurs are named after the best known of their group, *Stegosaurus*.

- **They are often called** 'plated dinosaurs', from the large, flat plates or slabs of bone on their backs.

- **Stegosaurs probably** first appeared in eastern Asia, then spread to other continents, especially North America and Africa.

- ***Kentrosaurus was*** a 5-m-long stegosaur and weighed an estimated one tonne. Its name means 'spiky reptile'. It lived about 155–150 mya in East Africa.

DID YOU KNOW?

In 2006, fossils of Stegosaurus were identified in Portugal, which is the first evidence that this dinosaur lived in Europe.

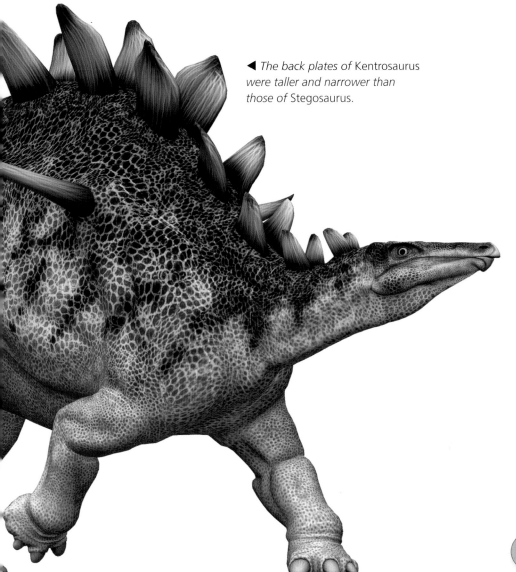

Most stegosaurs lacked teeth at the front of the mouth, but had horny beaks, like those of birds, for snipping off leaves. They chewed food with small, ridged cheek teeth.

◀ *The back plates of* Kentrosaurus *were taller and narrower than those of* Stegosaurus.

Stegosaurus

- *Stegosaurus* **was the largest** of the stegosaur group. Its fossils were found mainly in present-day Colorado, Utah and Wyoming, USA.

- **Like most of its group**, *Stegosaurus* lived towards the end of the Jurassic Period, about 155–150 mya.

- *Stegosaurus* **was about 8–9 m long** from nose to tail and probably weighed more than 4 tonnes.

- **Its most striking features** were the large, roughly diamond-shaped, leaf-shaped or triangular bony plates along its back.

- **The name *Stegosaurus*** means 'roof reptile'. This is because it was first thought that its bony plates lay flat on its back, overlapping like the tiles on a roof.

- **It is now thought** that the back plates stood upright in two long rows.

- **The plates may have been** for body temperature control, allowing the dinosaur to warm up quickly if it stood side-on to the sun's rays.

- **The back plates** may have been covered with brightly coloured skin, possibly to intimidate enemies – they were too flimsy to provide much protection.

- **Armed with four large spikes**, *Stegosaurus* probably used its tail for swinging at enemies in self-defence.

◀ Stegosaurus' *short front limbs meant that it ate low-growing plants.*

Tuojiangosaurus

- *Tuojiangosaurus* **was part** of the stegosaur group. It lived during the Late Jurassic Period, about 170–155 mya.

- **The first nearly complete** dinosaur skeleton to be found in China was of a *Tuojiangosaurus*, and fossil skeletons are on display in several Chinese museums.

- **The name *Tuojiangosaurus*** means 'Tuo River reptile'.

- *Tuojiangosaurus* **was 7 m long** from nose to tail and probably weighed about 3–4 tonnes.

- **Like other stegosaurs,** *Tuojiangosaurus* had tall plates of bone on its back.

- **The back plates** were roughly triangular and probably stood upright in two rows that ran from the neck to the middle of the tail.

- *Tuojiangosaurus* **plucked** low-growing plants with its beak-shaped mouth, and partly chewed them with its ridged cheek teeth.

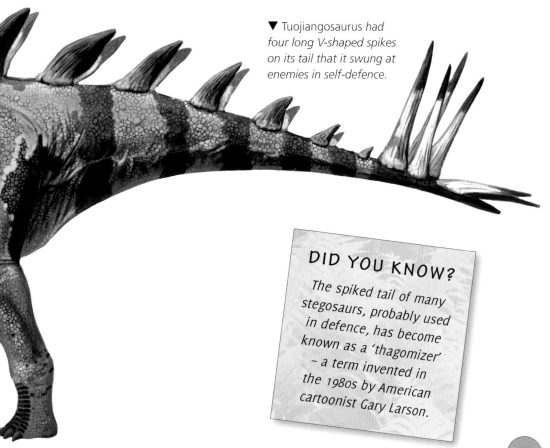

▼ Tuojiangosaurus *had four long V-shaped spikes on its tail that it swung at enemies in self-defence.*

DID YOU KNOW?

The spiked tail of many stegosaurs, probably used in defence, has become known as a 'thagomizer' – a term invented in the 1980s by American cartoonist Gary Larson.

Ankylosaurs

🐾 **Ankylosaurs had** a protective armour of bony plates.

🐾 **Unlike the armoured nodosaurs**, ankylosaurs had a large lump of bone at the end of their tail, which they used as a hammer or club.

🐾 **One of the best known ankylosaurs**, from the preserved remains of about 40 individuals, is *Euoplocephalus*.

🐾 **The hefty *Euoplocephalus*** was about 6 m long and weighed 2 tonnes or more. It lived about 76–75 mya in Alberta, Canada, Montana, USA and other places.

🐾 ***Euoplocephalus* had bony shields** on its head and body, and even had bony eyelids. Blunt spikes ran along its back.

🐾 **Specimens of *Euoplocephalus*** are usually found singly, so it probably didn't live in herds.

🐾 **The ankylosaur *Pinacosaurus*** had bony nodules like chainmail armour in its skin, and rows of blunt spikes from neck to tail.

🐾 **Ankylosaurs had small**, weak teeth, and probably ate soft, low-growing ferns and horsetails.

◄ *The tail club of* Euoplocephalus *was made from pieces of bone that had fused (stuck) together.*

DID YOU KNOW?

Pinacosaurus was about 5 m long and lived in Asia some 80–75 mya.

227

Scelidosaurus

- *Scelidosaurus* **was** a medium-sized armoured dinosaur, perhaps an early member of the ankylosaur or stegosaur group.

- **Very well-preserved fossils of** *Scelidosaurus* have been found in Dorset, in southern England. It lived during the Early Jurassic Period, about 190 mya.

- **From nose to tail**, *Scelidosaurus* was about 4 m long.

- *Scelidosaurus* **probably moved** about on four legs, although it could perhaps rear up to gather food.

- **A plant-eater**, *Scelidosaurus* snipped off its food with the beak-like front of its mouth, and chewed it with its simple, leaf-shaped teeth.

- *Scelidosaurus* **is one of the earliest** dinosaurs known to have had a set of protective, bony armour plates.

- **A row of bony plates**, or scutes, stuck up from *Scelidosaurus'* neck, back and tail. It also had rows of conical bony plates along its flanks, resembling limpets on a rock.

- *Scelidosaurus* **was described** and named in 1859 and 1861 by Richard Owen, who also invented the name 'dinosaur'.

▼ Scelidosaurus *was a forerunner of bigger, more heavily armoured dinosaur types, with bony plates called scutes.*

Nodosaurs

- **Nodosaurs were a subgroup** of armoured dinosaurs in the main ankylosaur group.

- **The nodosaur subgroup** included *Edmontonia*, *Sauropelta*, *Polacanthus* and *Nodosaurus*.

- **Nodosaurs were slow-moving**, heavy-bodied plant-eaters with thick, heavy nodules, lumps and plates of bone in their skin for protection.

- **Most nodosaurs lived** during the Late Jurassic and Cretaceous Periods, 160–66 mya.

- *Edmontonia* **lived** in North America during the Late Cretaceous Period, 75–66 mya.

- **It was about 7 m long**, but its bony armour made it very heavy for its size, at 4–5 tonnes.

- **Along its neck**, back and tail *Edmontonia* had rows of flat and spiky plates.

- **The nodosaur** *Polacanthus* was about 5 m long and lived 130–120 mya.

Fossils of *Polacanthus* come from the Isle of Wight, England, and perhaps from North America, in South Dakota, USA.

◀ Edmontonia, *one of the last dinosaurs, was covered in many sharp lumps and spikes of bone that gave it some protection from its enemies.*

Sauropelta

- *Sauropelta* **was a nodosaur** – a type of armoured dinosaur.

- **The name** *Sauropelta* means 'shielded reptile', from the many large, cone-like lumps of bone – some almost as big as dinner plates – on its head, neck, back and tail.

- **The larger lumps of bone** on *Sauropelta* were interspersed with smaller, fist-sized bony studs.

DID YOU KNOW?

Sauropelta *lived* 115–110 mya, in present-day Montana and Wyoming, USA.

🐾 *Sauropelta* **was about** 5 m long, including the tail, and probably weighed almost 2 tonnes.

🐾 *Sauropelta* **had a row** of sharp spikes along each side of its body, from just behind the eyes to the tail. The spikes decreased in size towards the tail.

🐾 **The armour** of *Sauropelta* was flexible, almost like lumps of metal set into thick leather, so the dinosaur could twist and turn, but was unable to run fast.

🐾 **Pillar-like legs** supported *Sauropelta's* weight.

🐾 **Using its beak-like mouth,** *Sauropelta* probably plucked its low-growing plant food.

◄ If attacked, Sauropelta *probably crouched down low to protect its soft belly. It may have swung its head to jab at enemies with its long neck spines.*

233

Heterodontosaurus

🦶 ***Heterodontosaurus* lived** about 200–195 mya, at the beginning of the Jurassic Period.

🦶 **A very small dinosaur** at only one metre in length (about as long as a large dog), *Heterodontosaurus* would have stood knee-high to a human.

🦶 **Probably standing partly upright** on its longer back legs, *Heterodontosaurus* would have been a fast runner.

🦶 **Fossils of *Heterodontosaurus*** come from Lesotho in southern Africa and Cape Province in South Africa.

🦶 **Most dinosaurs had teeth** of only one shape in their jaws, but *Heterodontosaurus* had three types of teeth.

🦶 **The front teeth** were small, sharp and found only in the upper jaw. They bit against the horny, beak-like lower front of the mouth.

▶ Small and slim, Heterodontosaurus *looked similar to meat-eaters such as* Compsognathus, *although it was probably an omnivore (eating anything, plant or animal matter).*

🦶 **The four middle teeth** of *Heterodontosaurus* were long and curved, similar to the tusks of a wild boar, and may have been used for fighting rivals or in self-defence.

🦶 **The back teeth** were long and had sharp tops, or cusps, for chewing.

DID YOU KNOW?
Heterodontosaurus *means* 'different-toothed reptile'.

235

Pegomastax

- *Pegomastax*, which means 'thick or strong jaw', dates back to 200–190 mya and has some very unusual features.

- **It belonged to the *Heterodontosaurus* group**, most members having different-shaped teeth, with two or four enlarged as long, fang-like canines.

- **In *Pegomastax*, these fangs** in the lower jaw were relatively long, giving a vampire-like appearance.

- *Pegomastax* **also had a parrot-like horny beak** at the front of its mouth for pecking and slicing.

- **Another strange feature** was a covering of long bristles that have been likened to those of a porcupine.

- **The long teeth may have been used** to rip fruit, stab small animal victims, slash at enemies, display open-mouthed to rivals, or even dig for food.

- *Pegomastax* **was very small**, hardly more than 60 cm long.

- **Its fossils come from Early Jurassic rocks** in South Africa and were first excavated in the 1960s, but not named until recently, in 2012.

▼ *The tough body bristles of* Pegomastax *may have worked as protection, not only from enemies, but while scurrying through thick, thorny undergrowth.*

Fruitadens

- *Fruitadens* **is named** not after a fruit-eating diet, but the place where its fossils were dug up, Fruita in Colorado, USA.

- **Living about 150–145 mya**, in the Late Jurassic Period, *Fruitadens* was one of the last of the small dinosaur group known as heterodontosaurs.

- **Fossil parts** of about four or possibly five individuals are known, together representing jaws, backbones and some front and rear limb bones.

- **These fossils were collected** from the 1970s but only assembled and described in 2010.

- **Like other heterodontosaurs**, *Fruitadens* had two longer teeth called canines, one on either side near the front of the lower jaw.

- *Fruitadens* **was very small** and lightly built, less than 80 cm long and weighing less than one kilogram.

- **It had long but well-muscled legs** and probably relied on speed and agility for survival.

- *Fruitadens* **would dart on its back legs** into the undergrowth or among rocks to escape from predators.

- *Fruitadens* **was probably an omnivore**, eating any small items such as leaves, seeds, tubers, insects, eggs and worms.

► Fruitadens *was one of the smallest of all known non-bird dinosaurs.*

Iguanodon

- **Part of the ornithopod group**, *Iguanodon* was a large plant-eating dinosaur. It lived during the Early to Middle Cretaceous Period, 130–125 mya.

- **Numerous fossils** of *Iguanodon* have been found in several countries in Europe, especially Belgium, with similar fossils from England, Germany and Spain.

- *Iguanodon* **measured** about 10–11 m from nose to tail. It probably weighed the same as a large elephant – 4–5 tonnes.

- *Iguanodon* **probably walked** and ran on its large, powerful back legs for much of the time, with its body held horizontal.

- **A cone-shaped spike** on the thumb may have been used as a weapon for jabbing at rivals or enemies.

- **The three central fingers** on the hands had hoof-like claws for occasional four-legged walking.

- **The fifth, or little finger**, was able to bend across the hand for grasping objects, and was perhaps used to pull plants towards the mouth.

DID YOU KNOW?
Iguanodon was one of the very first dinosaurs to be given an official scientific name in 1825.

▶ *The thumb spike was used in defence and the fingers grasped food.*

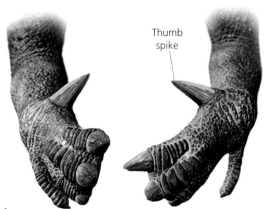

Thumb spike

▼ Iguanodon *is well known from the fossils of many individuals.*

Duckbills

- **The common name** for the hadrosaur group of dinosaurs is 'duckbills'.

- **Hadrosaurs were big plant-eaters** that walked mainly on their two large, powerful rear legs. They were one of the last main dinosaur groups to appear on Earth, less than 100 mya.

- **Hadrosaurs were named** after *Hadrosaurus*, the first dinosaur of the group to be discovered as fossils, found in 1858 in New Jersey, USA.

- **Most hadrosaurs** had wide mouths that were flattened and toothless at the front, like a duck's beak.

- **Large numbers** of cheek teeth filled the back of the hadrosaur's mouth, arranged in rows called batteries. They were ideal for chewing tough plant food.

- **Some hadrosaurs** had tall, elaborate crests or projections of bone on their heads, notably *Corythosaurus*, *Saurolophus* and *Parasaurolophus*.

- **Hadrosaurs that lacked bony crests** and had low, smooth heads included *Anatosaurus*, *Bactrosaurus*, *Kritosaurus* and *Edmontosaurus*.

- **The name *Hadrosaurus*** means 'big reptile'.

Long, relatively narrow tail with a muscular base to swish tail from side to side

DID YOU KNOW?

Edmontosaurus may have had a loose bag of skin on its nose that it blew up like a balloon to make a honking or trumpeting noise – perhaps a breeding call.

▼ *Hadrosaurs such as Corythosaurus are often shown feeding on water plants with their wide, duck-like beaked mouths.*

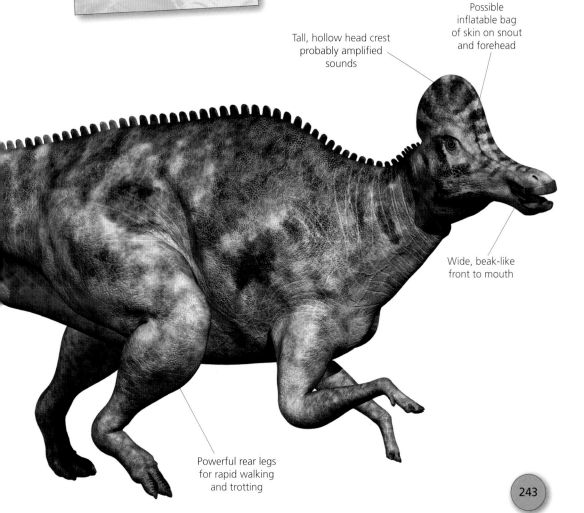

Possible inflatable bag of skin on snout and forehead

Tall, hollow head crest probably amplified sounds

Wide, beak-like front to mouth

Powerful rear legs for rapid walking and trotting

243

Brachylophosaurus

- *Brachylophosaurus* **was a hadrosaur** or duckbill that lived in what are now Alberta, Canada, and Montana, USA, in North America.

- **With a length of around 9 m**, and a weight of 2–3 tonnes, *Brachylophosaurus* was average size for the hadrosaur group.

- **Its bony head crest** was not upright, but like a shield or plate lying flat on the top of the forehead region, behind the eyes.

- **The head crest of *Brachylophosaurus*** does not seem to be strong enough for headbutting rivals or enemies. It may have been a visual sign of adulthood, maturity and readiness to breed.

- **The toothless front of the mouth** of *Brachylophosaurus* was wide and flat, and one of the most 'duck-bill-like' of the duckbills.

- **The rear of the mouth** had hundreds of teeth arranged in ranks called batteries, for powerful thorough chewing of tough plant food.

- **In life**, the cheeks were probably fleshy pouches that kept the food in the mouth while it was chewed.

- *Brachylophosaurus* **lived** towards the end of the Age of Dinosaurs, some 76–75 million year ago.

- **One of the best-preserved dinosaurs** ever found was a *Brachylophosaurus* nicknamed 'Elvis'.

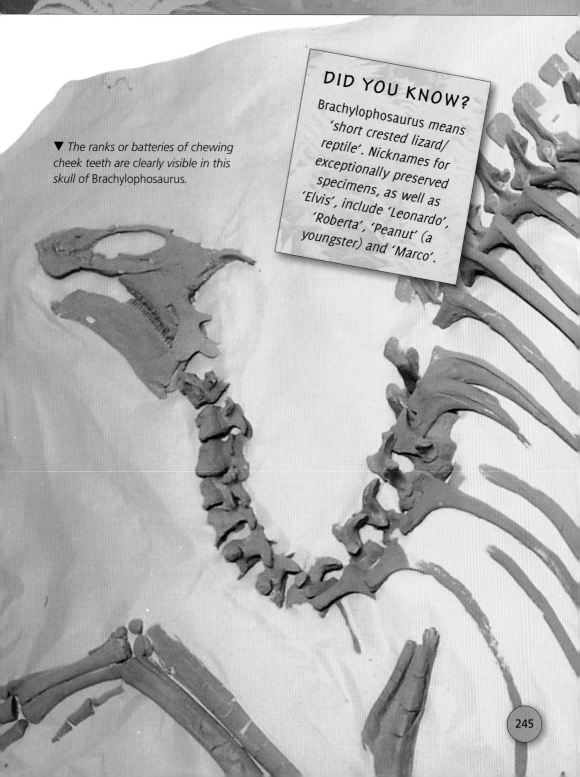

▼ The ranks or batteries of chewing cheek teeth are clearly visible in this skull of Brachylophosaurus.

DID YOU KNOW?

Brachylophosaurus means 'short crested lizard/ reptile'. Nicknames for exceptionally preserved specimens, as well as 'Elvis', include 'Leonardo', 'Roberta', 'Peanut' (a youngster) and 'Marco'.

245

Latirhinus

- *Latirhinus* **is one** of the most recently discovered hadrosaurs, named in 2012.

- **Its fossils are from** the Late Cretaceous Period, 80-70 mya, when many kinds of hadrosaurs were evolving.

- **The remains of** *Latirhinus* were dug from the Cerro del Pueblo Formation in Coahuila, Northern Mexico.

- **These rocks have also yielded fossils** of other hadrosaurs, horned dinosaurs (ceratopsians), pterosaurs and turtles.

- *Latirhinus* **is one of the most southern** of all hadrosaurs, most of which came from northern lands.

- **One of its main features** was its extra-large nose or snout, making up almost half of the head's length.

- **The name** *Latirhinus* means 'wide or broad nose'.

- **This very large nose** could have had a flap of loose skin that was blown up like a balloon, to make sounds or for visual display.

- **From similar hadrosaurs,** the size of *Latirhinus* was about 9 m long and 3 tonnes in weight.

▼ Latirhinus *may have used its nose flap to make honking sounds or to inflate like a balloon and attract mates at breeding time.*

Psittacosaurus

- *Psittacosaurus* **was a plant-eater**, and an early relative of the group known as ceratopsians, or 'horn-faced' dinosaurs.

- **Appearing in the Middle Cretaceous Period**, different species of *Psittacosaurus* lived from 125 to 100 mya.

▼ *In one fossil discovery, an adult* Psittacosaurus *was found with more than 30 young, which it may have been looking after.*

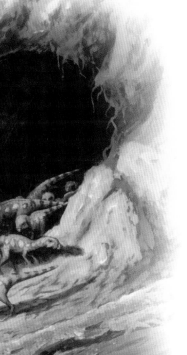

- *Psittacosaurus* **was named** in 1923 from fossils found in Mongolia, Central Asia. Fossils have been found at various sites across Asia, including Russia, China and Thailand.

- **The rear legs** of *Psittacosaurus* were longer and stronger than its front legs, suggesting that this dinosaur may have reared up to run fast on its rear legs, rather than running on all four legs.

- *Psittacosaurus* **measured** about 2 m long, weighed around 20 kg and had four toes on each foot.

- **The name** *Psittacosaurus* means 'parrot reptile', after the dinosaur's beak-shaped mouth, like that of a parrot.

- **Inside its cheeks**, *Psittacosaurus* had many sharp teeth capable of cutting and slicing through tough plant material.

DID YOU KNOW?

Fossil evidence shows that when newly hatched from their eggs, baby Psittacosaurus were hardly longer than a human hand.

249

Ceratopsians

- **Ceratopsians were large plant-eaters** that appeared less than 120 mya.

- **Ceratopsian fossils** come from Europe, North America and Asia.

- **Ceratopsian means 'horn-face'**, after the long horns on the dinosaurs' snouts, eyebrows or foreheads.

- **Most ceratopsians** had a neck shield or frill that swept sideways and up from the back of the head to cover the upper neck and shoulders.

- **Well known ceratopsians** include *Triceratops*, *Styracosaurus*, *Centrosaurus*, *Pentaceratops*, *Anchiceratops*, *Chasmosaurus* and *Torosaurus*.

- **The neck frills** of some ceratopsians, such as that of *Chasmosaurus*, had large gaps or 'windows' in the bone.

- **The windows in the neck frill** were covered in thick, scaly skin.

- **Ceratopsians had no teeth** in the fronts of their hooked, beak-like mouths.

- **Using rows** of powerful cheek teeth, ceratopsians sheared off their plant food.

DID YOU KNOW?
Torosaurus had one of the longest skulls of any land animal, at about 2.6 m from the front of the snout to the rear of the neck frill.

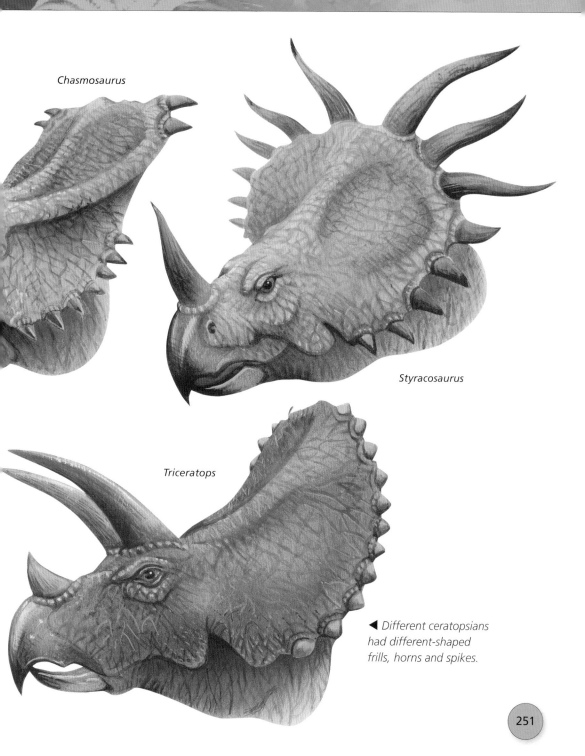

Chasmosaurus

Styracosaurus

Triceratops

◀ Different ceratopsians had different-shaped frills, horns and spikes.

Protoceratops

- *Protoceratops* **was an early kind** of horned dinosaur or ceratopsian, living some 77–70 mya.

- **It has some features** of its ancestors, and also some of the later ceratopsians, such as a neck frill or shield.

- **However the nose horn** of *Protoceratops* was hardly developed, unlike other ceratopsians.

- **The neck frill was not solid** but had gaps or 'windows' probably to save weight, which in life would be filled in with skin.

- *Protoceratops* **was about the size of a pig**, around 1.8 m long and weighed 150 kg.

- **Lots of fossils** found near each other suggest *Protoceratops* lived and travelled in herds.

- **Remains of *Protoceratops*** come from east Asia, especially Mongolia.

- **They were first dug out** in 1922 by a group of American palaeontologists and adventurers who were hoping to find fossils of early humans or 'ape-men'.

DID YOU KNOW?

People in ancient Asia who found Protoceratops fossils may have started the legend of the mythical griffin – a lion-sized beast with four legs and an eagle-like beak that made its nest on the ground.

- **One find of dinosaur nests and eggs** – the first ever to be identified – was said to have been laid by *Protoceratops*.

- **However later studies showed** they belonged to the beaked theropod *Oviraptor*.

▼ *One fossil find shows how* Protoceratops *(right) may have battled with the meat-eater* Velociraptor *(left)*.

253

Spinops

- **Spinops is one of the latest ceratopsians**, or horned dinosaurs, to receive a name, in 2011.

- **It is also one of the dinosaurs** with the longest time span between its fossils being collected and their official description and naming – almost 100 years.

- **The remains were collected** in Alberta, Canada in 1916, from the well-known Red Deer River 'bonebed' rocks.

- **The collectors** were the famous Sternberg family, led by father Charles H Sternberg.

- **They sent the fossils** to London's Natural History Museum, and two years later received a letter saying the remains were 'nothing but rubbish'.

- **Mainly parts of the skull** of *Spinops* were found, but they are enough for it to be identified, through recent study, as a new kind of ceratopsian.

- **The Sternbergs dug up fossils** of dozens of kinds of dinosaurs, fish and other prehistoric creatures.

- **Using information** from similar but more complete finds, *Spinops* is estimated at about 6 m long and weighing 1–2 tonnes.

> **DID YOU KNOW?**
>
> The Sternberg family became so famous that a museum with almost four million specimens is dedicated to them – the Sternberg Museum of Natural History, Hays, Kansas, USA.

🐾 **On each side of *Spinops*' frill** was one long slightly curved horn pointing up and back, and one smaller, curved, hook-shaped horn facing forwards and down.

▼ *The full name of this ceratopsian is* Spinops sternbergorum, *in honour of the Sternberg family.*

Ajkaceratops

- *Ajkaceratops* **was one** of the smallest ceratopsians or horned dinosaurs, probably less than one metre long.

- **Its fossils were found** near the town of Ajka, Hungary, leading to the name 'horn-face of Ajka', which was given in 2010.

- **The discovery of** *Ajkaceratops* extended the known range of ceratopsians from North America and Asia into Europe.

- **The toothless front part** of the mouth, shaped like a parrot beak, is usually easily recognized as typical for a ceratopsian.

- **But in the case of** *Ajkaceratops*, the curved bone forming part of the lower jaw was at first identified as a toe bone of a hoofed mammal, an ungulate.

- **Then turning the bone around,** the palaeontologists realized it came from the jaw of a small horn-faced dinosaur.

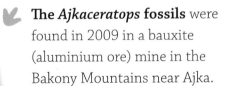

> **DID YOU KNOW?**
>
> Fossils found with those of Ajkaceratops include those of meat-eating dinosaurs, crocodiles, pterosaurs, birds, lizards, turtles and fish.

- **The** *Ajkaceratops* **fossils** were found in 2009 in a bauxite (aluminium ore) mine in the Bakony Mountains near Ajka.

The **remains are from 85 mya**, when parts of Europe were flooded, forming a series of large islands.

As sea levels rose and fell, it seems that ceratopsian dinosaurs and other animals 'island-hopped' from Asia and evolved into new types in their new homes.

▼ Ajkaceratops *probably used its beak to snip off low vegetation, which was chewed by its batteries of cheek teeth.*

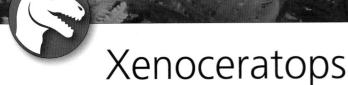

Xenoceratops

- **Officially named in 2012**, the fossils of *Xenoceratops* or 'strange horn face' were originally dug up in 1958.

- **The fossils of *Xenoceratops*** come from Alberta, Canada, and are about 80–75 million years old.

- **These are the oldest remains** of any horn-faced, or ceratopsian dinosaur, found in Canada.

- ***Xenoceratops* was a fairly standard size** for a ceratopsian, at about 6 m long and scaling some 2 tonnes.

- **Even though it was quite early** in the evolution of large ceratopsians, *Xenoceratops* already had a large neck frill with horns and bumps.

- **In particular it had two long**, stout, spike-like horns on either side at the top of the frill, pointing up and slightly outwards.

- **There may have also been** smaller, cone-shaped lumps further down the edge of the frill.

- **Experts studying the fossils** recently realized they had never been officially described or named, and that they represented a new kind of ceratopsian.

- **Then came the discovery of a 'field jacket'**, a plaster casing containing fossils to protect them during excavation and transport, which was over 50 years old.

- **The jacket contained** more remains identified as belonging to *Xenoceratops*.

◀ The exact position of the front horns of Xenoceratops, plus the bony mound or boss in front of them, are not certain.

Triceratops

- **Many fossil remains** of *Triceratops* have been found. It is one of the most-studied and best known dinosaurs, and lived at the very end of the Age of Dinosaurs, 68–66 mya.

- *Triceratops* **was the largest** of the plant-eating ceratopsians, or 'horn-faced' dinosaurs.

- **Fossils of more than** 100 *Triceratops* have been discovered in North America, though no truly complete skeletons.

- *Triceratops* **was about 9 m** long and weighed up to 10 tonnes – as big as the largest elephants of today.

- **As well as a short nose horn** and two one-metre eyebrow horns, *Triceratops* also had a wide, sweeping frill that covered its neck like a curved plate.

- **The neck frill** may have been an anchor for the dinosaur's powerful chewing muscles.

- **Acting as a shield**, the bony neck frill may have protected *Triceratops* as it faced predators head-on.

- **The neck frill** may also have been brightly coloured to impress rivals or enemies – or even potential mates.

- **The beak-like front** of *Triceratops'* mouth was toothless, but it had sharp teeth for chewing in its cheeks.

▲ *The beak, head and neck frill of* Triceratops *made up almost a quarter of its length.*

Pachycephalosaurs

🐾 **Pachycephalosaurs were one of** the last dinosaur groups to appear. Most lived 80–66 mya.

🐾 **They are named after** one of the best known members of the group, *Pachycephalosaurus*.

🐾 *Pachycephalosaurus* **means 'thick-headed reptile'**, due to the domed and hugely thickened bone on the top of its skull – like a cyclist's crash helmet.

DID YOU KNOW?

Pachycephalosaurs are often known as the 'bone-heads', 'dome-heads', or 'helmet-heads'.

▶ *Typical of its group,* Pachycephalosaurus *had a thickened layer of bone on the top of its head.*

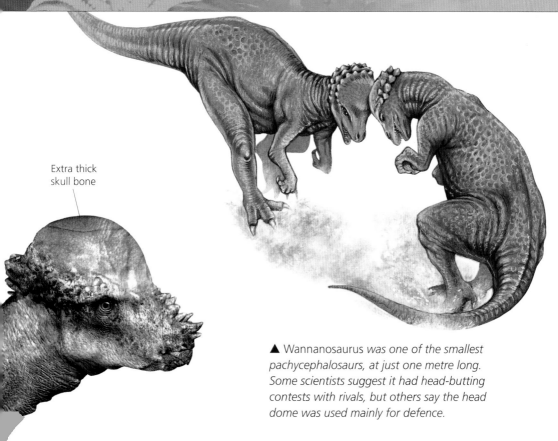

Extra thick skull bone

▲ Wannanosaurus *was one of the smallest pachycephalosaurs, at just one metre long. Some scientists suggest it had head-butting contests with rivals, but others say the head dome was used mainly for defence.*

About 4.5 m long from nose to tail, *Pachycephalosaurus* lived in the American Midwest.

Stegoceras, also from the American Midwest, was about 2 m long with a body the size of a goat.

Homalocephale, **about 2 m long**, lived in Asia 80 mya. It had a flatter skull, but some experts think it was a young *Prenocephale*.

Pachycephalosaurs may have defended themselves by lowering their heads and charging at their enemies.

At breeding time, the males may have tried to butt each other, but how and where is not clear.

Prenocephale

- *Prenocephale* **was one** of the last of the 'bone-heads' or pachycephalosaur dinosaurs, and indeed one of the last of all dinosaurs, living around 70 or less mya.

- **It was quite small**, around 1.8 to 2.5 m long and between 80 and 140 kg in weight.

- **The size of** *Prenocephale* is vague because it is estimated, since limited amounts of its fossils have been found, in East Asia.

- **However there are enough** *Prenocephale* remains to show it was similar in body shape to other, better-known bone-heads.

- *Prenocephale* **had a thickened**, egg-shaped upper skull, like a smooth dome.

- **Around the lower edges of the dome**, like the brim of a hat stretching down to the front of the snout, were a row of small lumps, bumps and spikes.

- **The eyes of** *Prenocephale* were large and faced partly forwards to see in detail and judge distances.

- **The eating habits of** *Prenocephale*, and most pachycephalosaurs, are not clear. Most experts think they ate soft plant material, with perhaps small worms and bugs and eggs, but their teeth were small and not very strong.

- **Fossils of** *Prenocephale* were discovered during an expedition by Polish, Mongolian and Russian fossil experts to the Gobi Desert.

- **The name** *Prenocephale* was given in 1974 and means 'sloping head'.

▼ *A herd of* Prenocephale *scatter in panic as they are attacked by the giant carnivore* Tarbosaurus *(which may be the Asian form of* Tyrannosaurus*).*

Estimating size

- **The biggest dinosaurs** were the sauropods such as *Giraffatitan, Brachiosaurus* and *Argentinosaurus* – but working out how heavy they were when they were alive is very difficult.

- *Giraffatitan* **is known** from many remains, including almost complete skeletons, so its length is measured accurately – 22 m.

- **A dinosaur's weight** can be estimated from a model of its skeleton, which is 'fleshed out' with clay.

- **The clay represents** muscles, guts and skin, which are based on those of similar reptiles, such as crocodiles, for comparison. Or this is done using a virtual model on a computer. Results give weights of between 20 and 40 tonnes for *Giraffatitan*.

- **The size of the clay model** is estimated by immersing it in water to find its volume.

- **The volume of the model** is scaled up to find the volume of the real dinosaur when it was alive.

- **The sauropod *Apatosaurus*** is now well known from about 12 skeletons, which between them have almost every bone in its body.

- **Experts have 'fleshed out'** the skeleton of *Apatosaurus* by different amounts, so estimates of its weight vary from 15 tonnes to more than 40 tonnes.

- **The length of *Apatosaurus*** is known accurately to have been 21 m in total.

Long neck allowed head to browse widely

▼ *African Giraffatitan had very long front legs, like its North American cousin Brachiosaurus.*

DID YOU KNOW?

The weights and volumes of reptiles alive today are used to calculate the probable weight of a dinosaur when it was alive.

Skin

- **Several fossils of dinosaur skin** have been found, revealing that dinosaurs had scales like today's reptiles.

- **As in crocodiles**, dinosaur scales were embedded in the thick, tough hide, rather than lying on top of the skin and overlapping, as in snakes.

- **When the first fossils** of dinosaur skin were found in the mid- 1800s, scientists thought they were from giant prehistoric crocodiles.

- **Fossil skin** of the horned dinosaur *Chasmosaurus* reveals that larger bumps or lumps, called tubercles, were scattered among the normal-sized scales.

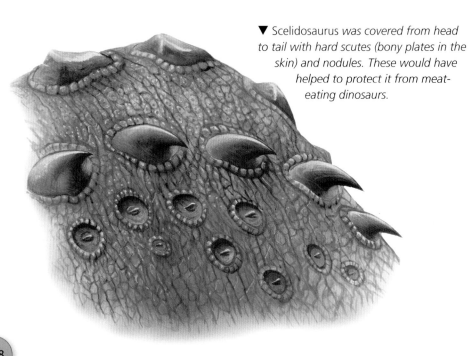

▼ Scelidosaurus *was covered from head to tail with hard scutes (bony plates in the skin) and nodules. These would have helped to protect it from meat-eating dinosaurs.*

▲ *Fossil skin, such as this from* Edmontosaurus, *is a relatively rare find.*

🦶 **Fossil skin** of the duckbilled hadrosaur *Edmontosaurus* has also been found.

🦶 *Edmontosaurus* **was covered** in thousands of small scales, like little pebbles, with larger lumps or tubercles spaced among them.

🦶 **Various specimens** of fossil skin show that the scales of *Iguanodon*-type dinosaurs were larger than those of same-sized, similar duckbill dinosaurs.

🦶 **Scaly skin** protected a dinosaur against the teeth and claws of enemies, accidental scrapes, and the bites of pests such as mosquitoes and fleas.

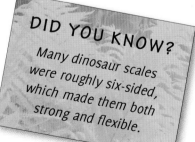

DID YOU KNOW?

Many dinosaur scales were roughly six-sided, which made them both strong and flexible.

Colours

- **No one knows for certain** what colours most dinosaurs were.

- **Some fossil specimens** of dinosaur skin show patterns or shading, but all are stone coloured, as fossils are living things that have turned to stone.

- **However recent detailed fossil finds** have allowed the study of microscopic details of structures called melanosomes in dinosaur feathers, that give clues to colours.

- **The feathered dinosaur *Sinosauropteryx*** probably had white and reddish ginger feathers.

- **According to some experts**, certain dinosaurs may have been bright yellow, red or blue, and possibly striped or patched, like some of today's lizards and snakes.

- **Some dinosaurs** may have been brightly coloured to frighten off predators or to intimidate rivals at breeding time. Colours may have also attracted potential mates.

- **Tall 'sails'** on the backs of the plant-eater *Ouranosaurus* and the meat-eater *Spinosaurus* may have been for visual display, as well as for temperature control.

- **The large, bony back plates** on stegosaurs may have been used for colourful displays to rivals and mates.

- **The large neck frills** of dinosaurs such as *Triceratops* may have been colourful and used for display.

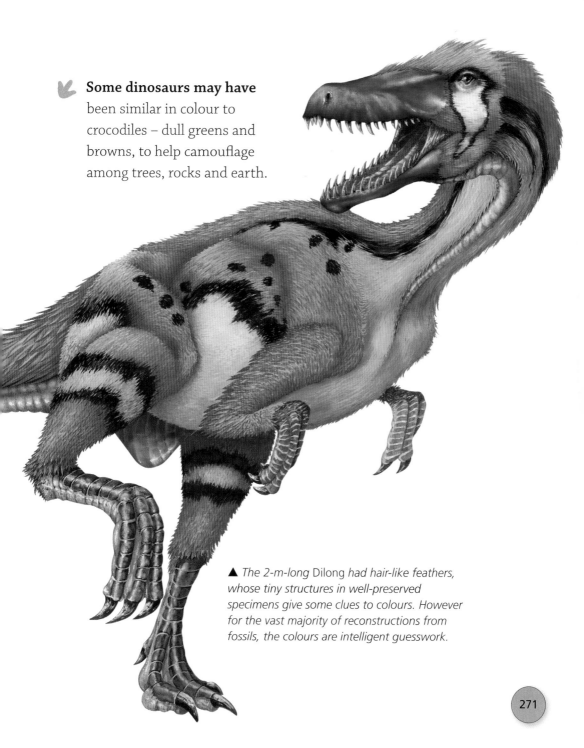

Some dinosaurs may have been similar in colour to crocodiles – dull greens and browns, to help camouflage among trees, rocks and earth.

▲ *The 2-m-long* Dilong *had hair-like feathers, whose tiny structures in well-preserved specimens give some clues to colours. However for the vast majority of reconstructions from fossils, the colours are intelligent guesswork.*

Armour

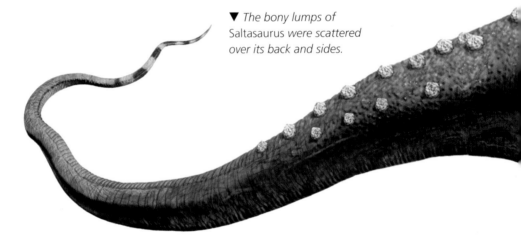

- **Many kinds of dinosaurs** had protective 'armour'.

- **Some armour** took the form of bony plates, or osteoderms, embedded in the skin.

- **A dinosaur with armour** might weigh twice as much as a same-sized dinosaur without armour.

- **Armoured dinosaurs** are divided into two main groups – the ankylosaurs and the nodosaurs.

▼ *The bony lumps of* Saltasaurus *were scattered over its back and sides.*

- **The large sauropod** *Saltasaurus*, unusual for its group, had a kind of armour in the form of hundreds of small, bony lumps packed together in the skin of its back.

- **On its back**, *Saltasaurus* also had about 50 larger pieces of bone, each one the size of a human hand.

- *Saltasaurus* **is named** after the Salta region of Argentina, where its fossils were found. Its fossils have also been found in Uruguay, South America.

- *Saltasaurus* **was 12 m long** and weighed about 6–8 tonnes.

273

Horns

- **A dinosaur's horns got bigger** as the animal grew. Each horn had a bony core and an outer covering of a tough material formed mainly from keratin – the same substance that makes up human hair and fingernails.

- **Horns were most common** among plant-eating dinosaurs. They were probably used for defence and to protect young against predators.

- **The biggest horns** belonged to the ceratopsians or 'horn-faces', such as *Triceratops*.

- **In some ceratopsian horns**, the bony core alone was about one metre long. This did not include the outer sheath, so the whole horn would have been longer.

- **The ceratopsian *Styracosaurus*, or 'spiked reptile',** had a series of long horns around the top of its neck frill, and a very long horn on its nose.

- **Horns may have been used** in head-swinging displays to intimidate rivals and make physical fighting less likely.

DID YOU KNOW?
Dinosaurs may have used their horns to push over plants or dig up roots for food.

- **In battle**, male dinosaurs may have locked horns in a trial of strength, as antelopes do today.

- **Armoured dinosaurs** such as the nodosaur *Panoplosaurus* had horn-like spikes along the sides of the body, especially in the shoulder region.

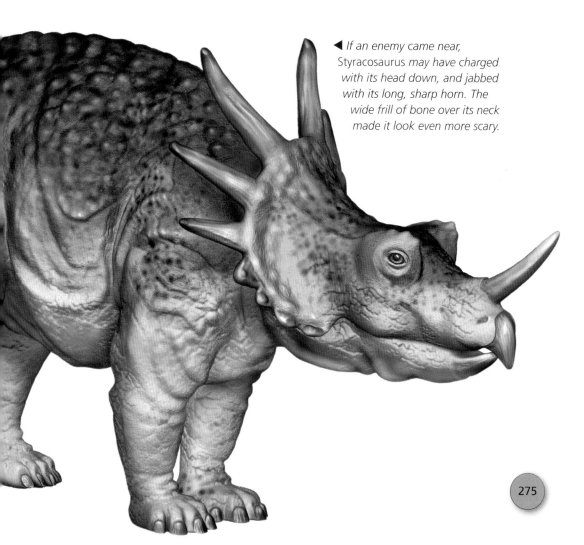

◀ If an enemy came near, *Styracosaurus* may have charged with its head down, and jabbed with its long, sharp horn. The wide frill of bone over its neck made it look even more scary.

275

Head crests

- **Many dinosaurs had lumps**, plates, ridges or other shapes of bone on their heads, called head crests.

- **Head crests** may have been covered with brightly coloured skin for visual display.

- **Meat-eaters with head crests** included *Carnotaurus* and *Dilophosaurus*.

- **The dinosaurs with the largest** and most complicated head crests were the hadrosaurs.

- **The largest head crest** was probably a long, hollow, tubular shape of bone belonging to the hadrosaur *Parasaurolophus*.

- **The head crests of hadrosaurs** may have been involved in making sounds.

- **Some years ago**, the hadrosaur *Tsintaosaurus* was thought to have a very unusual head crest – a hollow tube sticking straight up between the eyes, like a unicorn's horn.

- **The so-called head crest** of *Tsintaosaurus* was then thought to be from another hadrosaur, *Tanius*.

DID YOU KNOW?
The head crests of some large Parasaurolophus, perhaps full-grown males, reached an incredible 1.8 m in length.

Then another *Tsintaosaurus* specimen was found with a similar crest, but more paddle-shaped, so this dinosaur is again regarded as being crested.

▼ *The long crest of* Parasaurolophus *may have had a flap of skin behind it, attached to the lower back of the head.*

277

Teeth

- **Some of the most common** fossil remains are of dinosaur teeth – the hardest parts of their bodies.

- **Dinosaur teeth** come in a huge range of sizes and shapes – daggers, knives, shears, pegs, combs, rakes, file-like rasps, crushing batteries and vices.

- **In some dinosaurs**, up to three-quarters of a tooth was fixed into the jaw bone, so only one-quarter showed.

- **The teeth of plant-eaters** such as *Iguanodon* had angled tops that rubbed past each other in a grinding motion.

▼ Tyrannosaurus *had 50-plus 'banana' teeth. They were long and strong for tearing flesh and crushing bone.*

- **Some duckbill dinosaurs** (hadrosaurs) had more than 1000 teeth, all at the back of the mouth.

- **Like modern reptiles**, dinosaurs probably grew new teeth to replace old, worn or broken ones.

- **Some of the largest teeth** of any dinosaur belonged to 9-m-long *Daspletosaurus*, a tyrannosaur-like meat-eater. They measured up to 18 cm in length.

▼ Edmontosaurus *had no front teeth, only a flattened 'duck-bill'.*

Edmontosaurus had batteries of teeth for crushing plants

Beaks

🦶 **Several kinds of dinosaurs** had a toothless, beak-shaped front to their mouths.

🦶 **Beaked dinosaurs** included ceratopsians (horn-faces) such as *Triceratops*, ornithopods such as *Iguanodon* and the hadrosaurs (duckbills), stegosaurs, ankylosaurs (armoured dinosaurs) and fast-running ostrich dinosaurs.

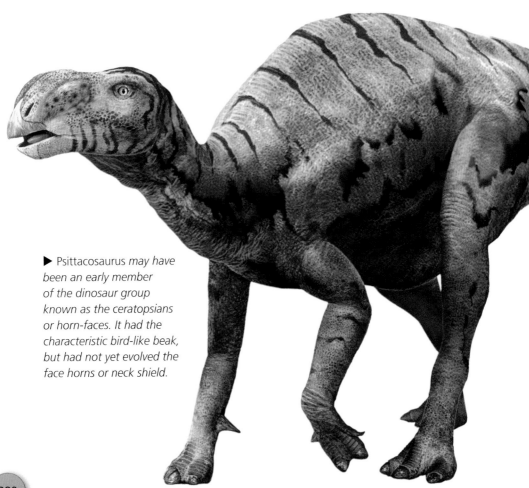

▶ Psittacosaurus *may have been an early member of the dinosaur group known as the ceratopsians or horn-faces. It had the characteristic bird-like beak, but had not yet evolved the face horns or neck shield.*

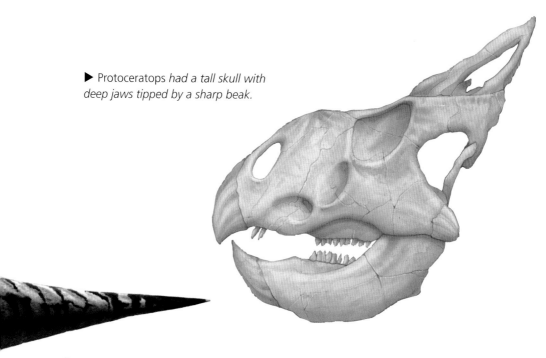

▶ Protoceratops *had a tall skull with deep jaws tipped by a sharp beak.*

🦶 **Most beaked dinosaurs** had chopping or chewing teeth near the backs of their mouths, in their cheeks, but ostrich dinosaurs had no teeth.

🦶 **A dinosaur's beak** was made up of the upper (maxilla) and the lower (dentary or mandible) jaw bones.

🦶 **The bones at the front** of a dinosaur's jaw would have been covered with horn, which formed the outer shape of the beak.

🦶 **Dinosaurs almost certainly used** their beaks for pecking, snipping, tearing and slicing their food. They may also have used their beaks to peck fiercely at any attackers.

DID YOU KNOW?

Some of the largest beaks in relation to body size belonged to Oviraptor and Psittacosaurus.

281

Noses

- **Dinosaurs breathed** through their mouths and/or noses, like many other creatures today.

- **Fossil dinosaur skulls** show that there were two nose openings, called nares, in the bone.

- **The nasal openings**, or nares, led to nasal chambers inside the skull, where the smell organs were located.

- **Some meat-eaters**, especially carnosaurs such as *Allosaurus* and *Tyrannosaurus*, had very large nasal chambers and probably had an excellent sense of smell.

- **In most dinosaurs**, the nasal openings were at the front of the snout, just above the upper jaw.

- **In some dinosaurs**, especially sauropods such as *Mamenchisaurus* and *Brachiosaurus*, the nasal openings were higher on the skull, between the eyes.

- **Fossils show** that air passages led backwards from the nasal chambers into the head for breathing.

DID YOU KNOW?
In hadrosaurs, the nasal passages inside the bony head crests were more than one metre long.

● **The nasal openings** led to external openings, or nostrils, in the skin.

● **New evidence from modern animals** suggests that a dinosaur's nostrils would have been lower down than the nares, towards the front of the snout.

▼ *The nares (nasal openings) at the snout tip of* Tyrannosaurus *were especially large.*

Nares

283

Eyes

No fossils have been found of dinosaur eyes because they were made of soft tissue that soon rotted away after death, or they were eaten by scavengers.

▼ Tyrannosaurus rex *had large eyes that were set at an angle so they looked more to the front rather than to the sides. This allowed* T rex *to see an object in front with both eyes and so judge its distance well.*

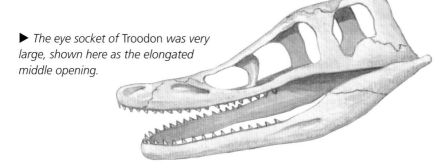

▶ *The eye socket of* Troodon *was very large, shown here as the elongated middle opening.*

🐾 **The main clues** to dinosaur eyes come from the bowl-like hollows, or orbits, in the skull where the eyes were located.

🐾 **The orbits** in fossil skulls show that dinosaur eyes were similar to those of reptiles today.

🐾 **The 6-m-long sauropod** *Vulcanodon* had tiny eyes relative to the size of its head.

🐾 **Small-eyed dinosaurs** probably only had good vision in the daytime.

🐾 **The eyes of many** plant-eating dinosaurs, such as *Vulcanodon*, were on the sides of their heads, giving them all-round vision.

🐾 **The small meat-eater** *Troodon* had relatively large eyes, and it could probably see well, even in dim light.

🐾 *Troodon's eyes* were on the front of its face and pointed forwards, allowing it to see detail and judge distance.

🐾 **Dinosaurs that had large bulges**, called optic lobes, in their brains – detectable by the shapes of their skulls – could probably see very well, perhaps even at night.

DID YOU KNOW?

The plant-eater Leaellynasaura had large optic lobes, and probably had good eyesight.

Brains

- **There is a broad link** between the size of an animal's brain compared to the size of its body, and the level of intelligence it shows.

- **Some fossil dinosaur skulls** have preserved the hollow where the brain once was, revealing its approximate size and shape.

- **In some cases**, a lump of rock formed inside a fossil skull, taking on the size and shape of the brain.

- **The tiny brain** of *Stegosaurus* weighed about 70–80 g, while the whole dinosaur weighed perhaps 4 tonnes.

- **The brain** of *Stegosaurus* was only 1/50,000th of the weight of its whole body (in a human it is 1/50th).

- ***Brachiosaurus'* brain** was perhaps only 1/100,000th of the weight of its whole body.

- **The brain of the small meat-eater** *Troodon* was about 1/100th the weight of its body, which means that *Troodon* was probably one of the most intelligent dinosaurs.

- **The brain-body size comparison** for most dinosaurs is much the same as that of living reptiles.

- **Small- and medium-sized** meat-eaters such as *Troodon* may have been as 'intelligent' as parrots or rats.

- **It was once thought** that *Stegosaurus* had a 'second brain' in the base of its tail. Now this lump is thought to have been a nerve junction.

▶ Camarasaurus *had one of the smallest brains for its body size of any dinosaur – about the size of a human fist.*

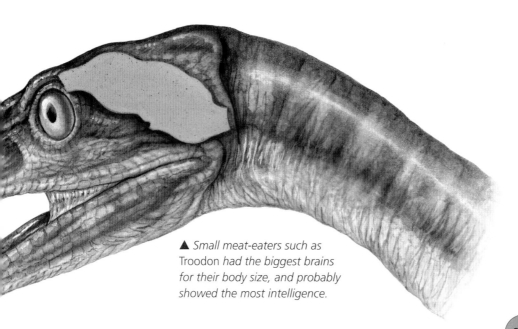

▲ *Small meat-eaters such as* Troodon *had the biggest brains for their body size, and probably showed the most intelligence.*

Stomach stones

- **Some dinosaur fossils** are found with smooth, rounded stones, like seashore pebbles, jumbled up among or near them.

- **Smooth pebbles occur** with dinosaur fossils far more than would be expected by chance alone.

- **These stones** are mainly found with or near the remains of large plant-eating dinosaurs, especially prosauropods such as *Massospondylus*, *Plateosaurus* and *Riojasaurus*, sauropods such as *Brachiosaurus* and *Diplodocus*, the parrot-beaked *Psittacosaurus* and the stegosaurs.

- **Some plant-eating dinosaurs** may have used smooth stones to help process their food.

- **The smooth pebbles** associated with dinosaur remains are known as gastroliths.

- **Gastroliths were stones** that a dinosaur deliberately swallowed.

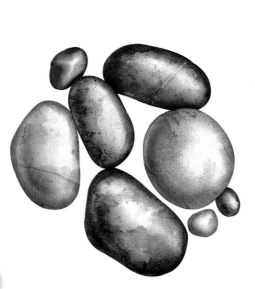

◄ *Gastroliths as small as a pea and as large as a football have been found.*

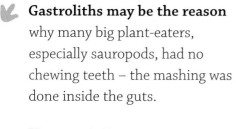

In the stomach, gastroliths acted as 'millstones', crushing and churning food, and breaking it down into a soft pulp for better digestion.

As gastroliths churned and rubbed inside a dinosaur's guts, they became very rounded, smoothed and polished.

Gastroliths may be the reason why many big plant-eaters, especially sauropods, had no chewing teeth – the mashing was done inside the guts.

▼ Sauropods, like Barosaurus, swallowed stones that ground up their food in a part of the digestive system called the gizzard. This meant that no feeding time was wasted in chewing.

KEY

1 Gullet
2 Crop
3 Windpipe
4 Heart
5 Liver
6 Lung
7 Gizzard (stomach)
8 Small intestine
9 Large intestine
10 Kidney

289

Sails

- **Long, bony extensions**, like rods or spines, stuck up from the backs of some dinosaurs.

- **These extensions** may have held up a large area of skin, commonly called a back sail.

- **Dinosaurs with back sails** included the meat-eater *Spinosaurus* and the plant-eater *Ouranosaurus*.

- *Spinosaurus* and *Ouranosaurus* both lived over 100 mya.

- **Fossils of *Spinosaurus*** and *Ouranosaurus* were found in North Africa.

- **The skin on a back sail** may have been brightly coloured, or may even have changed colour, like the skin of a chameleon lizard today.

- **Colours and patterns** could be used to startle enemies, deter rivals, and impress mates at breeding time.

- **A back sail** may have helped to control body temperature. Standing sideways to the sun, it would absorb the sun's heat and allow the dinosaur to warm up quickly.

- **Standing in the shade**, a back sail would lose warmth and help the dinosaur to avoid overheating.

▶ *Apart from its back sail,* Ouranosaurus *was similar to its close cousin, the plant-eater* Iguanodon.

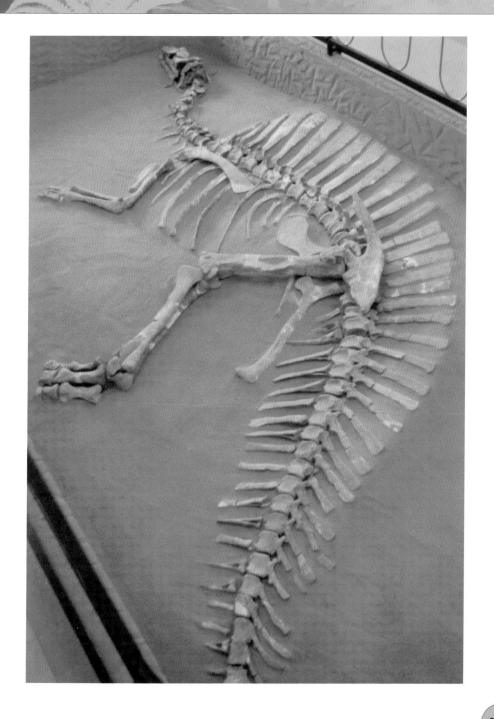

Hips

- **All dinosaurs are classified** in one of two large groups, according to the design and shape of their hip bones.

- **One of these groups** is the Saurischia, meaning 'reptile-hipped'.

- **In a saurischian dinosaur**, the pubis bones (the lower front pair of rod-shaped bones in the pelvis) project down and forwards.

- **Almost all meat-eating dinosaurs** belonged to the Saurischia.

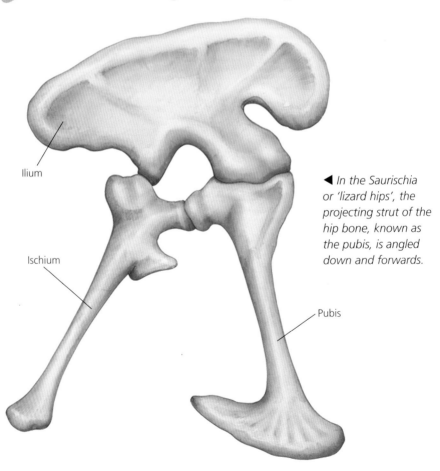

Ilium

Ischium

Pubis

◀ In the Saurischia or 'lizard hips', the projecting strut of the hip bone, known as the pubis, is angled down and forwards.

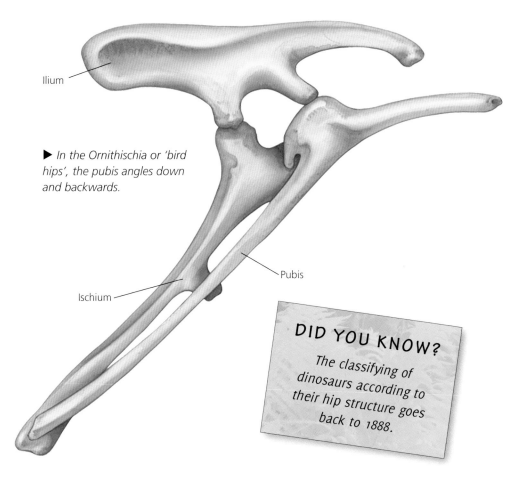

Ilium

▶ In the Ornithischia or 'bird hips', the pubis angles down and backwards.

Ischium

Pubis

DID YOU KNOW?

The classifying of dinosaurs according to their hip structure goes back to 1888.

🐾 **The biggest dinosaurs**, the plant-eating sauropods, also belonged to the Saurischia.

🐾 **The second group** is the Ornithischia, meaning 'bird-hipped'.

🐾 **In an ornithischian dinosaur**, the pubis bones project down and backwards, lying parallel with another pair, the ischium bones.

🐾 **All dinosaurs** in the Ornithischia group, from small *Heterodontosaurus* to huge *Triceratops*, were plant-eaters.

Legs and posture

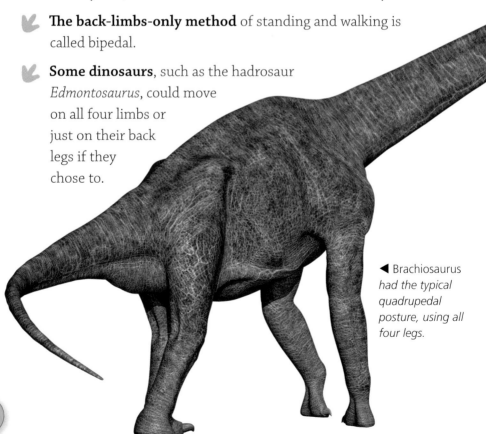

● **All dinosaurs had four limbs.** Unlike some other reptiles, such as snakes and slow-worms, they did not lose their limbs through evolution.

● **Some dinosaurs**, such as the massive, plant-eating sauropod *Janenschia*, stood and walked on all four legs nearly all the time.

● **The all-fours method** of standing and walking is called 'quadrupedal'.

● **Some dinosaurs**, such as the nimble, meat-eating dromaeosaur *Deinonychus*, stood and walked on their back limbs only.

● **The back-limbs-only method** of standing and walking is called bipedal.

● **Some dinosaurs**, such as the hadrosaur *Edmontosaurus*, could move on all four limbs or just on their back legs if they chose to.

◀ Brachiosaurus *had the typical quadrupedal posture, using all four legs.*

▲ Tarbosaurus, *an Asian type of* Tyrannosaurus, *was a bipedal dinosaur that ran and walked on its back legs. Its strong rear legs contrasted hugely to its puny front arms, which were too small to be used.*

The two- or four-legs method of standing and walking is called 'bipedal/quadrupedal'.

Reptiles such as lizards and crocodiles have a sprawling posture, in which the upper legs join the body at the sides.

Dinosaurs had an upright posture, with the legs directly below the body.

The more efficient upright posture and gait may be one major reason why dinosaurs were so successful compared to other animals of the time.

Feet

- **Dinosaur feet differed**, depending on the animal's body design, weight and lifestyle.

- **A typical dinosaur's front feet** had metacarpal bones in the lower wrist or upper hand, and two or three phalanges bones in each digit (finger or toe), tipped by claws.

- **The rear feet** of a typical dinosaur had metatarsal (instead of metacarpal) bones in the lower ankle.

- **Some dinosaurs** had five toes per foot, like most other reptiles (and most birds and mammals).

- **Sauropods probably had feet** with rounded bases supported by a wedge of fibrous, cushion-like tissue.

▲ *A Tyrannosaurus had three clawed toes per foot.*

- **Most sauropods had claws** on their first two or three toes, and smaller, blunter 'hooves' on the other two toes.

- **Ostrich dinosaurs** such as *Gallimimus* had very long feet and long, slim toes for running fast.

- **Many fast-running dinosaurs** had fewer toes, to reduce weight – *Gallimimus* had three toes per back foot.

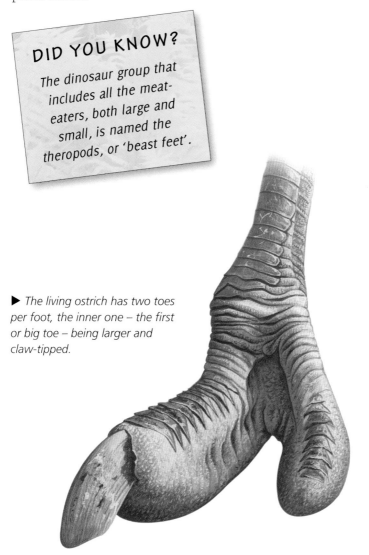

The ornithopod, or 'bird feet' dinosaur group, includes *Iguanodon*, duckbilled dinosaurs, *Heterodontosaurus* and many other plant-eaters.

DID YOU KNOW?

The dinosaur group that includes all the meat-eaters, both large and small, is named the theropods, or 'beast feet'.

▶ The living ostrich has two toes per foot, the inner one – the first or big toe – being larger and claw-tipped.

Claws

- **Like reptiles today**, dinosaurs had claws or similar hard structures at the ends of their digits (fingers and toes).

- **Dinosaur claws** were probably made from keratin – the same hard substance that formed their horns, and from which our own fingernails and toenails are made.

- **Claw shapes and sizes** relative to body size varied greatly between dinosaurs.

- **In many meat-eating dinosaurs** that ran on two back legs, the claws on the fingers were long and sharp, similar to a cat's claws.

- **A small, meat-eating dinosaur** such as *Troodon* probably used its finger claws for grabbing small mammals and lizards, and for scrabbling in the soil for insects and worms.

- **Larger meat-eating dinosaurs** such as *Allosaurus* may have used their hand claws to hold and slash their prey.

- **Huge plant-eating sauropods** such as *Diplodocus* had claws on its elephant-like feet that resembled nails or hooves.

- **Many dinosaurs** had five-clawed digits on their feet, but some, such as *Tyrannosaurus*, had only three.

- **The largest animal claws** belonged to the 'scythe lizards' or therizinosaur dinosaurs – some were more than one metre long.

▲ *The fingers and claws of* Deinonychus *were especially long and strong.*

Deinonychus **had long claws** on its hands and feet that it used to slash at prey. Its name means 'terrible claw' and it lived in the Mid-Cretaceous Period.

299

Tails

- **All dinosaurs** evolved with tails – though some individuals may have lost theirs in attacks or accidents.

- **The length of the tail** relative to the body, and its shape, thickness and special features, gives many clues as to how the dinosaur used it.

- **The longest tails**, at more than 17 m, belonged to the giant plant-eating sauropods such as *Diplodocus*.

- **Some sauropods** had a chain of more than 80 separate caudal vertebrae (bones in the tail) – more than twice the usual number.

▼ Compsognathus *had a long tail that helped it to balance and turn quickly when it was running fast.*

▶ *The 10-m sauropod* Shunosaurus *lived in China 170 mya. It had a tail club with added spikes, which would have made a powerful weapon for self-defence.*

Sauropods may have used their tails as a whip to flick at enemies.

Many meat-eating dinosaurs that stood or ran on their back legs had thick-based tails to balance the weight of their bodies.

Small meat-eaters, such as *Compsognathus*, used their tails for balance when leaping and darting about.

The meat-eater *Ornitholestes* had a tail that was more than half of its 2-m length. It was used as a counterbalance and rudder to help it turn corners at speed.

Armoured dinosaurs called ankylosaurs had two huge lumps of bone at the ends of their tails, which they swung at their enemies like a club.

The tails of duckbilled dinosaurs (hadrosaurs) may have been swished from side to side in the water as an aid to swimming.

Male and female

- **In dinosaur fossils**, the shapes of the hip bones and head crests can indicate if the creatures were male or female.

- **Head crest fossils** of different sizes and proportions belonging to the hadrosaur (duckbilled dinosaur) *Lambeosaurus* have been found.

- **Some *Lambeosaurus*** had short, rounded main crests with small, spike-like spurs pointing up and back.

- **Other _Lambeosaurus_** had a large, angular main crest with a large spur pointing up and back.

- **The head crest differences** in _Lambeosaurus_ fossils may indicate that males and females looked different.

- **Remains of the hadrosaur** _Corythosaurus_ show two main sizes of head crest, perhaps one belonging to females and the other to males.

- **New studies** in the variations of head crests led to about ten different species of these dinosaurs being reclassified as just two species of _Corythosaurus_.

> **DID YOU KNOW?**
>
> In Parasaurolophus specimens, some head crests were twice as long as others – probably a male-female difference.

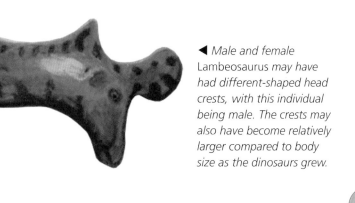

◀ Male and female Lambeosaurus _may have had different-shaped head crests, with this individual being male. The crests may also have become relatively larger compared to body size as the dinosaurs grew._

303

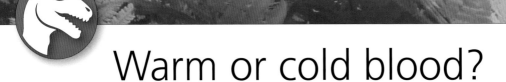

Warm or cold blood?

- **If dinosaurs were cold-blooded**, like reptiles today, they would have been slow or inactive in cold conditions.

- **If dinosaurs were warm-blooded**, like birds and mammals today, they would have been able to stay warm and active in cold conditions.

- **Experts once believed** that all dinosaurs were cold-blooded, but today there is much disagreement.

▼ *The 'Willo' specimen in 1993 was identified as the fossilized heart of a small plant-eating dinosaur,* Thescelosaurus, *with similarities to a bird or mammal heart. However it may well be simply a natural rock formation.*

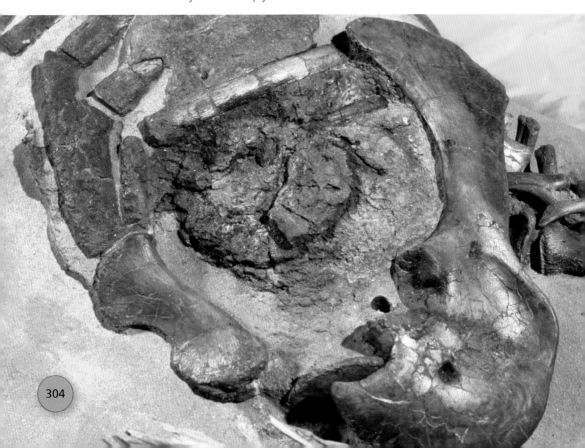

▶ *Crocodiles, which were around even in the very earliest dinosaur period (the Triassic) are cold-blooded.*

Some evidence for warm-bloodedness comes from the structure of fossil bones.

The structure of some dinosaur bones is more like that of warm-blooded creatures than of reptiles.

Some small meat-eating dinosaurs very probably evolved into birds. As birds are warm-blooded, these dinosaurs may have been warm-blooded too.

If some dinosaurs were warm-blooded, they would probably have needed to eat at least ten times more food than if they were cold-blooded, to 'burn' food energy to make heat.

In a 'snapshot' count of dinosaur fossils, the number of predators compared to prey is more like the comparisons seen in mammals than in reptiles.

Many small meat-eaters are now known to have had feathers. One reason could be as insulation, to keep in body heat if the dinosaur was warm-blooded.

Speed

- **The fastest dinosaurs** had long, slim, muscular legs and small, lightweight bodies.

- **Ostrich dinosaurs** were probably the speediest, perhaps attaining the same top speed as today's ostrich – 70 km/h.

- **The main leg muscles** of the ostrich dinosaur *Struthiomimus* were in its hips and thighs.

- **The hip and leg design** of ostrich dinosaurs meant they could swing their limbs to and fro quickly, like those of a modern racehorse.

- **Large, powerful, plant-eating dinosaurs**, such as the duckbill *Edmontosaurus*, may have pounded along on their huge back legs at 40 km/h.

- **Plant-eaters** such as *Iguanodon* and *Muttaburrasaurus* may have trotted along at 10–12 km/h for many hours.

- **Some experts** once suggested that the great meat-eater *Tyrannosaurus* may have been able to run at 50 km/h.

- **Other experts think** *Tyrannosaurus* was a relatively slow runner at 20 km/h.

- **The slowest dinosaurs** were giant sauropods such as *Brachiosaurus*, which probably plodded at 4–6 km/h (about human walking speed).

- **The fastest land animal today**, the cheetah, would beat any dinosaur with its maximum burst of speed of more than 100 km/h.

▼ *In 2007, computer predictions based on data taken from fossils suggested that the top speed of* Tyrannosaurus *may have been about 28 km/h.*

Coprolites

- **Coprolites are the fossilized droppings**, or dung, of animals from long ago, such as dinosaurs. Like other fossils, they have become solid rock.

- **Thousands of dinosaur coprolites** have been found at fossil sites across the world.

- **Cracking or cutting** open coprolites may reveal what the dinosaur had eaten.

- **Coprolites produced** by large meat-eaters such as *Tyrannosaurus* contain bone from their prey.

- **The microscopic structure** of the bones found in coprolites shows the age of the prey when it was eaten. Most victims were very young or old, as these were the easiest creatures for a predator to kill.

- **Coprolites produced** by small meat-eaters such as *Compsognathus* may contain the hard bits of insects, such as the legs and wing cases of beetles.

- **Huge piles** of coprolites found in Montana, USA, were probably produced by the large plant-eater *Maiasaura*.

- *Maiasaura* **coprolites** contain the remains of cones, buds and the needle-like leaves of conifer trees, showing that these dinosaurs had a diet of tough plant matter.

▶ *Fossilized dinosaur dung may provide clues as to the kind of food eaten by dinosaurs.*

DID YOU KNOW?

One of the largest dinosaur coprolites found measures 44 cm in length and was probably produced by *Tyrannosaurus*.

Footprints

Fossilized dinosaur footprints have been found all over the world.

Some dinosaurs left footprints when they walked on the soft mud or sand of riverbanks. Then the mud baked hard in the sun, and was covered by more sand or mud, which helped preserve the footprints as fossils.

Some footprints were made when dinosaur feet left impressions in soft mud or sand that was then covered by volcanic ash, which set hard.

Many footprints have been found together in lines, called 'trackways'. These suggest that some dinosaurs lived in groups, or used the same routes regularly.

The **distance between** same-sized footprints indicates whether a dinosaur was walking, trotting or running.

Footprints of big meat-eaters such as *Tyrannosaurus* show three toes with claws, on a forward-facing foot.

In big plant-eaters, such as *Iguanodon*, each footprint shows three separate toes, but less or no claw impressions, and the feet point slightly inwards.

In giant plant-eating sauropods, each footprint is rounded and has indentations of nail-like 'hooves'.

Some sauropod footprints are more than one metre across.

DID YOU KNOW?
In 2009 sauropod footprints 1.7 m across were found in the Jura region of France.

▲ *Fossilized footprints are called trace fossils because they are signs or prints made by dinosaurs, or other creatures, rather than actual body parts.*

311

Herds

- **When fossils of many individuals** of the same dinosaur type are found together, there are various possible causes.

- **One reason is because** their bodies were swept to the same place by a flood, although they may have originally been living in different places.

- **The dinosaurs may have died** in the same place if they had lived there as a group or herd.

- **There is much evidence** that various dinosaur types lived in groups or herds, examples being *Diplodocus*, *Triceratops* and *Iguanodon*.

- **Many fossil footprints** found together heading the same way also suggest that some dinosaurs lived in herds.

- **Some fossil groups** include dinosaurs of different ages, from babies to youngsters and adults.

- **Footprints of a plant-eating dinosaur** have been found with the prints of a meat-eater to one side of them – perhaps evidence of a hunter pursuing its victim.

- **Prints all pointing** in the same direction indicate a herd travelling together to the same place.

- **Sometimes larger footprints** are found to the sides of smaller ones, possibly indicating that adults guarded their young between them.

- **Many jumbled prints** in what was once mud suggests a group of dinosaurs came to drink at a riverbank or lakeside.

▶ *A mixed-age herd would have left similar footprints of different sizes.*

DID YOU KNOW?

At Peace River Canyon, British Columbia, Canada, some 1700 footprints were found.

Migration

🐾 **Today, almost no land reptiles** go on regular, long-distance journeys, called migrations.

🐾 **Over the past 30 years**, some scientists have suggested that certain dinosaurs regularly migrated.

🐾 **Evidence for migrating dinosaurs** comes from the positions of the continents at the time. In certain regions, cool winters would have prevented the growth of enough plants for dinosaurs to eat.

🐾 **Fossil evidence suggests** that some plants stopped growing during very hot or dry times, so some dinosaurs would have migrated to find food.

🐾 **The footprints or tracks** of many dinosaurs travelling in herds is possible evidence that some dinosaurs migrated.

🐾 **Dinosaurs that may have migrated** include *Pachyrhinosaurus*, sauropods such as *Diplodocus* and *Camarasaurus*, and ornithopods such as *Iguanodon* and *Muttaburrasaurus*.

🐾 **One huge fossil site** in Alberta, Canada, contains the fossils of about 1000 *Pachyrhinosaurus* – perhaps a migrating herd that got caught in a flood.

🐾 **In North America**, huge herds of horned dinosaurs may have migrated north for the brief sub-Arctic summer.

🐾 **In 2012, teeth from *Camarasaurus*** suggested they migrated perhaps 300 km each way to avoid the dry season.

▶ *Fossils of* Pachyrhinosaurus *have been found in parts of Alaska that were inside the Arctic Circle at the end of the Cretaceous Period. It is possible they migrated here from farther south.*

DID YOU KNOW?
Migrating Centrosaurus may have walked 100 km a day.

Hibernation

- **Dinosaurs may have** gone into an inactive state called torpor or 'hibernation' during cold periods, as many reptiles do today.

- **The plant-eater** *Leaellynasaura*, found at Dinosaur Cove, Australia, may have become torpid due to the yearly cycle of seasons there.

- **Dinosaur Cove** was nearer the South Pole when dinosaurs lived there, 110–105 mya. At this time, the climate was relatively warm, with no ice at the North or South Poles.

- **Dinosaurs living** at Dinosaur Cove would have had to cope with periods of darkness in winter. They may have become torpid to survive the cold.

- **The eye and brain shapes** of *Leaellynasaura* suggest it had good eyesight, which would have helped it to see in the winter darkness, or in dim forests.

- **Dinosaur fossils** have been found in the Arctic region near the North Pole.

- **Arctic dinosaurs** either became torpid in winter, or migrated south to warmer regions.

▼ Leaellynasaura *may have slept through the cold season, perhaps protected in a burrow. This 3-m dinosaur had a longer tail, in proportion to size, than almost any other dinosaur.*

DID YOU KNOW?

Leaellynasaura means 'Leaellyn's lizard/reptile', named after Leaellyn Rich, the young daughter of the palaeontolgists who discovered its fossils.

Sounds

🦕 **Few reptiles today** make complicated sounds, except for simple hisses, grunts, coughs and roars.

🦕 **Fossils suggest** that dinosaurs made a variety of sounds in several different ways.

🦕 **The bony, hollow head crests** of duckbills (hadrosaurs) may have been used for making sounds.

🦕 **The head crests** of some hadrosaurs contained tubes called respiratory airways, which were used for breathing.

🦕 **Air blown forcefully** through a hadrosaur's head crest passages could have made the whole crest vibrate.

🦕 **A vibrating head crest** may have made a loud sound like a honk, roar or bellow – similar to an elephant trumpeting with its trunk.

🦕 **Fossil skulls** of some hadrosaurs, such as *Edmontosaurus* and *Kritosaurus*, suggest that there was a loose flap of skin, like a floppy bag, between the nostrils and the eyes.

DID YOU KNOW?

By blowing through models of hadrosaur head crests, a wide range of sounds can be made – similar to those of brass and wind instruments!

▶ Inside the mostly hollow head crest of the hadrosaur Lambeosaurus, the airways or nasal passages followed a winding route.

Kritosaurus may have inflated its loose nasal flap of skin like a balloon to make a honking or bellowing sound, as some seals do today.

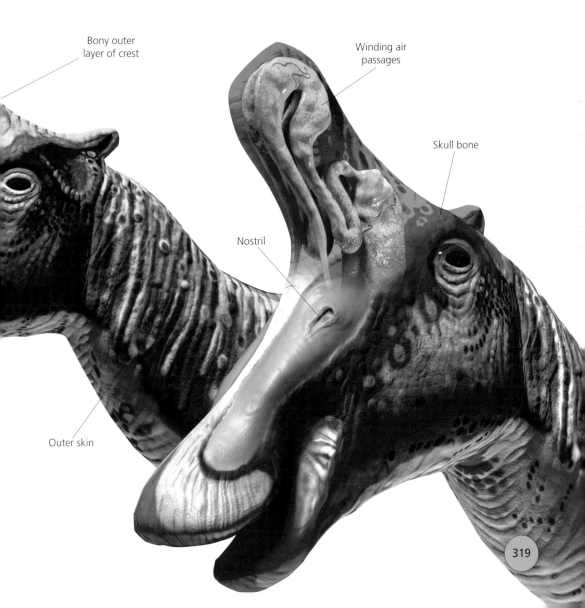

Bony outer layer of crest

Winding air passages

Skull bone

Nostril

Outer skin

Nests

- **There are hundreds** of discoveries of fossil dinosaur eggs and nests, found with the parent dinosaurs.

- **Eggs and nests** of the plant-eater *Protoceratops*, an early kind of horned dinosaur, were found in 2011.

- **Some of the nests** once thought to be of *Protoceratops* are now believed to belong to *Oviraptor*.

- **Many of these nests** were found in a small area, showing that these dinosaurs bred in colonies.

- **The nests were shallow**, bowl-shaped pits about one metre across, scraped in the earth.

- **The eggs were probably covered** with earth and incubated by the heat of the sun.

- **New nests had been made** on top of old ones, showing that the colony was used year after year.

- **Nests and eggs** of the plant-eater *Orodromeus* have been found in Montana, USA.

- **In each nest**, about 20 *Orodromeus* eggs were neatly arranged in a spiral, starting with one in the centre and working outwards.

▼ *Various clues from fossil evidence show that the hadrosaur* Maiasaura *may have brought food back to its newly hatched young in the nest. Whether one parent or both did is not known.*

DID YOU KNOW?

Some preserved nests of Maiasaura babies contain traces of fossil buds and leaves – perhaps food brought to them by a parent.

Hatchling

Unhatched egg

Eggs

- **Fossil finds since the 1970s** show that some dinosaurs may have looked after their young.

- **Fossils of the small** parrot-beaked dinosaur *Psittacosaurus* suggest one adult may have guided and guarded many young.

- **These fossils were probably preserved** when the adult and young sheltered in a cave that collapsed on them all.

- **Many fossils** of adult *Maiasaura* have been found, together with its nests, eggs and hatchlings (newly hatched young).

- **Fossils of *Maiasaura*** come mainly from Montana, USA and are about 75 million years old. The main fossil area is nicknamed 'Egg Mountain'.

- **There are remains of** more than 100 *Maiasaura* specimens of different ages.

- **The teeth of *Maiasaura*** babies found in the nest are slightly worn, suggesting that they had eaten food.

- **The leg bones and joints** of the *Maiasaura* babies were not quite fully formed, showing that they were not yet able to move about to gather their own food.

- **Evidence from the *Maiasaura*** nesting sites shows the nests were about 7 m apart, which would just allow room for a 9–m adult. Each nest had up to 40 eggs laid in spiral pattern.

- **The name *Maiasaura*** means 'good mother reptile' and was given in 1979 by US palaeontologists John 'Jack' Horner and Robert Makela.

▲ *A cast of a baby* Maiasaura *duckbill dinosaur, among the fossil remains of a nest site. These fossils were discovered in Montana, USA.*

Growth

 In very well-preserved fossils sometimes fine details can be seen as lines, rings and other marks relating to how the dinosaur or other animal grew through the seasons and years.

 The spacing of the marks may show slow or limited growth due to food shortage, disease or severe climate conditions. Marks farther apart indicate faster growth, for example, with plentiful food.

 More than 60 dinosaur bones have been studied in this way to assess growth speed at different ages.

 The bones included *Tyrannosaurus* and its smaller cousins *Albertosaurus*, at up to 2 tonnes, and *Daspletosaurus* at 2–3 tonnes.

 Results show all three kinds of dinosaurs grew especially fast in adolescence.

 Albertosaurus* and *Daspletosaurus had growth spurts at around 11–15 years of age, when they put on an estimated 0.3–0.5 kg of weight – every day.

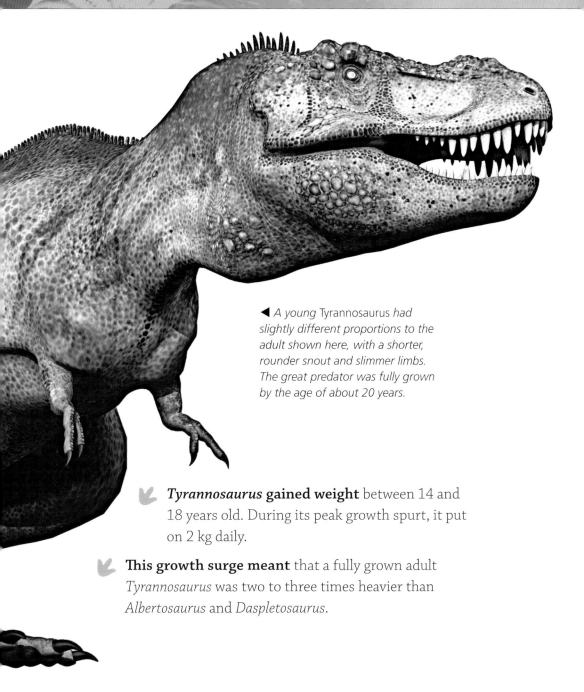

◀ *A young* Tyrannosaurus *had slightly different proportions to the adult shown here, with a shorter, rounder snout and slimmer limbs. The great predator was fully grown by the age of about 20 years.*

Tyrannosaurus **gained weight** between 14 and 18 years old. During its peak growth spurt, it put on 2 kg daily.

This growth surge meant that a fully grown adult *Tyrannosaurus* was two to three times heavier than *Albertosaurus* and *Daspletosaurus*.

Age and lifespan

- **Detailed studies of the growth lines** and rings in very well-preserved fossils reveal how long dinosaurs and other prehistoric creatures lived.

- **Analysis of *Tyrannosaurus* bones** showed that by 20 years of age, and weighing around 5 tonnes, they almost stopped growing during adulthood.

- **The oldest and biggest specimen** of *Tyrannosaurus*, nicknamed 'Sue', died at 28 years of age.

- **Other estimates of dinosaur growth** rates and ages come from comparisons with today's birds, mammals and reptiles.

- **Some reptiles today** continue to grow throughout their lives, although their growth rate slows with age, while birds reach adult size in one or two years, then do not grow any more.

- **Like many animals today**, a dinosaur's growth rate probably depended largely on its food supply, the temperature, disease and other factors.

- **Small meat-eating dinosaurs** such as *Compsognathus* may have lived to be only five to eight years old.

- **A giant sauropod probably lived** to be 50 years old, or even more than 100 years old.

- **During its lifetime**, a big sauropod such as *Brachiosaurus* would have increased its weight 2000 times (compared to 20 times in a human).

DID YOU KNOW?

The longest-lived land animals today are reptiles – the giant tortoises and other tortoise species. There are several recorded ages of 150–200 years, with a few claims for over 250 years.

▼ Crocodiles frequently exceed 50 years of age, and some may reach 100, while alligators have been recorded at 50–60 years old.

Europe

- **The first dinosaur fossils** ever discovered and given official names were found in England in the 1820s.

- **One of the first** almost complete dinosaur skeletons found was that of the big plant-eater *Iguanodon*, in 1871, in southern England.

- **Some of the most numerous** early fossils found were those of *Iguanodon*, discovered in the Belgian village of Bernissart in 1878.

- **About 155–145 mya**, Solnhofen in southern Germany was a mosaic of lush islands and shallow lagoons – ideal for many kinds of life.

- **At Solnhofen**, amazingly detailed fossils of tiny *Compsognathus* and the first-known bird *Archaeopteryx* have been found preserved in sandstone.

◄ *The dots indicate just a few of the dinosaur fossil sites found in Europe.*

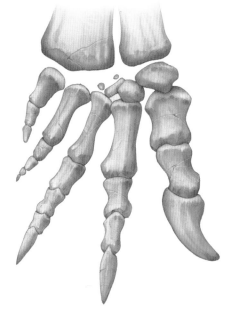

- Fossils of *Compsognathus* were also found near Nice in southern France.

- **Many fossils** of *Plateosaurus* were recovered from Trossingen, Germany, in 1911–12, 1921–23 and 1932.

- **Some of the largest fossil eggs**, measuring 30 cm long, were thought to have been laid by *Hypselosaurus* near Aix-en-Provence in southern France.

- **The Isle of Wight** off southern England has provided so many dinosaur fossils that it is sometimes known as 'Dinosaur Island'.

- Fossils of *Hypsilophodon* have been found in eastern Spain, and those of *Camptosaurus* on the coast of Portugal.

▲ *One of the first really big dinosaurs was* Plateosaurus, *or 'flat reptile'. Its front feet could be hyper-extended. This flexibility meant that* Plateosaurus *may have been able to grasp branches while feeding.*

▶ *During the Jurassic Period, much of Europe would have looked like this. There was a much more tropical climate where ferns, ginkgoes, horsetails and cycads flourished alongside forests of conifers and tree ferns.*

Africa

🐾 **The first major discoveries** of dinosaur fossils in Africa were made in 1907, at Tendaguru, present-day Tanzania. They included *Giraffatitan*, *Dicraeosaurus*, and the stegosaur-like *Kentrosaurus*.

🐾 **Remains of *Cetiosaurus*** were found in Morocco, north Africa.

🐾 ***Nigersaurus***, a 9-m, 10-tonne plant-eater, is known from fossils found in Niger. It had huge numbers of teeth, more than 500 at any one time.

🐾 **Fossils of *Spinosaurus***, the largest meat-eating dinosaur, come from Morocco and Egypt.

🐾 **The sail-backed *Ouranosaurus*** is known from remains found in Niger.

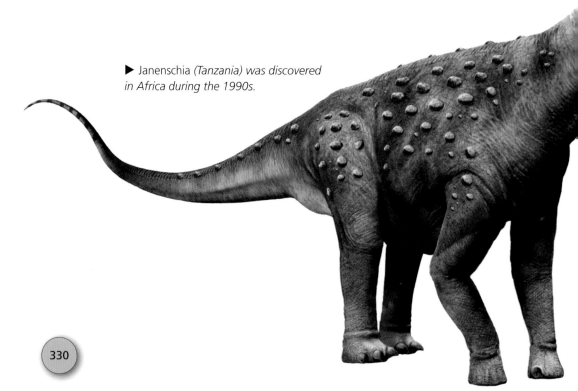

▶ Janenschia *(Tanzania) was discovered in Africa during the 1990s.*

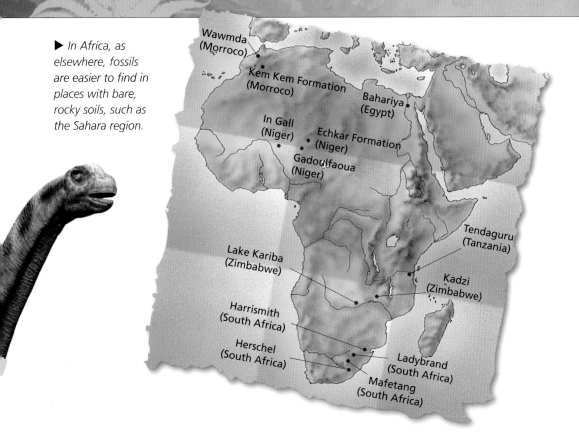

► In Africa, as elsewhere, fossils are easier to find in places with bare, rocky soils, such as the Sahara region.

Wawmda (Morroco)
Kem Kem Formation (Morroco)
Bahariya (Egypt)
In Gall (Niger)
Echkar Formation (Niger)
Gadoulfaoua (Niger)
Tendaguru (Tanzania)
Lake Kariba (Zimbabwe)
Kadzi (Zimbabwe)
Harrismith (South Africa)
Herschel (South Africa)
Ladybrand (South Africa)
Mafetang (South Africa)

🐾 **Many sauropod fossils** were uncovered at African sites, including *Tornieri* from Tanzania, and *Vulcanodon* in Zimbabwe.

🐾 **Remains of *Massospondylus*,** a plant-eating prosauropod, were extracted from several sites in southern Africa.

🐾 **Fossils named as *Gyposaurus*** have been found in Orange Free State, South Africa.

🐾 **During the 1908–12** fossil-hunting expedition to Tendaguru, more than 250 tonnes of fossil bones and rocks from dinosaurs such as *Giraffatitan* were carried 65 km to the nearest port, for transport to Germany.

Asia

🦶 **Hundreds of kinds** of dinosaurs have been discovered on the continent of Asia.

🦶 **In Asia**, most of the dinosaur fossils that have been found so far were located in the Gobi Desert in Central Asia, and in present-day China. Some were also found in present-day India.

🦶 **Remains of *Titanosaurus***, the huge plant-eating sauropod, were uncovered near Umrer, in India. It lived about 70 mya, and was similar in shape to its cousin of the same time, *Saltasaurus*, from South America.

🦶 ***Titanosaurus* was about** 12 m long and weighed 10–15 tonnes.

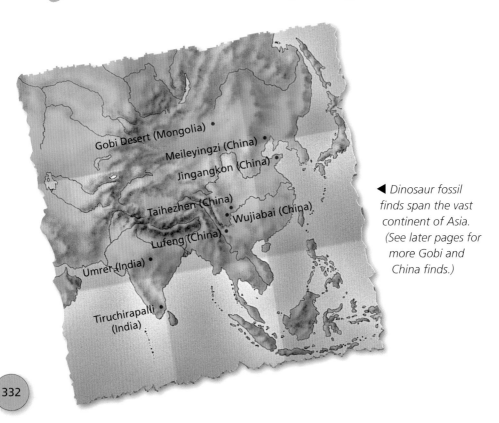

Gobi Desert (Mongolia)

Meileyingzi (China)

Jingangkon (China)

Taihezhen (China)

Wujiabai (China)

Lufeng (China)

Umrer (India)

Tiruchirapalli (India)

◀ *Dinosaur fossil finds span the vast continent of Asia. (See later pages for more Gobi and China finds.)*

▲ *The fossils of* Saltasaurus *(shown here) and* Titanosaurus *are very similar, and some experts consider them to be the same type of dinosaur.*

🦶 **Fossils of the sauropod** *Barapasaurus* were found in India and described and named in 1975.

🦶 ***Barapasaurus* was 14 m long** and probably weighed more than 10 tonnes. It is one of the first sauropods known from anywhere in the world, living around 190–180 mya.

🦶 **Fossils of** *Dravidosaurus*, once thought to belong to the stegosaur group, were found near Tiruchirapalli in southern India. Further studies suggest they are actually from a type of sea reptile.

Gobi Desert

The Gobi Desert covers much of southern Mongolia and parts of northern China.

The first fossil-hunting expeditions to the Gobi Desert took place in 1922–25, and were organized by the American Museum of Natural History.

The expeditions set out to look for fossils of early humans, but instead found amazing dinosaur remains.

▼ Gallimimus *fossils were found in the early 1970s in the Nemegt region of the Gobi, which has yielded many exciting remains. There are parts of skeletons of many individuals, ranging from youngsters to adults.*

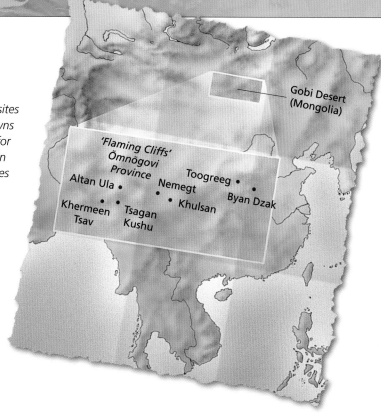

▶ *The Gobi's fossil sites are far from any towns or cities. Searching for fossils is hard work in extreme temperatures and dust storms.*

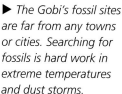

The first fossil dinosaur eggs were found by the 1922–25 expeditions.

Velociraptor, Avimimus* and *Pinacosaurus were discovered in the Gobi.

Russian expeditions to the Gobi Desert in 1946 and 1948–49 discovered new armoured and duckbilled dinosaurs.

More expeditions in the 1960s–70s found the giant sauropod *Opisthocoelicaudia* and the helmet-headed *Prenocephale*.

Other Gobi dinosaurs include *Gallimimus* and *Oviraptor*. In the 1990s–2000s more expeditions uncovered therizinosaurs.

China

- **For centuries**, dinosaur fossils in China were identified as belonging to folklore creatures such as dragons.

- **The first fossils** studied scientifically in China were uncovered in the 1930s.

- **From the 1980s**, dinosaur discoveries in almost every province of China have amazed scientists around the globe.

- **A few exciting dinosaur finds** in China have been fakes, such as part of a bird skeleton that was joined to the part-skeleton of a dinosaur along a natural-looking crack in the rock.

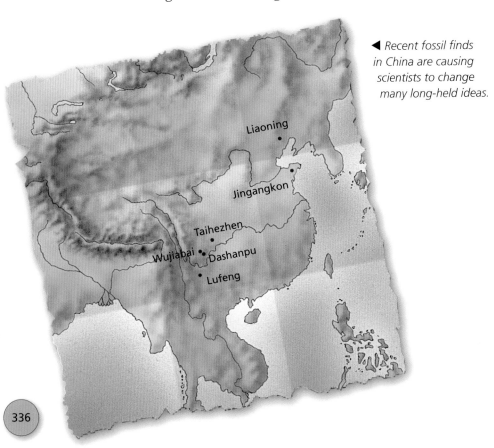

◀ Recent fossil finds in China are causing scientists to change many long-held ideas.

Liaoning

Jingangkon

Taihezhen

Wujiabai • Dashanpu

Lufeng

◀ When officially named in 2000, Microraptor, from the Early Cretaceous Period, was the only dinosaur with feathers on its body, arms and legs.

🐾 **Some better-known Chinese finds** include *Mamenchisaurus*, *Psittacosaurus*, *Tuojiangosaurus* and *Avimimus*.

🐾 **Remains of the prosauropod** *Lufengosaurus* were uncovered in China's southern province of Yunnan, in 1941.

DID YOU KNOW?
Only the USA probably has more fossil dinosaurs than China.

🐾 **China's *Lufengosaurus*** lived during the Early Jurassic Period, and measured about 6–7 m in length.

🐾 **Many recently found fossils** in China are of feathered dinosaurs such as *Caudipteryx*, *Sinosauropteryx* and *Microraptor*.

337

Anchiornis

- *Anchiornis*, **or 'near bird'**, was a tiny dinosaur that lived 160–150 mya. Its fossils were found in Liaoning in China, and were named in 2009.

- **A member of the troodontid group**, *Anchiornis* was almost completely covered in feathers.

- *Anchiornis* **was only 40 cm long** and probably weighed less than 0.2 kg. Its head, four legs, body and tail were all covered in feathers.

- **The leg and tail-end feathers** had central quills with vanes branching off, similar to a modern bird's flight feathers.

- **The head, body and upper tail** had plume-like or downy feathers, soft and flexible.

- *Anchiornis* **fossils were so detailed** that scientists could see tiny parts called melanosomes, which make the coloured substances, or pigments, for the feathers.

- **The shapes, sizes and positions** of melanosomes were compared with those of modern birds, to show the colours and patterns of Anchiornis feathers.

- *Anchiornis* **had a brown head crown**, a dark face with brown patches, and legs with rows of blackish-grey and white feathers, giving a striped effect.

- **Perhaps** *Anchiornis* **glided** from tree to tree and also used its feather patterns for display, such as to frighten rivals from its territory, or attract a mate.

DID YOU KNOW?

Anchiornis had more than 80 flight feathers on its limbs, and even most parts of its feet were feather-covered.

▲ The colours of Anchiornis in life are known from the microscopic details of its feathers – except for the tail, which was not preserved.

Australia

- **In the past 50 years**, some of the most exciting discoveries of dinosaur fossils have come from Australia.

- **Remains of the large plant-eater** *Muttaburrasaurus* were found near Muttaburra, Queensland.

- *Muttaburrasaurus* was about 8 m long and similar in some ways to the well known plant-eater *Iguanodon*.

- **Fossils of *Rhoetosaurus***, a giant plant-eater, were found in 1924 in southern Queensland.

DID YOU KNOW?
Dinosaur Cove is difficult to reach, and many of the fossils are in hard rocks in the middle of sheer cliffs with pounding waves far beneath.

▲ Muttaburrasaurus *lived 110–100 mya in what is now New South Wales, Australia. It could walk on two or four legs. A cousin of* Iguanodon, *it weighed 3 tonnes.*

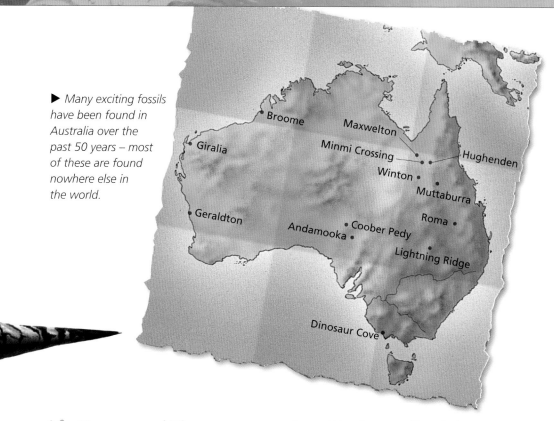

▶ *Many exciting fossils have been found in Australia over the past 50 years – most of these are found nowhere else in the world.*

🦶 **The sauropod *Rhoetosaurus*** was about 15 m long and lived about 180–160 mya.

🦶 **Near Winton, Queensland**, more than 3300 footprints show where about 130 dinosaurs once passed by.

🦶 **One of the major fossil sites** in Australia is Dinosaur Cove, on the coast near Melbourne, Victoria.

🦶 **Fossil-rich rocks** at Dinosaur Cove are part of the Otway-Strzelecki mountain ranges, and are 120–110 million years old.

🦶 **Remains found** at Dinosaur Cove include *Leaellynasaura*, a smaller version of the huge meat-eater *Allosaurus*, and the 3-m, 120-kg plant-eater *Atlascopcosaurus*.

341

Diamantinasaurus

- *Diamantinasaurus* **was** named in 2009 from fossils found near Diamantina River in south-west Queensland, Australia.

- **The fossils included** a shoulder blade, some ribs, front chest bone, and parts of the front and rear legs and hips.

- *Diamantinasaurus* **was a medium-sized sauropod**, a plant-eater from the Early Cretaceous Period some 105–100 mya.

- *Diamantinasaurus* **belonged** to the subgroup of sauropods known as titanosaurs, found mainly in the southern continents of South America and Australia, and Africa.

- **It was a well-built dinosaur** about 15 m long and 20 tonnes in weight.

- **Unusually for its group**, rather than the usual hoof-like nail found on all its other toes, *Diamantinasaurus* had a claw on the first digit of its front leg – its thumb.

- **Only one fossil specimen** of *Diamantinasaurus* has been found so far, nicknamed 'Matilda'.

- **The full two-part scientific name** is *Diamantinasaurus matildae*.

- **The second or species part of the name** is from the well-known Australian folk song 'Waltzing Matilda'.

↙ **'Waltzing Matilda' was written in 1895** by Andrew 'Banjo' Paterson, who at the time was staying near the town of Winton, in the area where the fossils were uncovered.

▼ *Remains of* Diamantinasaurus *were found along with fossils of fish, shellfish, turtles, crocodiles and pterosaurs, suggesting an ancient lake.*

343

North America

🦖 **North America** is the continent where most dinosaur fossils have been found.

🦖 **Most of these fossils** come from the West region, which includes the US states of Montana, Wyoming, Utah, Colorado and Arizona and Alberta in Canada.

Colville (Alaska)

Peace River (Canada)

Bay of Fundy (Canada)

Mt Tom (USA)

Drumheller (Canada)

Dinosaur Provincial Park (Canada)

Choteau (USA)

Hell Creek (USA)

Haddonfield (USA)

Billings (USA)

Lance Creek (USA)

Como Ridge (USA)

Dinosaur Nat. Monument (USA)

Cleveland-Lloyd Dinosaur Quarry

San Juan River (USA)

Garden Park (USA)

Ghost Ranch (USA)

Paluxy River (USA)

Moreno Hills (USA)

Coahuila State (Mexico)

▲ This map shows some of the most important fossil sites of North America. Remains of some of the most famous dinosaurs have been found at these locations, including Allosaurus, Tyrannosaurus, Diplodocus, Triceratops and Stegosaurus.

▲ Coelophysis *was discovered in New Mexico, USA, in 1881. In the 1940s, another expedition found dozens of skeletons at a single site*

Several fossil-rich sites in North America are now national parks.

The US Dinosaur National Monument, on the border of Utah and Colorado, was established in 1915.

The Cleveland-Lloyd Dinosaur Quarry in Utah contains fossils of stegosaurs, ankylosaurs, sauropods and meat-eaters such as *Allosaurus*.

Along the Red Deer River in Alberta, a large area containing thousands of dinosaur fossils has been designated the Dinosaur Provincial Park.

Fossils found in Alberta include those of the meat-eater *Albertosaurus*, armoured *Euoplocephalus* and the duckbill *Lambeosaurus*.

The Dinosaur Provincial Park in Alberta is a United Nations World Heritage Site – an area of outstanding natural importance.

A huge, 20-m-long plant-eater was named *Alamosaurus* from the Ojo Alamo rock formations, now known as Kirtland Shales, in New Mexico, USA.

Dinosaur National Monument

- **Dinosaur National Monument** is a protected area in the southwest of America, spanning the border between the states of Colorado and Utah.

- **It was one of the first sites** in the world to be given special protection for having valuable fossils, back in 1915.

- **Dinosaur National Monument today** covers more than 85,000 hectares.

- **The rocks** at Dinosaur National Monument were originally the banks and bed of a river, where animal bodies were washed during floods, and preserved.

- **The area contains** not only the fossil-rich Dinosaur Quarry, but also surrounding beautiful areas of the Uinta Mountains and the Yampa and Green Rivers.

- **Today's harsh climate** at the Dinosaur National Monument area means many rocks are bare and wear away, or erode, to reveal thousands of fossils.

- **Remains of more than 20 kinds** of dinosaurs and similar creatures have been found here, including the meat-eaters *Allosaurus* and *Ceratosaurus*.

▶ *A field worker carefully excavates fossil bones on a sloping rock layer at Dinosaur National Monument.*

🦶 **There are also fossils** of the 'ABCD' plant-eating sauropods *Apatosaurus*, *Barosaurus*, *Camarasaurus* and *Diplodocus*, and plate-backed *Stegosaurus*.

🦶 **Dinosaur National Monument** receives up to half a million visitors each year.

🦶 **At Dinosaur Wall** in the Quarry visitor centre, people can see jumbled fossil bones and other remains sticking out of the rocks.

South America

- **Many of the most important** discoveries of dinosaur fossils in the last 30 years were made in South America.

- **Dinosaur fossils** have been found from the north to the south of the continent, in the countries of Brazil and Argentina.

- **Most dinosaur fossils** in South America have been found on the high grassland, scrub and semi-desert of southern Brazil and Argentina.

- **Some of the earliest known dinosaurs**, such as *Herrerasaurus* and *Eoraptor*, lived more than 225 mya in Argentina.

- **Some of the last dinosaurs**, such as the sauropods *Saltasaurus* and *Titanosaurus*, also lived in Argentina.

- **Fossils of the meat-eating predator** *Piatnitzkysaurus* come from Cerro Condo in southern Argentina.

◄ Saltasaurus *is named after the region in Argentina where its fossils were discovered – Salta Province.*

▶ *Dinosaur fossils found in South America since the 1970s reveal unique kinds of meat-eaters, among the biggest predatory dinosaurs, some of the earliest members of the dinosaur group, and possibly the largest of all dinosaurs, Argentinosaurus.*

Boyacá
(Columbia)

Cerro Rajada
(Argentina)

El Breté (Argentina)

Santa Maria (Brazil)

Neuquén
(Argentina)

Ischigualasto
(Argentina)

Cerro Condor (Argentina)

Santa Cruz (Argentina)

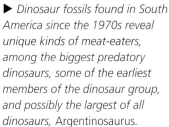

DID YOU KNOW?

Some of the biggest dinosaurs, including the large meat-eater Giganotosaurus and the vast sauropod Argentinosaurus, come from Argentina.

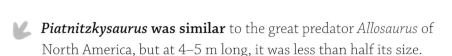

Piatnitzkysaurus was similar to the great predator *Allosaurus* of North America, but at 4–5 m long, it was less than half its size.

Like many dinosaurs in Argentina, *Piatnitzkysaurus* lived during the Middle–Late Jurassic Period.

Remains of about ten huge *Patagosaurus* sauropods were found in the fossil-rich region of Chubut, Argentina, from 1977.

Antarctic dinosaurs

- **The huge continent of Antarctica** has not always been ice-covered at the South Pole.

- **Through parts of prehistory**, Antarctica was joined to Australia, and the climate was much warmer, allowing forests with trees and bushes to grow.

- **This happened** during the Early Jurassic Period, 201–174 mya, and again in the Early Cretaceous Period, 145–100 mya.

- **At this time**, insects, worms, reptiles such as dinosaurs and crocodiles and flying pterosaurs, mammals and many other creatures lived in Australia, and fossils of some have been found on Antarctica.

- **Finding fossils** on Antarctica is very difficult, with intense cold, bitter winds, blizzards, and rocks covered with ice and snow for most of the year.

- **The first dinosaur fossils** found on Antarctica were dug out in 1986 on James Ross Island, at the tip of the Antarctic Peninsula, south of South America.

- **The dinosaur**, of the ankylosaur or armoured dinosaur group, was named *Antarctopelta*, meaning 'Antarctic shield'.

- *Antarctopelta* **was about 4 m long**, weighed up to one tonne, and lived about 70 mya.

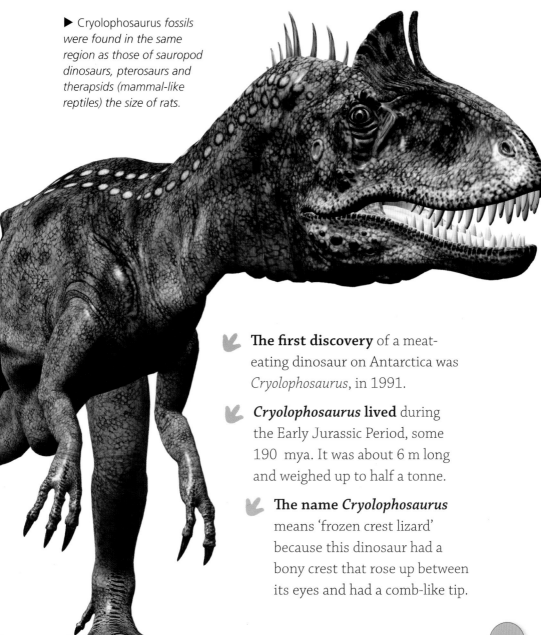

▶ Cryolophosaurus *fossils were found in the same region as those of sauropod dinosaurs, pterosaurs and therapsids (mammal-like reptiles) the size of rats.*

The first discovery of a meat-eating dinosaur on Antarctica was *Cryolophosaurus*, in 1991.

Cryolophosaurus **lived** during the Early Jurassic Period, some 190 mya. It was about 6 m long and weighed up to half a tonne.

The name *Cryolophosaurus* means 'frozen crest lizard' because this dinosaur had a bony crest that rose up between its eyes and had a comb-like tip.

Dinosaur fossil hunters

- **Many dinosaurs** were found in the USA in the 1870s–90s by Othniel Charles Marsh and Edward Drinker Cope.

- **Marsh and Cope** were great rivals, each one trying to find bigger, better and more dinosaur fossils than the other.

- **Between 1877 and 1897**, Cope and Marsh found and described about 130 new kinds of dinosaurs.

- **Joseph Tyrrell** discovered fossils of *Albertosaurus* in 1884, in what became a very famous dinosaur region, the Red Deer River area of Alberta, Canada.

- **Lawrence Lambe** found many North American dinosaur fossils, such as *Centrosaurus* in 1904.

- **German fossil experts** Werner Janensch and Edwin Hennig led expeditions to east Africa in 1908–12, and discovered *Giraffatitan* and *Kentrosaurus*.

- **From 1933**, Yang Zhong-jiang (also called CC Young) led many fossil hunting expeditions in China.

- **José Bonaparte** from Argentina has found many fossils in that region, including *Carnotaurus* in 1985.

- **Paul Sereno** from the University of Chicago has discovered and named huge dinosaurs and crocodiles from South America and North Africa.

◀ ▼ *Othniel Charles Marsh and Edward Drinker Cope had a rivalry between them that came to be known as the 'Bone Wars'. Allegedly, this began when Marsh pointed out a mistake that Cope had made with the reconstruction of a plesiosaur skeleton. Cope never forgave him, but the rift led to the discovery of almost 140 new dinosaur species.*

Othniel Charles Marsh
(1831–99)

Edward Drinker Cope
(1840–97)

Dinosaur names 1

- **Every dinosaur** has a scientific name, usually made up from Latin or Greek, place names or person names, and written in *italics*.

- **Many dinosaur names** end in *-saurus*, which some scientists say means 'reptile' and others say means 'lizard' – but dinosaurs were not lizards.

- **Names often refer** to a unique feature a dinosaur had. *Baryonyx*, for example, means 'heavy claw', from the massive claw on its thumb.

- **Many dinosaur names** are real tongue-twisters, such as *Opisthocoelicaudia*, pronounced 'owe-pis-thowe-see-lee-cord-ee-ah'. The name means 'posterior tail cavity', and refers to the joints between the backbones in the dinosaur's tail.

- **Some dinosaurs** are named after the place where their fossils were found. *Minmi* was found near Minmi Crossing, Queensland, Australia.

- **The fast-running ostrich dinosaurs** are named ornithomimosaurs, which means 'bird-mimic reptiles'.

▶ *In 1988, an almost complete specimen of the meat-eater* Herrerasaurus *was excavated in Argentina. It was named after Victorino Herrera, the farmer who discovered it.*

DID YOU KNOW?

Some dinosaur groups are named after the first discovered or major one of its kind, such as the tyrannosaurs or stegosaurs.

Dinosaur names 2

- **More than 150 types** of dinosaur have been named after the people who first discovered their fossils, dug them up, or reconstructed the dinosaur.

- **The large duckbill (hadrosaur)** *Lambeosaurus* was named after Canadian fossil expert Lawrence Lambe.

- **Lambe worked mainly** during the early 1900s, and named one of his finds *Stephanosaurus*.

- **In the 1920s**, *Stephanosaurus* was renamed, along with *Didanodon*, as *Lambeosaurus*, in honour of Lambe's work.

- **The full name** of the 'heavy claw' meat-eater *Baryonyx* is *Baryonyx walkeri*, after Bill Walker, the discoverer of its massive claw.

- **Part-time fossil hunter** Bill Walker found the claw in a clay pit quarry in Surrey, England.

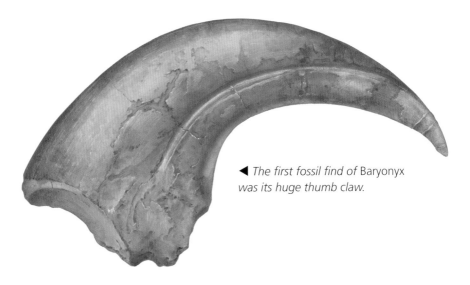

◀ *The first fossil find of Baryonyx was its huge thumb claw.*

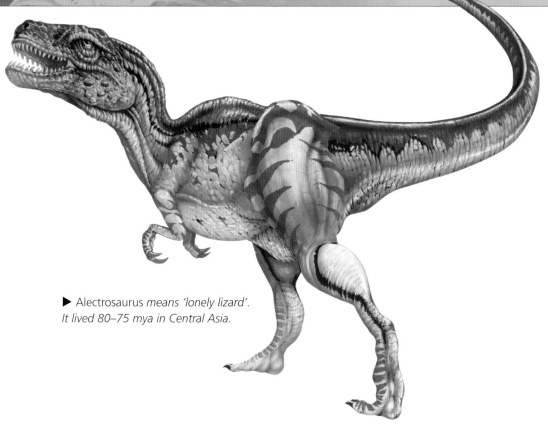

▶ Alectrosaurus *means 'lonely lizard'.*
It lived 80–75 mya in Central Asia.

Some dinosaur names are quite technical, such as *Diplodocus*,
which means 'double beam'. It was named for its tail bones, which
have two long projections like a pair of skis.

The 4-m-long plant-eater *Othnielia* was named after
19th-century fossil hunter Othniel Charles Marsh.

Parksosaurus, a 2.5-m-long
plant-eater, was named in
honour of Canadian dinosaur
expert William Parks.

DID YOU KNOW?
One of the shortest
dinosaur names is Kol,
a tiny meat-eater known
from only one fossil foot.

357

Reconstructions

- **No complete fossilized dinosaur**, with its skin, muscles, guts and other soft body parts, has ever been found.

- **Most dinosaurs are reconstructed** from the fossils of their teeth, bones, horns and claws.

- **The vast majority** are known from only a few fossil parts, such as several fragments of bones.

- **Fossil parts** of other, similar dinosaurs are often used in reconstructions to 'fill in' missing bones, teeth, and even missing heads, limbs or tails.

- **Soft body parts** from modern reptiles, such as lizards, are used as a guide for the reconstruction of a dinosaur's muscles and guts.

- **On rare occasions**, remains are found of a dinosaur body that dried out rapidly so that quite a few parts were preserved as mummified fossils.

- **One of the best known** of the best-preserved dinosaur fossils is of *Brachylophosaurus*, a 9-m hadrosaur (duck-bill) from about 75 mya.

▶ This fossil skeleton of an ankylosaur, *Euoplocephalus, has been restored with soft parts inside, then muscles and finally the skin covering with scales and horns.*

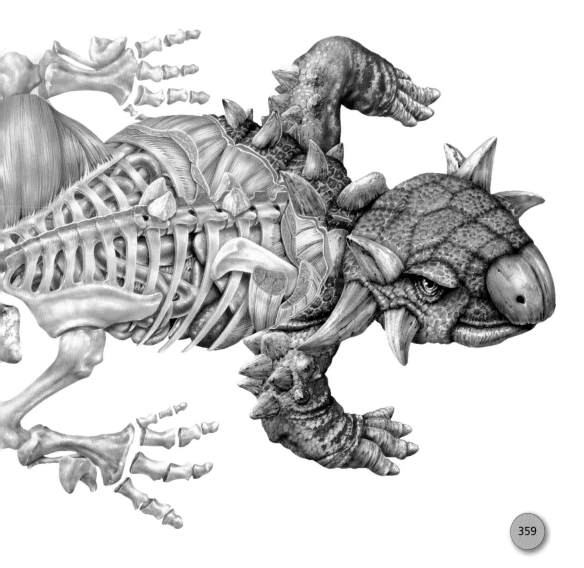

🦶 **Nicknamed 'Elvis'**, this amazing fossil was discovered in 1994 by fossil hunter Nate Murphy in Montana.

🦶 **In 2000 Murphy** found an even better *Brachylophosaurus*, which was called 'Leonardo'.

Birds

Birds and dinosaurs

● **In 1868 Thomas Henry Huxley**, English biologist and supporter of Charles Darwin's theory of evolution, examined newly discovered fossils of the early bird *Archaeopteryx*.

● **Huxley saw how similar** these fossils were to those of small meat-eating dinosaurs such as *Compsognathus*.

● **However, his suggestion that birds evolved** from small dinosaur meat-eaters gradually fell out of favour for almost a century.

● **Since the 1970s** new fossil discoveries of small meat-eating dinosaurs and early birds have shown that the two are closely related.

● **The common features shared by both groups** include hollow lightweight bones, the arrangement of bones in the chest, shoulder, arm and wrist, feathers, and also behaviours such as nest-building and care of young.

● **Today, most experts accept** that birds evolved from the small meat-eating dinosaur group known as maniraptorans, meaning 'hand snatchers'.

● **The maniraptoran group includes** the dromaeosaurs or raptor dinosaurs, and the troodontids.

● **However feathers are not unique** to maniraptorans and birds – they are known from several other groups of dinosaurs.

▶ *Creatures like* Anchiornis *show how difficult it is to separate birds from other groups of dinosaurs, which is why the main modern view is that birds are a subgroup of dinosaurs.*

DID YOU KNOW?

The most likely direct ancestors of birds were the troodontids, a group that includes Troodon, Anchiornis, Mei and Saurornithoides.

Bird fossils

- **There are far fewer fossils** of birds than other animals because birds have very delicate skeletons.

- **Some species** of prehistoric birds are only revealed by the fossil impression of a feather or a fossilized footprint.

- **One of the most famous** bird fossils is that of *Archaeopteryx*, which was discovered in Solnhofen, Germany, in 1861.

- **Lime-rich muds** slowly formed the limestone rock of Solnhofen. This process ensured *Archaeopteryx* was preserved in amazing detail, right down to the clear outline of its feathers.

- **Other famous bird fossil sites** have included the Niobrara Chalk of Kansas, and mudstone rocks of Utah and Wyoming.

- **The fossil site** at Messel in Germany also contains the skeletons of long-extinct birds as well as ones resembling flamingos, swifts, owls and nightjars.

- **The Messel bird fossils** are around 47 million years old and date from the Middle Paleogene Period.

- **Flamingo fossils** at Messel proved that the modern flamingo is related to wading birds called avocets rather than ducks and storks, since they share a similar skeleton.

- **One quick way** fossil hunters can identify bird bones is because they are hollow – unlike the bones of many prehistoric reptiles.

DID YOU KNOW?

An example of a fossilized egg is one belonging to the extinct elephant bird, Aepyornis. The egg was also huge – it could hold 8.5 litres of liquid.

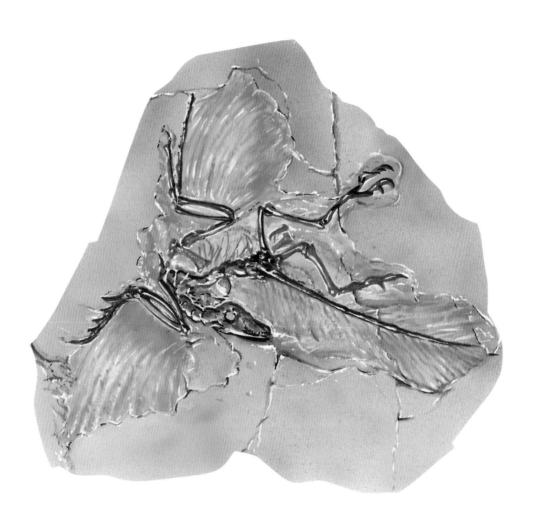

▲ *Fossils of Archaeopteryx are some of the most famous fossils of all. They show the bird's feathers, clawed fingers, teeth-filled beak and long tail.*

Archaeopteryx

- **The earliest known bird** for which there is good fossil evidence, and which lived during the Age of Dinosaurs, is known as *Archaeopteryx*, meaning 'ancient wing'.

- ***Archaeopteryx* lived** in Europe during the Late Jurassic Period, about 150–147 mya.

- **At about 50–60 cm** from nose to tail, *Archaeopteryx* was about the size of a large crow.

- ***Archaeopteryx* resembled** a small, meat-eating dinosaur in many of its features, such as the teeth in its long, beak-like mouth, and its long, bony tail.

- **In 1951**, a fossilized part-skeleton was identified as a small dinosaur similar to *Compsognathus*, but in the 1970s it was re-studied and named *Archaeopteryx* – showing how similar the two creatures were.

- **Three clawed fingers** grew halfway along the front of each of *Archaeopteryx*'s wing-shaped front limbs.

- **The flying muscles** were anchored to its large breastbone.

- ***Archaeopteryx* probably flew**, but not as fast or as skillfully as today's birds.

> **DID YOU KNOW?**
>
> Archaeopteryx was covered with feathers that had the same detailed designs found in those covering flying birds today.

Clawed digits on
leading edge of
wing

Small teeth
in jaws

Strong rear legs
for running

Flight feathers suited
to agile manoeuvres
in the air

▶ Some reconstructions of
Archaeopteryx *show feathers
only on the limbs and tail,
where they formed air-proof
flying surfaces. This bird could
probably glide, swoop and turn
as it pursued flying prey such
as dragonflies.*

Long bony tail

Confuciusornis

- *Confuciusornis* **is one of the earliest birds** known to have a horny beak with no teeth, like modern birds, and a very short bony tail, rather than the long trailing tail of vertebrae or backbones.

- *Confuciusornis* **lived** during the Early Cretaceous Period, 125–120 million years ago.

- **It was named in 1995** after the famous Chinese philosopher (scholar and thinker) Confucius, who lived about 2500 years ago.

- **Hundreds of detailed fossils** of *Confuciusornis* have been collected from the rocks known as the Jiufotang and Yixian Formations in China.

- *Confuciusornis* **weighed** about 0.5–1.5 kg and its wings measured up to 80 cm from tip to tip.

- **It had feathers on its head**, body, wings and upper legs.

- **The wing feathers were shaped** like those of a modern flying bird and were more than 20 cm long. They probably allowed for good gliding, and perhaps short bursts of powered flight.

- **Some specimens of *Confuciusornis*** had very long tail feathers called streamers, shaped like narrow flat tape, although most did not.

These tail streamers may show that the specimen was a certain sex, for example, male rather than female.

Possibly the streamers may show it was an adult rather than a youngster.

Lack of streamers could mean they had just been shed or moulted with the seasons.

DID YOU KNOW?

In 2012 a 2.5-m meat-eating feathered dinosaur called Sinocalliopteryx was discovered with the remains of three Confuciusornis – its last meals.

▲ Studies of the micro-details of Confuciusornis *feather fossils suggest it was coloured in patches of brown, white and black.*

369

Terror birds

- **After the large dinosaurs** became extinct (about 66 mya), huge flightless birds – known as terror birds – seized the opportunity to become the dominant predators of their day.

- *Gastornis* **was one** such terror bird. It had an enormous head and powerful legs, like those of its dinosaur ancestors, so it could outrun its prey.

- **Some experts believe** that *Gastornis* is a close cousin of ducks, geese and other related birds.

- **Even though these birds** were huge, they were also light-footed, fast runners. This is because, like all birds, they had hollow bones.

- **The diets of terror birds** included small and medium-sized mammals, such as prehistoric rodents and horses.

- **During the Late Eocene** and Oligocene Epochs (40–23 mya), the big carnivorous mammals became more powerful and better hunters. They became dominant, and took over.

- **However, in South America**, which was cut off from North America and the rest of the world for much of the past 66 million years, terror birds managed to stay dominant for a longer period of time.

- **One South American terror bird** was *Phorusrhacus*, which grew to be 2.5 m tall.

- *Titanis* **was one** of the few North American terror birds, and one of the biggest of all – it was 2.5 m tall and weighed 150 kg.

▶ Gastornis *attacks a small mammal of its time,* Leptictidium.

DID YOU KNOW?

Gastornis was named in 1855 after Gaston Planté, a fossil-hunter who turned to physics, and four years later invented the lead-acid battery used in cars and trucks.

371

Other flightless birds

- **Most prehistoric flightless birds** were giants, but not all of them were terror birds.

- **Much later giant birds** grew to incredible sizes. *Dinornis*, for instance, was the tallest flightless bird ever at 3.5 m tall.

- *Dinornis* **lived** in New Zealand. It first appeared about 2 mya and survived until perhaps 500 years ago!

- *Dinornis* **was one of a group** of birds known as moas. At various times there were probably about eight or nine different kinds of moas living on the two main islands of New Zealand.

- **The largest kinds of** *Dinornis* were the giant moas, which were extremely heavy, weighing over 200 kg.

- **The disappearance of the moas** was soon after humans reached New Zealand, and all moas were probably extinct by the end of the 15th century.

- **Another group** of enormous flightless birds lived on the island of Madagascar, and were called elephant birds.

- **At 450 kg**, the giant elephant bird *Aepyornis* was probably the heaviest bird ever to have lived. Like moas, the elephant birds became extinct within the last 500 years.

- **Both** *Dinornis* **and** *Aepyornis* were herbivores. Their diet consisted of seeds and fruit.

> **DID YOU KNOW?**
> Genetic studies show the closest living relative of moas is probably the ostrich of Africa.

◄ On Madagascar, in the absence of large mammal grazers and browsers, elephant birds evolved to become the biggest land herbivores.

Water birds

- *Ichthyornis* **was a prehistoric seagull,** which first appeared in the Late Cretaceous Period (100–66 mya).

- **It was similar in size** to a modern seagull, but had a much larger head and a beak full of very sharp teeth.

- *Presbyornis* **was related** to modern ducks. Like *Ichthyornis*, it evolved in the Late Cretaceous Period and was abundant in the Early Paleogene Period (66–40 mya).

- *Presbyornis* **was much bigger** than a modern duck – it stood between 0.5 m and one metre tall.

- **It had much longer legs** than its modern relative and so may have been a wading bird rather than a diving bird.

- *Presbyornis* **lived in large flocks** on lake shores, like modern flamingos.

- *Osteodontornis* **was a huge flying bird**, with a wingspan up to 6 m across.

- **It lived in the Miocene Epoch** (23–5 mya) and would have flown over the North Pacific Ocean.

- *Osteodontornis* **had a long bill**, lined with tooth-like bony spikes. Its diet probably included squid, seized from the surface of the sea.

▶ *Osteodontornis* was in the bird group called pseudotooths, where the 'teeth' were small bony points or spikes growing from the jaw bones, rather than true teeth.

DID YOU KNOW?

The skull of Presbyornis most closely resembles that of the living Australian duck Stictonetta.

Land birds

- **Land birds are flying birds** that fly in the skies over land and hunt or feed on the ground, unlike water birds.

- **Fossils of prehistoric land birds** are rare because their bones were light and would not have fossilized well.

- **As a result**, there are big gaps in palaeontologists' knowledge of the evolution of many species of birds. However, there are some early land birds they do know about.

- *Archaeopsittacus* **was an early parrot** of the Late Oligocene Epoch (28–23 mya) that lived in what is now France.

- *Ogygoptynx* **was one of** the first known owls. It lived in the Palaeocene Epoch (66–56 mya).

- *Aegialornis* **was an early** swift-like bird, which lived in the Eocene and Oligocene Epochs (56–23 mya). It may be the ancestor of swifts and hummingbirds.

- *Gallinuloides* **was an early member** of the chicken family. Its fossils have been found in Wyoming, USA, in rock strata of the Eocene Epoch (56–33 mya).

- **The earliest known vultures** lived in the Palaeocene Epoch (66–56 mya).

- **The earliest known hawks**, cranes, bustards, cuckoos and songbirds lived in the Eocene Epoch.

DID YOU KNOW?

Neocathartes was an early vulture-like bird. There are similarities between its skeleton and those of storks, which suggests vultures and storks are closely related.

▼ Vultures have been following the same scavenging way of life for more than 50 million years.

Argentavis

- **Argentavis magnificens** is the biggest known flying bird of all time, with wings measuring up to 7 m from tip to tip.

- **Its name means** 'magnificent Argentine bird' after the place where several sets of its fossils were found in Argentina.

- **Argentavis lived** in the late Miocene Epoch, about seven million years ago.

- **In overall shape** it resembled the vultures and condors of today, with wide wings for soaring.

- **Argentavis may have weighed** up to 75 kg – as much as an adult human.

- **It probably stood up to 2 m high**, had a head-body length of 1.3 m, and its main flight feathers were over 1.3 m long.

- **Like modern vultures**, Argentavis probably soared high on uprising air currents called thermals, so it rarely had to flap its enormous wings.

- **One idea is that Argentavis swooped** down to scavenge on sick, dying or dead large animals, tearing off pieces of flesh with its hooked beak.

- **However, a newer idea** is that its head, jaws and beak were not fully adapted to scavenging. Perhaps it pecked up small creatures like mice, young birds and lizards, and swallowed them whole.

▲ Argentavis, *also called the giant teratorn, could spot faraway food as it circled at height, then glided down to feast.*

Mammal fossils

◀ *Fur is still visible around the feet of Dima, the well preserved remains of a baby mammoth.*

Fossil finds of prehistoric mammals include skulls, teeth, jawbones, ear bones, horns, tusks and antlers.

There are few fossils of the earliest mammals because scavengers would usually have eaten their bodies.

However, coprolites (fossilized dung) of predators and scavengers sometimes contain undigested parts of the early mammals themselves, such as their teeth.

Palaeontologists can tell a lot from a mammal's molars (cheek teeth). They can work out its species and the period it lived in from the pattern of ridges and furrows on their surface.

Palaeontologists can also estimate the age of a mammal when it died by looking at the wear and tear on its teeth.

Some mammal fossils are preserved in tar pits – natural pools of thick, sticky tar, which ooze up from the ground in some places, such as forests and scrublands.

Tar pits at Rancho La Brea, near present-day downtown Los Angeles, USA, contained a perfectly preserved skeleton of the sabre-tooth carnivore *Smilodon*.

▲ *This enormous mammoth skull was found in South Dakota, USA. In Siberia, palaeontologists have also discovered the remains of mammoth skin, hair and other body parts.*

Freezing is another very effective way of preserving animals. Remains of frozen mammoths have been discovered in near-perfect condition in Siberia.

Explorers using dog sledges discovered some of the first frozen mammoths. Their remains were so well preserved that the dogs were able to eat the meat on the bones.

In 1977, an almost complete mammoth was discovered. 'Dima' is the name given to the frozen 40,000-year-old baby mammoth.

Mammal offspring

- **Mammals developed a very different way** of producing young, compared to reptiles and birds, which both lay eggs.

- **Instead, most mammals** are viviparous, which means they give birth to live young.

- **One unusual group of mammals**, the monotremes, defy this rule by laying eggs. There are five surviving monotremes – the duck-billed platypus and four species of echidna.

- **After the young of mammals are born**, their mothers feed them milk that is produced in their mammary glands.

- **The word 'mammal'** comes from the name for the mammary glands – the part of female mammals' bodies that secretes milk.

- **Early mammals**, such as *Megazostrodon*, *Eozostrodon* and *Morganucodon*, grew one set of milk teeth, which suggests that the young fed on milk.

- **Milk teeth** are temporary teeth that grow with the nutrients provided by milk, and prepare the jaw for later teeth.

- **Mammals can be divided** into three groups depending on how they rear their young – placentals, marsupials and monotremes.

- **In placental mammals**, the offspring grows inside its mother's body, in the womb, until it is a fully developed baby –at which point it is born.

- **Marsupial mammals** give birth to their offspring at a much earlier stage. The tiny infants then develop fully in their mothers' pouch, called a marsupium.

▼ Mammal mothers care for their young, as with Toxodon, which lived in South America as recently as 20,000 years ago.

Early mammals

- *Megazostrodon* was one of the first true mammals. It appeared at the start of the Early Jurassic Period (about 200 mya).

- **This shrew-like insectivore** (insect-eater) was about 12 cm long. It had a long body that was low to the ground, and long limbs that it held out to the side in a squatting position.

- *Eozostrodon* was another very early mammal, which emerged about the same time as *Megazostrodon*.

- **It had true mammalian teeth**, including two different sorts of cheek teeth – premolars and molars – which were replaced only once during its lifetime.

- **Its sharp teeth** suggest it was a meat-eater, and its large eyes suggest that it hunted at night.

- **Another early mammal** was *Morganucodon*. It too had premolars and molars and chewed its food in a circular motion, rather than the up-down motion of reptiles.

- *Sinoconodon* was yet another early mammal that lived in the Early Jurassic Period, about 190 mya. It was probably covered in fur.

- **These early mammals** had three middle ear bones, which made their hearing more sensitive than that of reptiles.

- **They also had whiskers**, which suggests they had fur. This in turn suggests that they were warm-blooded.

- **All true mammals** are warm-blooded, which means they maintain a constant body temperature. Fur helps mammals keep warm in cold conditions.

▼ *Among the best-preserved fossil mammals is* Leptictidium *from Germany's Messel Pit site, at 45 million years of age.*

Juramaia

- **Juramaia was a small, rat-shaped mammal** about 10–12 cm long. It lived towards the end of the Jurassic Period, 160 mya.

- **Fossils of Juramaia** were found in China, in rocks known as the Tiaojishan Formation.

- **These rocks**, in the area of Liaoning, northwest China, have provided many other beautifully preserved, highly detailed remains of mammals, dinosaurs, birds, insects and plants.

- **The main single specimen** of Juramaia has an almost complete set of fossil bones for the front of the skeleton, including the skull, teeth, upper backbone, ribs and front legs.

- **Juramaia probably lived** like a shrew of today, eating worms, bugs and other small prey.

- **Its feet show it was well adapted** to climbing and so it may have lived mainly in trees.

- **Clues from the jaws**, teeth, front legs and other parts show that Juramaia was in the mammal group called eutherians, which includes placental mammals – those whose young develop in the womb, nourished by the placenta (unlike the marsupial or egg-laying mammals).

- **Juramaia is the earliest known** placental mammal, living more than 30 million years before the previous first-known, Eomaia.

🐾 **The full name *Juramaia sinensis*** was given in 2011 and translates as 'Jurassic mother from China'. This means it was the first of the eutherian mammals, or 'mother of us all', and it lived in the Jurassic Period.

▼ Juramaia *was probably small and quick-moving, darting among rocks and undergrowth in search of small creatures to eat.*

Repenomamus

- **Before the discovery** of *Repenomamus*, 'reptile mammal', it was thought all mammals from the Age of Dinosaurs were smaller than today's pet cats or even brown rats.

- **Two different kinds of *Repenomamus*** have been discovered in the famous fossil-rich Yixian rocks in the province of Liaoning, northwest China.

- **Their fossils date back** to the Early Cretaceous Period, 130–125 mya.

- **The larger of the two kinds**, *Repenomamus giganticus*, was described and named in 2005.

- ***Repenomamus giganticus*** had a total length of over one metre and probably weighed more than 12 kg.

- **It had a build similar** to today's badger, with a stocky body and strong legs, but with a longer tail.

- **The second kind**, *Repenomamus robustus*, was described and named in 2000. It was similar to its larger cousin but around half the length, 50–60 cm, and weighed about 5 kg.

- **One fossil specimen** of *Repenomamus robustus* had some bones of a small dinosaur preserved with it, in the place where its stomach would have been.

This small dinosaur was *Psittacosaurus*, a young 'parrot-beak', that *Repenomamus* had probably eaten.

Both kinds of *Repenomamus* belonged to an early mammal group called eutriconodonts. The name of this group means 'true three-pointed tooth', and they died out by 70 mya.

▲ Repenomamus *fossil bones show it was a powerful, muscular mammal that relied on strength rather than speed and agility.*

Fruitafossor

- **This small mammal dated back** to the Late Jurassic Period, around 155–150 mya.

- *Fruitafossor* **was quite small**, around 15 cm long from head to tail, and weighed less than 40 g.

- *Fruitafossor* **was something of a surprise** when its fossils were dug up, studied and named in 2005.

- **Experts were surprised** by its several specialized features, which would have allowed it to dig and probably live in burrows, and feed on ants and termites.

- **Until the discovery of** *Fruitafossor*, most mammals from the Age of Dinosaurs were thought to be shrew-like with a diet of small creatures such as worms and bugs.

- **However** *Fruitafossor* **showed** that mammals of that time could be as specialized for different ways of life as modern mammals.

- **The teeth of** *Fruitafossor* were small and shaped like short pegs, very similar to the teeth of modern termite-eaters such as anteaters and aardvarks.

- **The front legs of** *Fruitafossor* were relatively large and strong, and used for digging up and scratching out its tiny prey. This gave it the nickname 'Popeye', after the strong cartoon sailor.

- *Fruitafossor* **means** 'Fruita's digger', from its digging and tunnelling adaptations.

DID YOU KNOW?
Fruitafossor was not named from any direct connection with fruits, but from the town where its fossils were discovered – Fruita, Colorado, USA.

▼ Fruitafossor *may have dug into termite and ant nests, and perhaps dug a burrow for its home.*

Marsupials

- **Marsupials are mammals** that give birth to their offspring at a very early stage in their development – when they are still tiny.

- **After being born**, the infant crawls through its mother's fur to a pouch called the marsupium, where it stays, feeding on milk, until it is big enough to leave.

- **Palaeontologists think** that the first marsupials evolved in Asia and then spread to the Americas and Australia.

- **An early marsupial** called *Alphadon,* meaning 'first tooth', emerged around 70 mya. It lived in North America.

- *Alphadon* **was 30 cm long** and weighed 300 g. It would have lived in trees, using its feet to climb, and fed on insects, fruit and small vertebrates.

- **When Australia became isolated** from the rest of the world, about 40 mya, its marsupials continued to evolve – unlike most other regions of the world, where they fell into decline.

- **Marsupials continued** to exist in South America, which was also isolated from the rest of the world during much of the last 66 million years, the Paleogene and Neogene Periods.

- **When South America** became reconnected with North America, from about 4 mya, the arrival of placental mammals from the north led many marsupials to extinction.

- **Today**, **there are only two surviving groups** of marsupials in the Americas – the opossums found throughout North America and the rat opossums found in South America.

Australia has many living marsupials, such as kangaroos and koalas. However it had a much greater marsupial population in the Paleogene and Neogene Periods – we know this from fossil sites such as Riversleigh in northwest Queensland.

▼ Thylacoleo, *the 'marsupial lion', was similar to a modern small puma (mountain lion), but with huge slashing thumb claws. Its remains have been discovered in Australia.*

Australian mammals

- **Australia has a unique natural history** because it became isolated from the rest of the world around 40 mya.

- **Australia's native mammals**, living and extinct, are mostly marsupials – mammals that give birth to tiny young, which then develop in their mother's outside pouch.

- **The earliest Australian marsupials** date from the Oligocene Epoch (34–23 mya). Many fossils come from the Miocene Epoch (23–5 mya) or later.

- **These fossils show** that there were giant kangaroos, called *Procoptodon*, as well as giant wombats, called *Diprotodon*.

- **Two marsupial carnivores** preyed on these giant herbivores. One was the lion-like *Thylacoleo*, the other was the smaller, wolf-like *Thylacinus*.

- **Palaeontologists** are very interested in *Thylacoleo* and *Thylacinus* because they demonstrate how different species can evolve to look very similar – the process known as evolutionary convergence.

- **Although they had different ancestors** and lived on different continents, *Thylacoleo* came to look like a placental lion, while *Thylacinus* came to look like a placental wolf.

- **The Miocene fossil site** in Riversleigh, northern Queensland, has revealed the extent and variety of prehistoric marsupials in Australia.

⮞ **Among the fossils** are many long-extinct marsupials. One of these was so unusual that at first palaeontologists called it a 'thingodont', although now it is known as *Yalkaparidon*.

⮞ *Thylacinus* **continued** to exist in Australia into the 20th century, as the thylacine. The last one died in a zoo in Tasmania in 1936.

◀ *At 3 m long, the giant wombat* Diprotodon *was probably the largest marsupial ever to have lived. It had tusks for its front teeth, but its cheek teeth were like a kangaroo's.*

South American mammals

- **South America was separated** from the rest of the world for much of the last 60 million years.

- **Like Australia**, South America's isolation meant that certain mammals only evolved there.

- **The main difference** between them was that South America had placental mammals as well as marsupials.

- **Placental mammals** included the giant ground sloths, such as *Megatherium*, and huge rodents the size of bears.

- **Marsupial mammals** included the marsupial carnivores, such as *Thylacosmilus*.

- **Evolutionary convergence**, when different species develop to look very similar, happened in South America just as in Australia. One example was *Thoatherium*, which looked very much like the small horses that were evolving in other parts of the world.

- **The formation** of the Panama isthmus (a strip of land) reconnected South America to North America from about 4 mya.

DID YOU KNOW?
A good example of evolutionary convergence was Pyrotherium, which had the trunk, cheek teeth and tusks of an early elephant – but it belonged to a different group.

■ **Many South American mammals** journeyed north. Some, such as armadillos, porcupines and guinea pigs, were very successful in their new homes.

■ **Others, like the glyptodonts**, eventually died out. This might be because of climate change – or because humans hunted them to extinction.

▼ *The South American hoofed mammal known as* Macrauchenia *used its short trunk to gather vegetation. It lived from about 6 million to 30,000 years ago.*

399

Megatherium

- **Also called the giant ground sloth**, *Megatherium* was one of the largest-ever land mammals not belonging to the elephant group.

- **It was up to 6 m long** and weighed over 4 tonnes.

- *Megatherium* **had long, curved claws** on its front feet, and so it probably walked on its knuckles when moving on all fours.

- **It could also sit upright** or even stand on two legs, using its tail as a support.

- **In this position**, *Megatherium* could reach up with its front legs to a height of perhaps 5 m.

- **It could then hook high branches** with its claws, down towards its mouth, to chop up with its sharp-edged teeth.

- *Megatherium* **lived in South America** from about 5 million to 10,000 years ago.

- **It may have died out** when humans spread through its range and hunted it to extinction with spears and other weapons.

- *Megatherium* **was named** more than 200 years ago, in 1796, by French animal and fossil expert Baron Georges Cuvier.

- **Its fossils were also collected** and studied in 1832 by English naturalist Charles Darwin, on his round-the-world voyage in the ship HMS *Beagle*.

▶ *Elephant-sized* Megatherium *was well armed with its long hand and toe claws – similar to its relatives, the tree sloths of today.*

Creodonts

- **Creodonts were the first** big flesh-eating mammals. They lived from the Paleocene to the Miocene Epochs (about 50–10 mya).

- **These mammals came** in many different shapes and sizes. Some were as small as weasels, others were bigger than bears.

- **Many creodonts** were flat-footed and walked on short, heavy limbs tipped with claws.

- **They hunted early herbivores** that, like these early carnivores, had not yet evolved into quick runners.

- **Creodonts had smaller**, more primitive brains than later carnivores – these were cleverer, faster hunters than the creodonts, and forced them into decline.

- **Another way** in which creodonts were less successful than later carnivores was their teeth, which were less effective at stabbing or slicing.

- **Creodonts were**, however, the top predators of their day. The wolf-sized *Hyaenodon* was particularly successful.

DID YOU KNOW?

Hyaenodon species ranged in size from 30 cm high at the shoulders to 1.2 m high – the size of a small rhinoceros.

Fossils of *Hyaenodon* skulls show that they had a very highly developed sense of smell, as well as powerful, bone-crushing jaws.

Fossils of male *Hyaenodon* teeth reveal grinding marks, which palaeontologists think means they ground their teeth to ward off rivals, like some modern animals.

▲ Hyaenodon *fossils are known from many regions including Europe, Asia, Africa and North America.*

Carnivores

- **The first carnivorous mammals** were the creodonts, which ranged in size from the cat-like *Oxyaena* to the wolf-like *Mesonyx*.

- **In the Late Eocene Epoch** (around 40 mya) large hoofed carnivores, such as *Andrewsarchus*, began to appear.

- **Modern carnivores** are descended from a separate group called miacids.

- **Modern carnivores** belong to the order Carnivora. This order had two subgroups – the feliforms, which include the cats, and the caniforms – the dog families and the pinnipeds (seals, sea lions and walruses). Some classification schemes put pinnipeds in their own mammal group, separate from the other carnivores.

- **In the Oligocene Epoch** (34–23 mya), carnivorans began to replace creodonts as the dominant carnivores.

- **Carnivorans were smarter**, faster, and deadlier than creodonts, and were the only predators that could catch the new fast-running herbivores.

- **Faster mammals** evolved in the Oligocene Epoch as thick forests changed into open woodlands, with more space to run after, and run from, other creatures.

DID YOU KNOW?

The pinniped Allodesmus was a prehistoric seal. It had flippers, large eyes and spiky teeth, which it used to impale fish.

- **As carnivorans evolved** they developed bigger brains, more alert senses, sharper claws and teeth, and stronger jaws and limbs.

- **The pinnipeds** are carnivorous mammals that, like whales and dolphins (and reptiles before them), reinvaded the seas.

▼ Andrewsarchus *is known only from a fossil skull, which suggests a huge beast with a head-body length of 3.5 m, a shoulder height of 1.7 m and a weight approaching one tonne.*

Cats

The most highly developed carnivores are cats. They are the fastest hunters, with the greatest agility, and with the sharpest claws and teeth.

Cats evolved along two lines. One group included the various kinds of sabre-tooths, of which *Smilodon* was one. This group is extinct today.

Sabre-tooths probably specialized in killing large, heavily built animals with thick hides, which explains their long canine teeth.

The other group of cats is the felines, which are the ancestors of all modern cats, from lions and cheetahs to pet cats.

▼ Dinofelis *was a muscular, heavily built predator with relatively short canines for a sabre-tooth cat.*

- **The felines were faster** and more agile than the sabre-tooths, which may have become extinct because their prey became faster and more able to outrun them. The felines, however, continued to be successful hunters.

- **One prehistoric feline** was *Dinictis*, a puma-sized cat that lived in the Oligocene Epoch (37–23 mya).

- **Later felines** were various types of *Dinofelis*, which lived between 5 and 1.3 mya across North America, Europe, Africa and Asia.

- **The name *Dinofelis*** means 'terrible cat'. It looked like a modern jaguar, but had stronger front legs that it used to press down on its victims before stabbing them with its teeth.

- ***Dinofelis' diet*** included baboons, antelope and perhaps australopithecines – our prehistoric human relatives.

DID YOU KNOW?

Prehistoric cats' ability to unsheathe and retract their claws provided them with one of their deadliest weapons – and one that cats still have.

407

Smilodon

- *Smilodon* **is often called** a sabre-tooth 'tiger', but it was not an especially close relative of today's tigers.

- **A better name is sabre-toothed cat**, since *Smilodon* was in the general cat group, felids, along with lions, tigers, cheetahs and wildcats.

- *Smilodon* **belonged** to the cat subgroup known as machairodonts, which have all died out.

- **Several kinds of *Smilodon*** lived in North and South America from around 2.6 million to 11,000 years ago.

- **The largest kind had a head-tail length** of 3.5 m, stood 1.2 m at the shoulder, and was heavily built, weighing over 350 kg.

- **The 'sabres' were canine teeth** in the upper jaw of *Smilodon* – up to 30 cm long, curved, very sharp and pointed, but not particularly strong.

- *Smilodon* **could open its mouth** very wide, so the teeth almost pointed forwards.

- *Smilodon* **probably used these long teeth** to slash and stab at its prey's throat very quickly, then it backed away and waited until the victim bled to death, before starting to feed.

- **Hundreds of *Smilodon***, along with many other animals such as bison, wolves and mammoths, were trapped and preserved in the La Brea natural tar pits in modern-day Los Angeles, USA.

▶ Snarling Smilodon *tracks a victim by scent, its huge canine teeth ready to deliver a deadly strike.*

Dogs

🐾 **Early dogs probably hunted** in a similar way to most modern wild dogs – in packs.

🐾 **Dogs developed** long snouts, which gave them a keen sense of smell, and forward-pointing eyes, which gave them good vision.

🐾 **Dogs also developed** a mixture of teeth – sharp canines for stabbing, narrow cheek teeth for slicing, and farther along the jaw at the back, flatter teeth for crushing.

🐾 **These different teeth** meant that dogs could eat a variety of different foods, including plants, which they might have had to eat if meat was in short supply.

🐾 **One of the ancestors** of dogs, as well as bears, was the bear-dog *Amphicyon*. Its name means 'in-between dog'.

🐾 *Amphicyon* **lived** between 20 and 10 mya.

🐾 **Trace fossils** of *Amphicyon's* footprints show that it walked like a bear, with its feet flat on the ground.

🐾 *Hesperocyon* was one of the earliest dogs, living between about 40 and 30 mya.

🐾 *Hesperocyon* was the size of a small fox. It had long legs and jaws, forward-pointing eyes and a supple, slender body.

DID YOU KNOW?
Hunting in packs allowed Hesperocyon to catch large animals that it would not have been able to kill on its own.

▶ *In North America a pack-leading, or alpha-male,* Hesperocyon *tackles an extinct relative of deer,* Synthetoceras.

Herbivores

- **The first specialist herbivores** (plant-eaters) appeared in the Late Palaeocene Epoch (around 60 mya).

- **They ranged in size** from the equivalent of modern badgers to pigs.

- **These early herbivores** were rooters or browsers – they foraged for food on the floor or among branches in their forest homes.

- **It was not until** the very end of the Palaeocene Epoch (56 mya) that the first large herbivores evolved.

- **Large herbivores** emerged before large carnivores. They must have had a peaceful life – for a while.

- **_Uintatherium_ was one** of the large early herbivores. It was the size of a large rhinoceros, with thick limbs to support its heavy body.

- **_Uintatherium_ had three pairs** of bony knobs protruding from its head. Males had very long, strong canine teeth, which they would have used if attacked by creodont carnivores.

- **The growth of grasslands** and the decline of forests in the Miocene Epoch (23–5 mya) sped up changes to herbivores' bodies.

- **Herbivores developed** faster legs to outrun carnivores in open spaces. They also developed better digestive systems to cope with the new, tough grasses.

- **The most important** requirements for a herbivore are complex teeth and digestive systems to break down plant food and release its energy.

▼ *Elasmotherium* was a huge rhinoceros, about the size of modern elephants, that lived 2–1 mya in Europe and Asia.

Rodents

- **In terms of their numbers**, variety and distribution, rodents are the most successful mammals that have ever lived.

- **Squirrels**, **rats, guinea pigs**, beavers, porcupines, voles, gophers and mice are all types of rodent.

- **Rodents have been** – and still are – so successful because they are small, fast-breeding and able to digest all kinds of foods, including substances as hard as wood.

- **One of the first known** rodents was *Paramys*, which appeared more than 50 mya.

- *Paramys* **was a squirrel-like rodent** that could climb trees. It was 60 cm long, and had a long, slightly bushy tail.

- **Modern squirrels evolved** around 40 mya. These mammals have one of the longest known ancestries for any living mammal group.

- **Another early rodent** was *Epigaulus*, which was a gopher with two horns. The horns were side by side on the top of its snout, pointing upward.

- *Epigaulus* **was 30 cm long** and lived in North America in the Miocene Epoch (23–5 mya). It probably used its horns for defence or digging up roots.

- **Prehistoric rodents** could be massive. *Castoroides* was an early beaver that was over 2 m long – almost the size of a black bear.

DID YOU KNOW?

Rabbits and hares are descended from rodents. Modern hares first appeared around 5 mya.

▼ Platypittamys *was a prehistoric, rat-like rodent. Rodents first became plentiful during the Oligocene Epoch (34–23 mya).*

415

Ruminants

- **Ruminants are a successful group** of plant-eating mammals that first appeared about 40 mya.

- **Modern ruminants** include cattle, sheep, deer, giraffes, antelopes and camels.

- **All these animals** can eat quickly, store plant material in the stomach, and then bring it back to their mouths again to chew it and break it down. This process is called 'chewing the cud'.

- *Archaeomeryx* **was an early**, rat-to-rabbit-sized ruminant, which lived in Asia. It was similar to the living chevrotain – a small, hoofed mammal also known as the mouse deer.

- *Archaeomeryx* **probably** had a three-chambered stomach, each of which broke down its plant food a little bit further.

- **Camels were the next** ruminants to evolve. One large prehistoric camel was *Aepycamelus*, which had a very long, giraffe-like neck.

- **They were followed** by cattle, sheep and deer, which were more advanced ruminants because they had four-chambered stomachs.

- **The four chambers** of ruminants' stomachs are called the rumen, the reticulum, the omasum and the abosmasum.

- **Ruminants' big advantage** over other plant-eaters was that they could decide when to digest their food. If they sensed a threat while they were eating they could run away and digest their meal later.

- **Camels and chevrotains** are the only surviving ruminants with three-chambered stomachs.

◀ Aepycamelus *was a large, giraffe-like prehistoric camel found in Colorado, North America, during the Miocene Epoch, 23–5 mya.*

Condylarths

- **Condylarths were among** the first hoofed mammals.

- **They lived in** the Paleogene Period, 66–23 mya.

- **All later hoofed mammals**, from horses to pigs, are probably descended from condylarths or similar animals.

- **The earliest condylarths** had claws as opposed to hooves.

- **Later species evolved** longer limbs, tipped with nails or hooves, for running away quickly from carnivores.

- **The first known condylarth** was *Protungulatum*, a rabbit-sized plant-eater, living 64–63 mya.

- **A slightly later condylarth** was *Phenacodus*, which palaeontologists think was an insectivore (an insect-eater).

- *Phenacodus* **was the size** of a small sheep, and had clearly developed hooves.

- **Condylarths spread** over most of the world, including Europe, Asia, South America and Africa.

DID YOU KNOW?

Early condylarths were also rabbit-sized. Later ones, however, were as big as bears.

▼ Arctocyon, *from about 50 mya, was probably 2 m long from head to tail. Muscle marks on fossils suggest it could climb trees.*

Perissodactyls

- **Perissodactyls are plant-eating**, hoofed mammals with an odd number of toes (either three or one) on their feet.

- **The three living groups** of perissodactyls are horses, tapirs and rhinoceroses.

▼ One branch of the rhinoceros family developed to be enormous animals. They roamed across Asia, browsing leaves and twigs from treetops. The biggest of these was Paraceratherium, *the largest land mammal ever.*

- **Two extinct groups** of perissodactyls are brontotheres and chalicotheres.

- **Brontotheres included** massive beasts, such as *Brontotherium*, which had elephant-like limbs and a blunt, bony prong jutting from its nose. It ate only soft-leaved plants.

- *Chalicotherium* was a chalicothere. It lacked front teeth, and ate by placing soft plant shoots in the back of its mouth, like a modern panda.

- **The earliest ancestors** of modern horses, tapirs and rhinos, appeared before 50 mya, probably as the Paleocene Epoch gave way to the Eocene, 56 mya.

- *Miotapirus* **was an early type** of tapir. It lived in North America about 20 mya and was similar in size to living tapirs, 1.5–2 m long.

- **Perissodactyls' feet** carried the weight of the animal on the middle toe, either in a single hoof, as in horses, or a big toe with one on each side, as in tapirs and rhinos.

- **For much of the Paleogene Period** (66–23 mya), perissodactyls were the most abundant form of hoofed mammals. They then declined, however, and artiodactyls (even-toed mammals) became dominant.

> **DID YOU KNOW?**
>
> Chalicotheres had long front legs and long curved claws, which they could not place flat on the ground. Instead, they walked on their knuckles, like apes.

Artiodactyls

- **Artiodactyls are hoofed mammals** with an even number (either two or four) of toes on their feet.

- **Pigs, camels, giraffes**, sheep, goats, cattle, hippopotamuses, deer, antelopes and their ancestors are all artiodactyls.

- **Like the perissodactyls**, artiodactyls first appeared about 55–50 mya.

- *Dichobune* **was an early artiodactyl**, which lived between 40 and 30 mya. It had short limbs and four-toed feet.

- **In smaller artiodactyls**, such as sheep and goats, the foot is often divided into two parts (toes).

- **In very heavy artiodactyls**, such as hippopotamuses, there are four toes to carry the animal's weight.

- **At least two** of the middle toes on artiodactyls' feet carry an equal weight.

- **During the Miocene Epoch** (23–5 mya), artiodactyls became the most successful hoofed mammals.

- **Their success** lay more in their stomachs than in their feet. Artiodactyls evolved more advanced digestive systems, which allowed them to process the tough grasses that had replaced the earlier, softer, forest plants.

- **Another difference** between artiodactyls and perissodactyls is their ankle bones. Artiodactyls' ankle bones have more rounded joints at both ends, which means they provide more thrust when they run.

▼ Synthetoceras *had a long forked nose horn, unlike any modern artiodactyl. However this horn was probably present only in males.*

Entelodonts

- **Entelodonts were large** pig-like mammals that lived in Asia and North America in the Eocene and Miocene Epochs (56–5 mya).

- **These mammals are also known as** 'terminator pigs' or 'hell pigs' because of their fearsome appearance.

- **One of the largest** entelodonts was *Daeodon* (*Dinohyus*). It stood almost 2 m tall at the shoulder with a skull that was around one metre long.

- *Daeodon* **probably fed** off plant roots or scavenged for prey.

- *Daeodon* **had** very distinctive teeth. Its incisors (front teeth) were blunt, but the teeth next to them, the canines, were sturdy and substantial, and could have been used for defence.

- **Another entelodont** was the scavenger *Entelodon*, the largest of which was about the same size as *Daeodon*.

- **There are severe wounds** in the fossils of some *Entelodon* skulls, such as a 2-cm-deep gash in the bone between its eyes. Palaeontologists think these were caused by the animals fighting among themselves.

DID YOU KNOW?

Entelodon's face had bony lumps all over it. One reason could be that they protected its eyes and nose during clashes with rivals.

- *Entelodon* **means** 'perfect-toothed'. This mammal had a thick layer of enamel on its teeth.

- **However, many fossil** remains of *Entelodon* have broken teeth – a result of the tough, varied diet of this scavenger.

▲ The fierce-looking Daeodon, formerly
known as Dinohyus, may well have
scavenged for its food like modern hyenas.
Its powerful neck muscles and large canine
teeth suggest it could have broken bones
and eaten flesh.

Bats

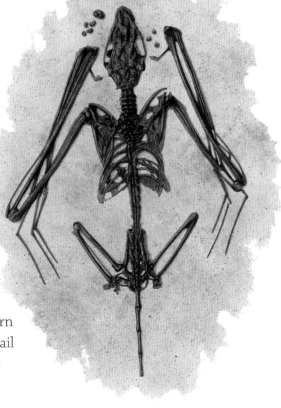

🐾 **Icaronycteris is one of** the earliest known bats. Its fossil remains are about 52 million years old.

🐾 **Despite its age**, Icaronycteris looks very similar to a modern bat. It has a bat's typically large ears, which it probably used as a sonar, like modern bats.

🐾 **One difference** from modern bats was that Icaronycteris' tail was not joined to its legs by flaps of skin.

🐾 **Palaeontologists think** that there must have been earlier, more primitive-looking bats from which Icaronycteris evolved.

▲ This very rare fossil of Icaronycteris shows its long, strong arm or wing bones and much smaller leg bones.

▶ The earliest bats belong to Microchiroptera mammal group. These are the smaller, insect-eating bats that are most numerous today. They are characterized by their large ears and noses, which they use during echolocation.

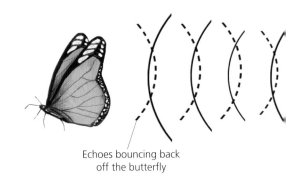

Echoes bouncing back off the butterfly

The chance of finding earlier prehistoric bat fossils is very small – like birds, bats have fragile skeletons that do not fossilize well.

Icaronycteris **ate insects**. Palaeontologists know this because they have found insect remains in the part of the fossil where its stomach would have been.

Icaronycteris **fossils** have been found in North America.

The fossil remains of another prehistoric bat, *Palaeochiropteryx*, have been found in Europe.

Like *Icaronycteris*, this bat seems to have been an insectivore (insect-eater).

Sound waves from the bat

Elephant evolution

- **Elephants and their ancestors** belong to an order of animals called Proboscidea, meaning 'long-snouted'. Another word for the elephant group is proboscideans.

- **The first elephants** appeared around 40 mya. They didn't have trunks and looked a bit like large pigs.

- *Moeritherium* **is one of the earliest** known animals in the elephant group. Its name comes from Lake Moeris in Egypt, where fossil-hunters discovered its remains.

- **The American palaeontologist** Henry Fairfield Osborn (1857–1935) described *Moeritherium* as 'a missing link' between elephants and other mammals.

- *Moeritherium* **was 3 m long**, weighed 200 kg, lived around 37 mya, and probably spent much of its life wallowing in rivers or shallow lakes, like a hippopotamus.

- **Another stage** in the development of elephants was *Phiomia*, which lived about 35 mya.

- *Phiomia* **had a shoulder height** of about 2.5 m. Its fossils come from North Africa and other remains found with them show it lived in swampy areas.

DID YOU KNOW?

Mammoths were giant elephants. The steppe mammoth was up to 4 m tall at the shoulder and probably weighed more than 15 tonnes.

🐾 **The deinotheres** were members of the elephant group, with one pair of enormous downward curving tusks in the lower jaw.

🐾 **The other groups** of the Proboscidea were the true elephants (which resembled living elephants) and the mammoths. These animals appeared in the Pliocene Epoch (5–2.5 mya).

▶ *Most elephants through time had a long trunk and enlarged teeth known as tusks.*

Moeritherium
50 mya

Palaeomastodon
35 mya

Primelephas
7 mya

429

Woolly mammoths

- **Woolly mammoths** (scientific name *Mammuthus primigenius*) first evolved over 200,000 years ago, probably in Asia.

- **They lived on the cold grasslands** of Asia, Europe and North America, and some survived to only 4000 years ago.

- **To survive** in these cold places, woolly mammoths were designed for warmth and insulation.

- **Their woolly coats** were made up of two layers of hair – an outside layer of long, coarse hairs, and a second layer of densely packed bristles.

- **Woolly mammoths also had** very tough skins – up to 2.5 cm thick – beneath which was a deep layer of fat.

- **Male woolly mammoths** could grow up to 3.5 m long and 2.9 m high at the shoulder, and weigh up to 6 tonnes.

- **They had long tusks** that curved forward, up and then back. They used their tusks to defend themselves against attackers and probably to clear snow and ice to reach low-lying plants.

- **Some cave paintings** by ice-age humans clearly depict woolly mammoths.

- **Many excellently preserved** woolly mammoth remains have been discovered in the permanently frozen ground of Siberia.

DID YOU KNOW?
People often think the woolly mammoth had red hair, but in fact this colour was a chemical reaction that happened after the animal died.

▼ *Woolly mammoths had thick, shaggy fur to keep them warm, small ears and enormous tusks.*

Rhinoceroses

- **Rhinoceroses were a very important group** of mammals in the Paleogene and Neogene Periods (66–2.6 mya).

- *Hyracodon* **was an early rhino-like mammal** that lived in North America about 30 mya.

- **Long, slender legs** meant that *Hyracodon* would have been a fast runner. It grew to about 1.5 m long.

- **Amynodonts were a group** of prehistoric rhinos that experts believed evolved from *Hyracodon*.

- *Metamynodon* **was** an amynodont rhino-like creature. It was as large as a hippopotamus and may have had a similar lifestyle to one, wading in rivers and lakes.

- **True rhinoceroses**, the ancestors of modern rhinos, were probably descended from early versions such as *Hyracodon*.

- **One of the first true rhinos** was *Trigonias*, which had four developed toes on its front feet but three on its hind feet. It lived about 35 mya in the Late Eocene or Early Oligocene Epoch.

- *Caenopus*, **another true rhino**, had three toes on all four feet. This was the pattern for all later rhinos.

- **The largest rhinoceros** horn of all time may have belonged to *Elasmotherium*, which lived in Europe possibly up to 50,000 years ago. The horn could have been a massive 2 m long.

🐾 **Rhinos became extinct** in North America between 5 and 2 mya, and later in Europe. But they survived in Asia and Africa and continue to do so today, although they are severely threatened by extinction.

◀ *The woolly rhino of the last great ice age died out less than 10,000 years ago.*

Paraceratherium

- *Paraceratherium* **was the biggest** known land mammal ever.

- **Several kinds of** *Paraceratherium* lived around 35–20 mya across Asia.

- **The biggest** *Paraceratherium* stood almost 5 m tall at the shoulder, with long, powerful legs and a long neck.

- **Its head and body were 8 m long**, and the total weight was over 15 tonnes, perhaps even 20 tonnes – heavier than the biggest-ever mammoth.

- **However** *Paraceratherium* **was not a mammoth** or other member of the elephant group – it was a kind of rhino, without a horn.

- **The head of** *Paraceratherium* was at a similar height to today's giraffe, around 6 m.

- *Paraceratherium* **probably fed** in a similar way to a giraffe, among trees at a height that no other ground-based animal could reach.

- *Paraceratherium* **had tusk-like front teeth** to pull and strip leaves, fruits and twigs from trees.

- *Paraceratherium* **was named** in 1911, from fossils discovered in present-day Pakistan.

- **Similar huge fossils** have been given various names over the years, such as *Baluchitherium*, *Indricotherium* and *Thaumastotherium*, but many experts suggest these should now all be called *Paraceratherium*.

◀ A mother and calf *Paraceratherium* cross a plain to reach woodland where they can feed.

Megacerops

- *Megacerops* **was formerly known** as *Brontotherium*, a large herbivore whose name means 'thunder beast'.

- **It lived in North America** and central Asia around 40–35 mya.

- *Megacerops* **was somewhere** between a rhinoceros and an elephant in size. It was 2.5 m tall at its shoulders.

- **It belonged to the group** of mammals called perissodactyls – hoofed mammals with an odd number of toes.

- *Megacerops* **had thick legs** and short, broad feet with four toes on its front feet and three toes on its hind feet.

- **On the top of its snout**, *Megacerops* had a thick, Y-shaped horn.

- **Palaeontologists think** that *Megacerops* used its horn to ward off predators and to fight rival males.

- *Megacerops* **lived in herds** on grassy plains and in forests.

- **It had big**, square molar teeth that crushed the soft leaves it fed on.

DID YOU KNOW?

Megacerops is a distant cousin of modern horses, tapirs and rhinoceroses.

▶ Male Megacerops *had larger two-pronged horns than females, which suggests that males used them for display and for fighting.*

The first horses

- **Horses have one of the best fossil records** of any animal. Palaeontologists have been able to trace their evolution from the earliest horse-like mammals to the modern horse.

- *Hyracotherium* **was an early horse**. It lived in forests in Europe in the Late Palaeocene and Early Eocene Epochs (58–50 mya).

▼ Hyracotherium *is the earliest known horse. Over time, horses became the best adapted of all hoofed animals for life on the open plains.*

- **Another name** for *Hyracotherium* used to be *Eohippus*, which means 'dawn horse', but *Eohippus* has now been given its own status as another type of early horse.

- *Hyracotherium* **was the size** of a small fox, with its head and body about 60 cm long. It had a short neck, a long tail and slender limbs. It also had three toes on its hind feet and four toes on its front feet.

- *Mesohippus* **was one of the horses** to evolve after *Hyracotherium*, between 40 and 30 mya. Its name means 'middle horse'.

- *Mesohippus* **had longer legs** than *Hyracotherium* and would have been a faster runner.

- **It would also have been better** at chewing food, because its teeth had a larger surface area.

- **An improved chewing ability** was important for horses and other plant-eaters as forests gave way to grasslands, and more abundant but tougher plants.

- *Mesohippus* **had also evolved** three toes on its front feet to match the three on its hind feet, and a longer face with elongated jaws.

- **As horses evolved**, they migrated from North America and Europe to Asia, Africa and South America.

Later horses

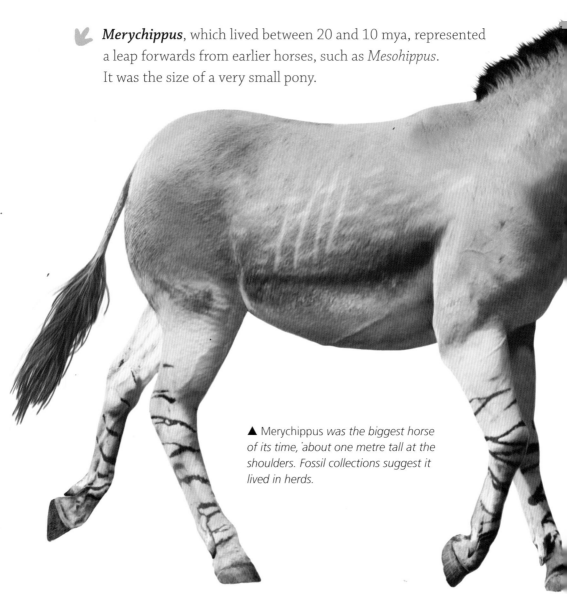

Merychippus, which lived between 20 and 10 mya, represented a leap forwards from earlier horses, such as *Mesohippus*. It was the size of a very small pony.

▲ Merychippus *was the biggest horse of its time, about one metre tall at the shoulders. Fossil collections suggest it lived in herds.*

- *Merychippus* **was the first horse** to eat mainly grass, and – to help it reach the grass – it had a longer neck and muzzle (snout) than earlier horses.

- *Merychippus'* **middle toe** had also evolved into a hoof, although this hoof did not have a pad on the bottom, unlike modern horses.

- **The legs of *Merychippus*** were designed for outrunning carnivores. Its upper leg bones were shorter than previous horses, while the lower leg bones were longer.

- **Shorter upper leg bones** meant that the horse's main leg-moving muscles could be packed in at the top of the leg – which translates into a faster-running animal.

- *Hipparion*, which means 'better horse', was a further advance on *Merychippus*. It had thinner legs and more horse-like hooves. *Hipparion* lived between 20 and 1 mya.

- **An even more advanced** horse was *Pliohippus*. The side toes that *Hipparion* still had became smaller. *Pliohippus* appeared about 5 mya.

- *Pliohippus'* **teeth** were similar to those of modern horses – they were long and had an uneven surface for grinding up grass.

- *Equus*, **the group that includes modern horses**, asses and zebras, is the latest stage in the evolution of the animal, first appearing around 4 mya.

The first whales

The very first whales looked nothing like the enormous creatures that swim in our oceans today.

Ambulocetus, one of the first members of the whale family, looked more like a giant otter. It lived about 50 mya.

Ambulocetus **means** 'walking whale', and it may have spent more time on land than in water.

▶ Pakicetus *could run fast and swim well. It probably lived alongside water and hunted animals both in and out of the water.*

Fossil remains show that *Ambulocetus* had webbed feet and hands, so it would have been a good swimmer.

An even earlier whale ancestor than *Ambulocetus* was *Pakicetus*, which lived about 52 mya.

Pakicetus **is named** after the country Pakistan, where a fossil of its skull was found in 1979.

Pakicetus **was around** 1.8 m long. *Ambulocetus*, at 3 m, was bigger.

Palaeontologists used to think that the whale and dolphin group, Ceracea, evolved from carnivorous hoofed mammals called mesonychids. A modern view is that the cetaceans are more closely related to the even-toed ungulates of hoofed mammals, the artiodactyls.

Around 40 mya, the first true whales evolved from their half-walking, half-swimming ancestors. They stayed in the ocean waters and didn't come onto land.

DID YOU KNOW?

Only the back of Pakicetus' skull and part of its lower jaw have been found. However, from this, palaeontologists can tell it was not able to dive very deeply.

443

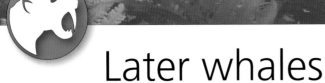

Later whales

- **First appearing** about 40 mya, *Basilosaurus* closely resembled the whales we are familiar with today, more so than its previous relatives, *Pakicetus* and *Ambulocetus*.

- **It was also enormous**. It measured between 20 and 25 m in length – the same as three elephants standing in a row.

- *Basilosaurus* **had a variety of teeth** in its mouth – sharp teeth at the front for stabbing, and saw-edged teeth at the back for chewing.

- **These whales ate large fish**, squid, and other marine mammals.

DID YOU KNOW?

Cetotherium was a prehistoric baleen whale that first appeared over 20 mya. Instead of teeth, these whales had hard plates in their mouths, called baleen, that filtered plankton and small fish.

There were some big differences between *Basilosaurus* and modern whales. For a start, it had a slimmer body.

Basilosaurus also lacked a blowhole, a nostril on the top of modern whales' heads that they breathe out of when they come to the surface. Instead, it had nostrils on its snout.

▲ The prehistoric whale Basilosaurus, which means 'king of the lizards', was so named because the first person to examine its remains thought it was a gigantic plesiosaur – a prehistoric marine reptile.

A more advanced whale than *Basilosaurus* was *Prosqualodon*. It lived between 30 and 20 mya and had a blowhole.

Prosqualodon may have been similar to the ancestor of toothed whales, a group that includes sperm whales, killer whales, beaked whales and dolphins.

Prosqualodon looked similar to a dolphin. It had a streamlined body about 2.5 m in length and a long, narrow snout, which was full of pointed teeth.

Early primates

- **The primates** are a group of mammals that include lemurs, bushbabies, tarsiers, monkeys, and apes such as gorillas, chimps and humans.

- **Primates have** a much greater range of movement in their arms, legs, fingers and toes than other mammals.

- **They also have** a more acute sense of touch because their fingers and toes end in flat nails, not curved claws – so the skin underneath evolved into a sensitive pad.

- **The ancestors of primates** were small insectivorous (insect-eating) mammals that looked like shrews.

- **One of the first known** primates was *Plesiadapis*, which lived about 57 mya in Europe and North America. It was a squirrel-like tree climber.

- **More advanced primates** developed about 5–10 million years later. They looked a bit like modern lemurs.

- *Notharctus* **was one** of these lemur-like primates. It ate leaves and fruit, had a head-body length of 40 cm, and a grasping thumb that would have gripped well around branches.

- **Other more advanced** – but still early – primates include *Smilodectes* and *Cantius*. They had larger brains and eyes, longer tails and smaller snouts than *Plesiadapis*.

- **These animals** were the early relatives of lemurs and lorises, but probably not the higher primates – the monkeys, apes and humans. Palaeontologists believe that role belongs to a different branch of primate evolution.

One early monkey was *Mesopithecus*, which lived about six mya in Greece and Turkey. It was similar to modern monkeys in many ways, but had a longer tail.

▼ *The early primate* Plesiadapis *had a long tail and claws on its fingers and toes – unlike later monkeys and apes, which had nails.*

449

Archicebus

- *Archicebus* **was one of the earliest** known primates, with fossils dating back to just after those of *Plesiadapis*.

- *Archicebus* **lived 55 mya** during the Eocene Epoch.

- **Its fossils** are from central China and were first dug up in 2003.

- *Archicebus,* **'ancient monkey'**, was officially described and named in 2013.

- **It was very small**, with a head-body length of only 7 cm, and a tail of perhaps 10 cm. It was also lightly built and weighed less than 30 g.

- *Archicebus* **had the typical** primate features of forward-facing eyes, flexible shoulders and hips, wrists and ankles that could bend and twist, and grasping hands and feet.

- *Archicebus* **was probably** very early on the evolutionary branch leading to tarsiers, just after it split from monkeys and apes.

- **In general appearance** *Archicebus* looked like today's bushbabies and tarsiers.

- **However it had smaller eyes** than these modern primates, so it may have been active by day (diurnal), rather than at night (nocturnal).

> **DID YOU KNOW?**
> The name primate means 'first or best' and was given in 1758 by Swedish expert on classifying life, Carl Linnaeus.

The teeth of Archicebus, especially the big, sharp canines near the front, indicate that it probably ate insects along with other small creatures.

▲ Archicebus *had long fingers and toes to hold twigs and branches.*

451

Darwinius ('Ida')

- ***Darwinius* was a primate** that lived 47 mya in what is now southwest Germany.

- **The remains of *Darwinius*** are amazingly complete, missing only a few small parts of the skeleton, and they include fur, and even plant parts that were probably its last meal.

- **The *Darwinius* fossils** come from the Messel Pits, well known for preserving fine details of many kinds of creatures, from bugs to fish, reptiles, birds and mammals.

- ***Darwinius* was named in honour** of the English naturalist Charles Darwin, who suggested the theory of evolution by natural selection in 1859.

- **The official name** *Darwinius* was give in 2009 – 200 years after Darwin's birth.

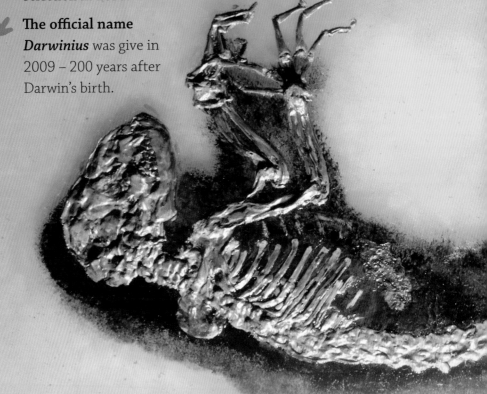

- **However the fossils** of *Darwinius* had been discovered 26 years earlier, in 1983.

- **For several years** these fossils had been involved in attempted forgery, sale to private collectors, secret purchase deals and other suspicious events.

- *Darwinius* **was a lemur-like mammal**, almost fully grown, with a head-body length of 25 cm, and a tail adding another 34 cm.

- **Experts do not agree** whether *Darwinius* was a very early ancestor of humans, or a relative of that ancestor, or from a different part of the primate group, after the human branch had split away.

◄ *Few fossil remains are as complete as the specimen of Darwinius, which was probably a female about four-fifths adult size.*

Apes

Apes are primates that have more complex brains than monkeys and no tails. They include lesser and great apes and humans.

Aegyptopithecus was one of the early pre-apes. It lived in Egypt in the Oligocene Epoch (34–23 mya). It was small and had a short tail.

An early ape that lived between 25 and 23 mya was *Proconsul*. Its body size varied from that of a small monkey to that of a female gorilla, and it had a larger brain than *Aegyptopithecus*.

▼ *The early ape* Dryopithecus *stood about one metre tall. It had the largest brain for its size of any mammal at the time, and it flourished in open grassland regions in Africa, Asia and Europe.*

- *Proconsul* **was a fruit-eater**. Palaeontologists think that it walked on four limbs with part of its weight supported by the knuckles of its hands, like modern chimpanzees and gorillas.

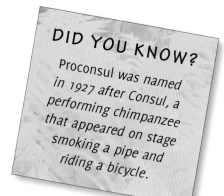

- **Several lines of apes** developed after *Proconsul*. They led to lesser apes or gibbons, the Asian great apes the orang-utans, and the African great apes, the chimpanzees, gorillas and humans.

- *Dryopithecus* **was a chimp-like ape** that evolved after *Proconsul* and lived in the Late Miocene Epoch (15–5 mya). It may have stood on two legs but climbed using all four.

- *Sivapithecus* **was an ape** that lived from about 12 to 8 mya. It is now thought to be part of the chain of evolution of Asian apes and is possibly an ancestor of the orang-utan. It was once also called *Ramapithecus*.

- **Australopithecines were a further step** in the evolution from apes to humans. Australopithecines (meaning 'southern apes') were found in Africa and some walked on two legs.

- **The biggest ape** was *Gigantopithecus*, which lived in China from about 8 to less than 1 mya. It may have been up to 2.5 m tall and weighed 300 kg.

Sahelanthropus

- *Sahelanthropus* **was an ape-like creature** whose fossils have been found in Chad, central North Africa.

- **The region where the remains were found** is called The Sahel, leading to the name *Sahelanthropus*, 'Sahel ape'.

- **Fossils of *Sahelanthropus*,** found in 2001–2002 and named in 2008, consist of parts of the skull, including bits of jaws and teeth.

- **These fossils** have been given that nickname 'Toumai', meaning 'Hope of Life' in the local language.

- **These remains are enough** to known that *Sahelanthropus* was a member of the ape group – gorillas, chimps, humans and orang-utans.

- **However the fossils are not complete** or detailed enough to show the relationship between *Sahelanthropus*, gorillas, chimps and humans.

- *Sahelanthropus* **lived at least 6 mya** and probably about 7 mya, although possibly even earlier.

- **Some fossil experts** say this is the time when the human line of evolution was separating from our closest living relatives, the chimpanzee line.

- *Sahelanthropus* **may have lived** just before this split, as the last common ancestor of chimps and humans.

- **Or *Sahelanthropus* may have existed** just after the split, as the earliest human-line ancestor, or less likely, on the other side of the split as an early chimp ancestor.

▼ *Fossils of* Sahelanthropus *are not complete enough to know whether it lived mainly in trees or on the ground.*

457

Orrorin

- **The name *Orrorin*** means 'Original Man' in the local language of the Tugen Hills in Kenya.

- **Several *Orrorin* fossils** were unearthed here from 2000, giving the nickname 'Millennium Human', and received their official name in 2001.

- ***Orrorin* fossils include** bits of thigh and upper arm bones, fingers, lower jaw and teeth.

- **Comparing these remains** to similar parts of other fossil and also living apes, *Orrorin* was probably about 1.4–1.5 m tall and weighed around 40–50 kg.

- **Dating *Orrorin* fossils** by various means gives an age of around 6 million years, that is, after *Sahelanthropus* but before *Ardipithecus*.

- **The shape of the thigh bones** found suggests *Orrorin* could stand and walk upright.

- **The teeth are also more similar** to modern humans, compared to certain other fossil apes.

- **These features have led** some experts to propose that *Orrorin* is a direct ancestor of modern humans.

- **If so, this could place** the extinct *Australopithecus* on a side branch of human evolution, rather than as our ancestor, as described later.

> **DID YOU KNOW?**
> Features of Orrorin fossils show it is more similar to modern humans than some later human-type primates – causing a real puzzle for experts.

However other bones of *Orrorin* are shaped more for tree-climbing than for upright walking.

▼ *About 20 fossils of* Orrorin *have been found in Kenya, East Africa.*

459

Ardipithecus

- **A possible early hominin** (humans and close relatives) was *Ardipithecus ramidus*, which lived about 4.5 mya.

- **It would have looked similar** to a chimpanzee in many ways, except for one major difference – *Ardipithecus ramidus* could walk on two legs.

- **It probably lived** in woods and forests, sleeping in trees at night, but foraging on the ground for roots during the day.

- **A full-grown** *Ardipithecus ramidus* was about 1.3 m tall and weighed up to 50 kg.

- **Archaeologists discovered** the teeth, skull and arm bone fossils of *Ardipithecus ramidus* in Ethiopia and it was named in 1994.

- **In 2001**, archaeologists in Ethiopia found the remains of an even older hominid, *Ardipithecus kadabba*, which lived between 5.6 and 5.8 mya.

- **The fossils** of *Ardipithecus kadabba* are similar to those of *Ardipithecus ramidus*, so it is possible they are very closely related.

- **The name *kadabba*** comes from the local language version of 'basal family ancestor'.

- ***Australopithecus anamensis*** is a later hominin than *Ardipithecus ramidus*. Its fossils date to between 4.2 and 3.9 million years old.

- **A fossil** of one of *Australopithecus anamensis'* knee-joints shows that it shifted its weight from one leg to the other when it moved – a sure sign that it walked on two legs.

▲ Ardipithecus ramidus. *Scientists chose its name from the Afar language of Ethiopia –* ardi *means 'ground' while* ramid *means 'root' – words that express its position at the base of human history.*

Australopithecus africanus

- **Australopithecus africanus**, which means 'the southern ape of Africa', was an early hominid that emerged between 3 and 2 mya.

- **This species** was the first australopithecine to be discovered.

- **The Australian-born** scientist Raymond Dart made the discovery of this important fossil in South Africa in 1924.

▼ This reconstruction of Australopithecus africanus show a projecting ape-like jaw but also a forehead that does not slope back so much as in modern apes.

- **The fossil** that Dart identified was found in a quarry near the village of Taung, on the edge of the Kalahari Desert.

- **It was the fossil** of a skull, belonging to a child around two or three years old. The fossil became known as the Taung child.

- **Many people** did not believe in Dart's discovery – they thought it was an ape, not a hominin. But one person did believe it – the archaeologist Robert Broom.

- **In 1947**, Broom himself found a skull of an adult *Australopithecus africanus*.

- **The adult skull** became known as 'Mrs Ples' because Broom first thought it belonged to a different species, *Plesianthropus transvaalensis*.

- **By the 1950s** other parts of *Australopithecus africanus*' skeleton had been unearthed, including a pelvis and a femur.

- **These fossils proved** beyond doubt that *Australopithecus africanus* was an upright-walking hominin.

DID YOU KNOW?
'Hominid' is used to refer to modern and extinct Great Apes and all their immediate ancestors. 'Hominin' is used to refer to modern and extinct humans and all their immediate ancestors.

Australopithecus afarensis

- **One of the most famous** of all fossils is 'Lucy'.

- **'Lucy' was a female** young adult *Australopithecus afarensis*, 'Southern Ape from Afar'.

- **Her remains were excavated** near Hadar in the Afar region of Ethiopia, northeast Africa, in 1974, and named in 1978.

- **About two-fifths of the skeleton** of 'Lucy' were preserved – a very large amount compared to other human fossils from such a long time ago. The hip bones show she was female.

- **Many other fossils** of *Australopithecus afarensis* have been found in East Africa. They include parts of a group of 13 individuals of various sizes known as the 'First Family' at Hadar in 1975, and a young girl about three years old, 'Selam', also near Hadar in 2000.

- *Australopithecus afarensis* lived between 4 and 3 mya.

- **Its spine, hips, legs and feet** show it could walk quite well, upright on two legs, while the shoulders, arms and hands were adapted to grasping, as when climbing in trees.

- **The typical height** of an adult *Australopithecus afarensis* was 1.1 m for females and 1.5 m for males, and a weight of 40 kg for males and 30 kg for females. Brain size was small, usually less than 400 cubic cm.

- *Australopithecus afarensis* may have been our direct ancestor, on the evolutionary line to modern humans, or a close relation of this ancestor.

▶ Fossils found with those of 'Lucy' and her kin indicate these creatures lived in a mixed habitat with water, trees and grasses.

465

Homo habilis

- **Homo habilis** is one of the earliest known members of the genus *Homo*, to which we also belong. It lived between 2.3 and 1.4 mya.

- **The archaeologists** Louis and Mary Leakey first discovered its remains at Olduvai Gorge in Tanzania, in 1960–61.

- **Fossils of Homo habilis** skulls have since been found around Lake Turkana in Kenya, one of the richest sites for hominid fossils in the world.

▲ *The first* Homo habilis *skull found by Louis and Mary Leakey in Tanzania. It had a bigger brain than any previous hominin.*

- **The skulls show** that *Homo habilis* had a flat face with prominent cheekbones, similar to australopithecines, which it would have lived alongside.

- **Homo habilis** was much more ape-like than its successors, such as *Homo ergaster*. It probably had body fur and lacked any form of language.

- **But it did have a bigger brain** than any australopithecine. It also had more flexible hands and straighter, more sensitive fingers.

- **Homo habilis** means 'handy man' – it could use its hands to gather fruit and it also created stone tools, known as Oldowan.

- **A fully grown** *Homo habilis* male was around 1.4 m tall and weighed about 50 kg.

▶ Homo habilis *showed the trend of jaws that protruded less compared to earlier relatives.*

DID YOU KNOW?
Homo habilis used stone tools to crack open animal bones so it could eat the nutritious marrow inside.

Homo erectus

- **About 1.8 million years ago** a new form of human appeared in Africa – *Homo erectus*. Some scientists think that a similar form, *Homo ergaster*, may have been a type of *Homo erectus*.

- **The body of *Homo erectus*** was very similar to that of a modern human, and was also tall, with some specimens standing 1.8 m in height.

- **The head was rather different** to that of modern humans, having a heavy ridge of bone over the eyes and protruding jaws that made it look more ape-like.

- **Some remains indicate** that *Homo erectus* was capable of building huts out of wood and brushwood. These were probably temporary shelters for a tribe on the move, not permanent homes.

- ***Homo erectus*** spread beyond Africa and settled in Europe and Asia.

DID YOU KNOW?

The 'Peking Man' fossils disappeared at the beginning of World War II and have never been found. They were confiscated by Japanese troops just when they were about to be shipped to the USA.

- **In the late 19th century**, Eugène Dubois discovered *Homo erectus* fossils on the Indonesian island of Java. At the time he named them *Pithecanthropus erectus*, which later changed to *Homo erectus*.

- **In the 1930s**, archaeologists found over 40 *Homo erectus* skeletons in China, naming them *Sinanthropus pekinensis*.

🐾 **For a long time**, people called the human to which the Chinese fossils belonged 'Peking Man'. It was much later that palaeoanthropologists realized it was in fact *Homo erectus*.

🐾 **Archaeologists have also found** evidence that *Homo erectus* used fire and practised cannibalism.

▼ *Stone hearths that were used by* Homo erectus *prove that it had mastered fire. Fire provided warmth, light, protection and the means to cook food.*

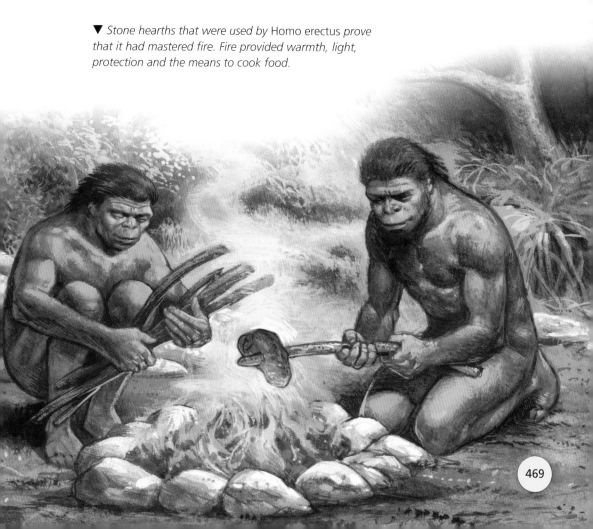

469

Homo heidelbergensis

- *Homo heidelbergensis* may well be the direct ancestor of our own species, *Homo sapiens*, and perhaps the Neanderthals as well.

- **This species is named** after a bone called the Heidelberg jaw, found in Germany in 1907 and officially described in 1908.

- **Thousands of similar fossils** have been found since across Europe, Western Asia and Africa, from Boxgrove in England to South Africa.

- *Homo heidelbergensis* probably appeared in Africa, perhaps evolving from *Homo erectus*, some 1,100,000 to 750,000 years ago, and then spread to other regions.

- **Although it was about as tall** and heavy as modern humans, *Homo heidelbergensis* had a slightly smaller brain size, around 1200–1300 cubic cm.

- **Many stone tools** are associated with *Homo heidelbergensis*, including hand axes, scrapers and spear points.

- **From the details** of preserved skull, ear and throat (hyoid) bones, *Homo heidelbergensis* may well have had some form of language.

- *Homo heidelbergensis* **may be** the same species as another fossil, *Homo rhodesiensis*, found only in Africa.

- **It seems that** *Homo heidelbergensis* had died out by 200,000 years ago, as Neanderthals appeared in Europe and modern humans appeared in Africa.

▼ Homo heidelbergensis *may well have hunted in cooperative groups using spears, clubs and similar simple weapons.*

Homo neanderthalensis

- *Homo neanderthalensis* – or Neanderthals – lived between around 300,000 and perhaps 30,000 years ago across Europe, West Asia and parts of the Middle East.

- The name *Homo neanderthalensis* means 'man from the Neander Valley', which is the site in Germany where the first of its fossil remains were found in 1865.

- **Neanderthals are our extinct cousins** rather than our direct ancestors – they are from a different branch of the human family.

- **They were about 30 percent heavier** than modern humans. Their bodies were more sturdy and they had shorter legs.

- **Neanderthals' shorter, stockier bodies** were better suited than modern humans to life in Europe, West Asia and parts of the Middle East during the ice ages of the Pleistocene Epoch (2.6 million to 12,000 years ago).

- **Their faces** were also different, with sloping foreheads and heavy brow ridges.

- **They buried their dead**, cooked meat and made various tools and weapons.

- **Neanderthals made** the first ever spears tipped with stone blades.

▶ *Neanderthals showed great skills in hunting, collecting plants and cooking foods.*

DID YOU KNOW?

Many people think that Neanderthals were slow and stupid, but in fact their brains were at least as big as modern humans' brains.

Towards Homo sapiens

All people alive today belong to the species *Homo sapiens*, 'Wise Human'.

More accurately, we belong to a subgroup or subspecies known as *Homo sapiens sapiens*, *H. s. sapiens*, anatomically modern humans or simply 'modern humans'.

Homo sapiens sapiens probably originated in Africa around 200,000 years ago.

Before that time, fossils show there were several other kinds of Homo sapiens with more ancient or primitive features, known by the general name of archaic *Homo sapiens*.

These primitive or archaic features included slightly different brain size, thicker skull bones, a sloped-back forehead, bony eyebrow ridges, projecting face and less protruding cheek bones.

Further archaic features compared to modern humans were bigger teeth, a sloped-back or rounded chin, and a skeleton that had a generally heavier or more robust build.

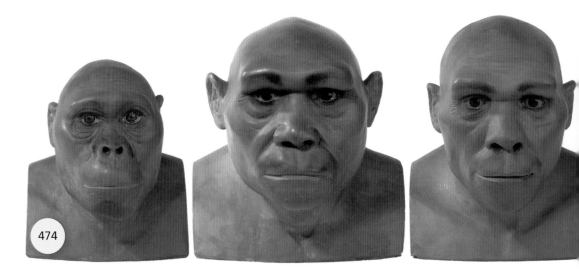

- **Some kinds of archaic *Homo sapiens*** have one or a few modern features mixed with the primitive ones, which makes it difficult to put them into precise, well-defined groups.

- **One version of the evolutionary line** leading to us goes from *Australopithecus* (probably *A. afarensis*), perhaps to *Homo habilis*, then *H. erectus* (*H. ergaster*), on to *H. heidelbergensis* (*H. rhodesiensis*), then archaic *H. sapiens*, and finally modern humans, *H. s. sapiens*.

- **In this version**, the whole evolution of *Homo* occurred in Africa.

- **However this sequence** is only one of many suggestions. Different experts have very different opinions and debate them with great passion.

▼ *Hominin reconstruction sequence. Model reconstructions of hominins in chronological order, from left to right:* Australopithecus, *early* Homo erectus *(Java Man), late* Homo erectus *(Peking Man),* Homo heidelbergensis *(Rhodesian Man),* Homo neanderthalensis *(Neanderthals) and early* Homo sapiens *(Cro-Magnons).*

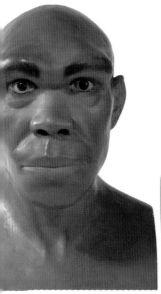
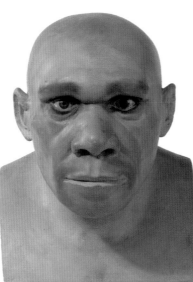
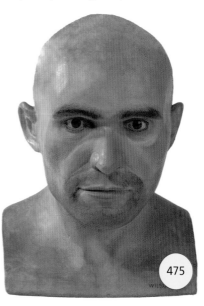

Modern humans

- **All people alive today** are (anatomically) modern humans, subspecies *Homo sapiens sapiens*.

- **Various evidence suggests** when and where modern humans appeared, including tools, fossil bones and teeth, genetic material (DNA) extracted from them, and genes from living people.

- **Most evidence shows** modern humans appeared around 200,000 years ago in East Africa.

- **The oldest fossils recognized** as modern humans come from Omo, in Ethiopia, dated to 195,000 years ago.

- **By 90,000 years ago**, modern humans had become established in Africa and started to spread into the Middle East. This migration is known as 'Out of Africa'.

- **From the Middle East**, modern humans spread into Europe by 40,000 years ago as 'Cro-Magnon People'.

- **They also spread east** into Asia, South East Asia and then Australia by 45,000 years ago.

- **Other modern humans** spread north-east through Asia into north-west North America by 15,000 years ago, and then south through the Americas.

- **As modern humans spread**, they replaced archaic *Homo sapiens* and other humans living in each region.

- **However modern humans** may have interbred with some of these other groups, such as the Neanderthals in Europe.

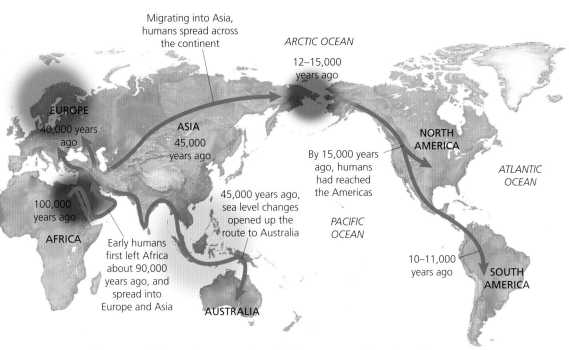

Migrating into Asia, humans spread across the continent

ARCTIC OCEAN

12–15,000 years ago

EUROPE
40,000 years ago

ASIA
45,000 years ago

NORTH AMERICA

By 15,000 years ago, humans had reached the Americas

ATLANTIC OCEAN

100,000 years ago

45,000 years ago, sea level changes opened up the route to Australia

PACIFIC OCEAN

AFRICA

Early humans first left Africa about 90,000 years ago, and spread into Europe and Asia

10–11,000 years ago

SOUTH AMERICA

AUSTRALIA

▲ Improved climate (green area) enabled humans to migrate into Europe and Asia from Africa. Changes in the sea level (orange area) opened up the route to Australia. Ice age glaciations (blue areas) limited migration north and east, but once established, the Americas were swiftly populated.

🐾 **Modern humans gradually** adapted to the climate and other conditions in each region, producing the variety of people around the world today.

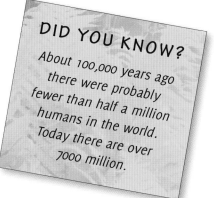

DID YOU KNOW?

About 100,000 years ago there were probably fewer than half a million humans in the world. Today there are over 7000 million.

Hobbit people

- **In 2003**, the bones of some very small people, hardly one metre tall yet living within the past 15,000 years, were found on the island of Flores, Southeast Asia.

- **Bones from several individuals** were found, including one partially complete skull. They showed a brain size of 400–450 cubic cm – one-third that of modern humans.

- **These remains were described** in 2004 as the species *Homo floresiensis*, 'Flores Human'.

- **The movie series *Lord of the Rings***, featuring small human-like hobbits, was released around this time, leading to the nickname 'Hobbit people' for *Homo floresiensis*.

- ***Homo floresiensis* bones** date from around 40,000 to 13,000 years ago. Stone tools found at the site are between 95,000 and 13,000 years old.

- **Experts argue** about whether *Homo floresiensis* was a separate species from modern humans, or a group of modern humans who were extra-small, perhaps because of genetic changes called mutations, or some form of disease.

- **Puzzling was the presence of stone tools** presumably made by *Homo floresiensis* when it had the brain size of a chimpanzee.

- **Recent studies show** *Homo floresiensis* had a curious mix of modern and primitive features which cannot easily be explained.

- ***Homo floresiensis* may have lived** on Flores alongside modern humans, perhaps in just the past few thousand years.

▲ Flores humans may have used their tools to kill and cut up pygmy elephants that also lived on their island.

Denisovan and Red Deer people

- **Denisovan humans** are named after Denisova Cave in the Altai Mountains of Central Asia.

- **Numerous kinds of fossils** were found here of three distinct kinds – Neanderthals, anatomically modern humans (*Homo sapiens sapiens*), and Denisovan people.

- **The Denisovan fossils** include pieces of finger and toe bones and teeth, from around 40,000 years ago.

- **Denisovan people** may have evolved separately from the line leading to modern humans around 800,000 years ago. They probably separated from the Neanderthal line 650,000 years ago.

- **However studies of genetic material** from fossils and living people show these three groups bred with each other at certain times, so that some modern humans from Asia and Australia have inherited certain Denisovan genes.

- **Red Deer Cave people** are known from preserved bones and teeth found in the cave of that name, in Yunnan, South China.

- **These fossils** have some differences from those of modern humans, yet the most recent date from only 11,500 years ago.

- **It is unclear** whether Red Deer people were a different species from modern humans, a result of interbreeding, or a regional variation of modern humans.

▶ *Palaeontologists carefully sift the cave for fossils of Denisovan humans, along with other animals and plants of their time, 40,000 years ago.*

DID YOU KNOW?

Discoveries such as Homo floresiensis, *Denisovans and* Red Deer *people show that in the last 50,000 years, and even 15,000 years, there were more kinds of humans than was once believed.*

Brains and intelligence

🐾 **Primates, including all the various** kinds of humans, had bigger brains in relation to their body size than other mammals.

🐾 **Primates developed** larger brains – and more intelligence – because living in and moving between trees required a high degree of balance, coordination and the skilful use of hands and feet.

🐾 **Once hominids' brains** started getting bigger, so their skulls began to change. Bigger brains led to the development of foreheads.

🐾 *Homo habilis'* **brain** was 50 percent bigger than its australopithecine predecessors. It had a brain capacity of 750 cubic cm.

🐾 **The structure of its brain** was different to that of earlier hominids. It had much bigger frontal lobes – the parts of the brain associated with planning and problem-solving.

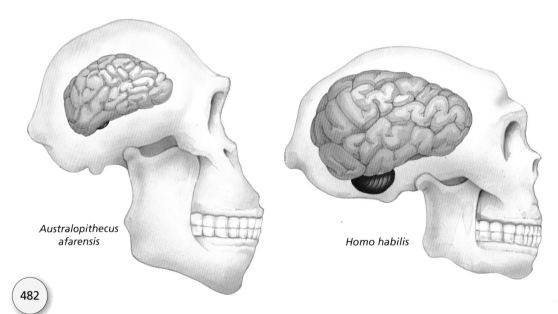

Australopithecus afarensis

Homo habilis

- **Homo habilis** put its greater intelligence to use in the quest to find meat, which it scavenged from other animals' kills to supplement its diet.

- **Eating more meat** allowed hominids' brains to get even bigger. Breaking down plant food uses up a huge amount of energy, so the fewer plants hominids ate, the more energy was available for their brains.

- **Homo ergaster** had an even bigger brain, with a capacity of around 1000 cubic cm. It could use this intelligence to read tracks left by animals – a major development in hunting.

- **The brain** of *Homo erectus* became larger during its existence. About one mya its brain capacity was 1000 cubic cm, 500,000 years later it was 1300 cubic cm.

- **The average human brain** capacity today is 1350–1450 cubic cm.

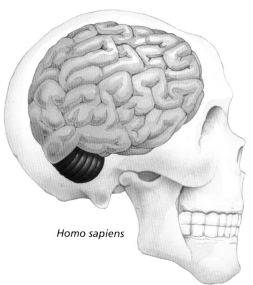

Homo sapiens

◀ Brain size is linked to intelligence, but size isn't everything. What makes humans and our ancestors intelligent is our brain's complex structure.

Language

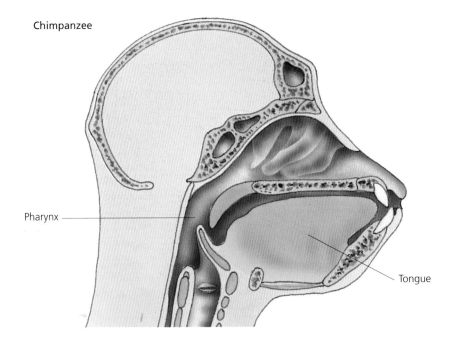

- **Language may go back** as far as *Homo erectus* or *Homo ergaster* – although this would probably have been a much simpler form of communication than we use today.

- **One reason** for language development was as a way of maintaining relationships within groups.

- **Language is different** from cries of alarm or mating calls. It involves a system for representing ideas and feelings.

- **An important feature** in speech is the pharynx – a tube in the neck, from the vocal cords (contained in the larynx) to the mouth.

- **In other primates** the pharynx is too short to produce complex modifications of sound.

- ***Homo erectus/ergaster*** probably had a longer pharynx than earlier hominins, suggesting it was able to produce basic speech.

Chimpanzee

Pharynx

Tongue

- **Homo heidelbergensis** had an even longer pharynx and would have been able to produce complex sounds. However, its speech would have differed from ours because of the different shape of its face.

- **Neanderthals would also** have been able to speak. The fossil remains of a Neanderthal hyoid bone, which supports the larynx, is almost identical to a modern human's.

- **Modern speech probably** only developed with the arrival of *Homo sapiens sapiens*.

- **Some experts think** that modern speech first developed around 150,000 years ago – others think it did not happen until less than 50,000 years ago.

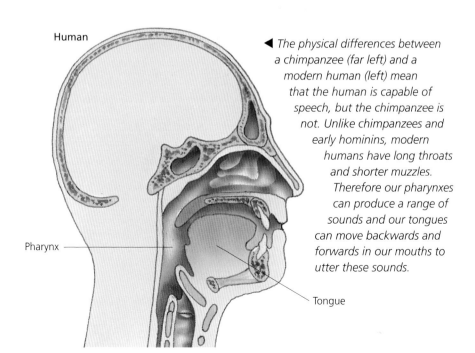

Human

Pharynx

Tongue

◀ *The physical differences between a chimpanzee (far left) and a modern human (left) mean that the human is capable of speech, but the chimpanzee is not. Unlike chimpanzees and early hominins, modern humans have long throats and shorter muzzles. Therefore our pharynxes can produce a range of sounds and our tongues can move backwards and forwards in our mouths to utter these sounds.*

Tools

▲ Homo habilis
produced flakes of
stone, such as this one,
by striking one stone
against another, called
a hammerstone.

🦶 **The greatest number** of *Homo habilis* tools has been found in the Olduvai Gorge in Tanzania. They include rocks that were used as hammers, flakers, choppers and scrapers.

🦶 *Homo habilis* used these tools to cut meat and, especially, to scrape open animal bones to eat the marrow inside.

🦶 **The stone tools** used by *Homo habilis* are crude and basic. This hominin was one of the the first tool-makers, but not a skilled one as yet.

🦶 **Making these early stone tools** was still a challenging task – the tool-maker needed to strike one rock with another so that it would produce a single, sharp flake rather than shattering into many pieces.

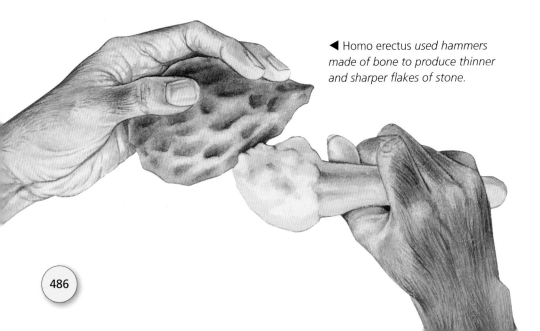

◀ Homo erectus *used hammers made of bone to produce thinner and sharper flakes of stone.*

🐾 **Tool-making requires** considerable intelligence. It involves the use of memory, as well as the ability to plan ahead and to solve abstract problems.

🐾 *Homo erectus'* **tools** were more advanced. This hominin made tear-drop shaped, symmetrical hand axes called Acheulean axes, after the place in France where similar axes have been discovered from a later period.

🐾 **Neanderthals developed** a method for producing razor-sharp flakes of stone, called Levallois flakes, which could be placed on the end of spears.

🐾 **This method** required great precision and dexterity. While modern humans have a much broader range of skills, most would be very hard pushed to produce such tools themselves.

🐾 **Modern humans** developed the greatest variety of tools. Cro-Magnon tools include knives, spearpoints and engraving tools.

🐾 **Cro-Magnon humans** also began to make tools from materials other than stone, including wood, bones, antlers and ivory.

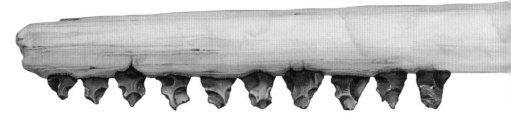

▲ Homo sapiens' *tools became more and more complex. They incorporated different materials, such as twine in the axe (top) and flint teeth held in place by resin in this saw (bottom).*

Hunting

- **One of the earliest** human hunters was *Homo erectus*. Other hominins that came before it, like *Homo habilis*, may have hunted small or lame animals, but probably they mostly scavenged other animals' kills.

- *Homo erectus* used fire to drive animals into traps. They also developed handaxes, which they used to kill animals or butcher them once they were dead.

- **In the 1990s**, finds of *Homo heidelbergensis* weapons in Boxgrove, England, showed the complete range of this species' hunting arsenal. It included axes, slicing knives, and blades for cutting and slashing.

- **A site at Schöningen, Germany**, preserved the remains of several polished wooden spears of spruce wood, probably made by *Homo heidelbergensis*.

- **Each of these spears** was over 2 m long, and was designed to be thrown like a javelin.

- **Hunting developed** into a way of providing not only food, but also clothing (animal skins) and materials for tools (bones, horns and hooves).

- **It was the Neanderthals** that excelled in hunting – a skill they developed during the ice ages of the Pleistocene Epoch (2.6–0.01 mya).

- **Neanderthals used nets** or spears to catch spawning fish. They also hunted seals by spearing them through holes in the ice or by throwing spears at them.

As well as hunting for meat, hominins also gathered wild fruits, vegetables and nuts.

Homo sapiens developed new weapons for hunting, including the bow and arrow, the blowpipe and the boomerang.

▼ *Various kinds of evidence show Neanderthal people hunted animals, lived in rock shelters, and held ceremonies to bury their dead.*

Rituals

- **One difference** between living humans and other animals is that we have complicated rituals and ceremonies.

- **These include** passing from childhood to adulthood, welcoming a new year or growing season, the birth of a baby, and mourning and burying our dead.

- **Fossils from Spain** and other sites suggest *Homo heidelbergensis* had burial ceremonies for their dead.

- **Bones from more than** 30 *Homo heidelbergensis* individuals were found at a site called La Sima de los Huesos, 'The Pit of Bones', near Atapuerca, northern Spain.

- **These bones are about 300,000 years old** and may be an ancient burial chamber – although it is also possible they were washed in by water or mudflows.

- **Evidence from about 80,000–40,000 years ago** from Spain to Iraq also suggests that Neanderthal people held ceremonies to bury their dead.

- **The evidence includes skeletons** carefully laid in certain positions, charred or burned wood and animal remains, cloth fibres and arranged rocks, all together in one small area.

- **At Shanidar Cave**, Iraq, detailed study showed many kinds of pollen grains associated with Neanderthal skeletons, suggesting flowers and other plants were laid for the dead.

▶ Homo heidelbergensis *prepare to commit one of their dead into 'The Pit of Bones', throwing in a hand axe perhaps as some kind of offering to the spirits.*

Cave art

- **Cro-Magnon people** produced many cave paintings.

- **One of the best examples** is the Grotte de Chauvet in the Ardeche, France, which was discovered in 1994.

- **The Grotte de Chauvet** caves contain more than 300 drawings of animals, from lions and deer to buffalos and woolly rhinoceroses.

- **People used to be very sceptical** that early humans could have produced cave paintings and thought they were hoaxes.

- **Another magnificent example** of cave painting is that of the Altamira cave in northern Spain, which has an 18-m-long ceiling covered with red-, black- and violet-coloured paintings of bison.

- **Most cave paintings** date from around 30,000 to 15,000 years ago, when Cro-Magnon man lived in Europe and elsewhere.

- **Other cave paintings** may be much older. Some archaeologists think that the Cave of El Castillo paintings in Spain are 40,000 years old.

- **Many cave pictures** appear to represent hunting scenes, but there are also many symbols in caves, including patterns of squares and dots.

- **Another very common image** in caves is that of a human hand.

> **DID YOU KNOW?**
>
> Cro-Magnon people made hand outlines by blowing a sooty pigment over their hand as they pressed it against the cave wall.

▶ A series of cave paintings known as the Great Hall of Bulls in Lascaux, southwest France. The paintings are around 17,000 years old.

Index

Index

Entries in **bold** refer to main entries; entries in *italics* refer to illustrations.

A

acanthodians **52**, *53*
Acanthostega 68, **70–72**, *70*
Acheulean axes 487
adders 94
Aegialornis **376**
Aegyptopithecus **454**
Aepycamelus **416**, *417*
Aepyornis 372
Africa,
  dinosaurs **330–331**, *331*
  fossil hunters 352
Aglaophyton 20
agnathans **50–51**
air, early Earth 12
Ajkaceratops **256–257**, *257*
Alamosaurus 345
Alaxasaurus **188**
Albertosaurus 345
  discovery 352
  growth **324**, *325*
Aldanotreta **40**
Alectrosaurus 357
algae,
  blue-green 13, 18, 19
  first plants 19
  lichens *18*
alligators 89, 170
  life span of *327*
Allodesmus 404
Allopleuron 104
Allosaurus **146–147**, *147*, **155**
  claws 298
  North America *344*, 345,
   346
  nose 282
Alphadon **394**
Amborella **27**, *27*
  A. trichopoda **27**, *27*

Ambulocetus **442–443**, 444
ammonites **44–45**, *44*, *45*
  prehistoric timescale *15*, *81*
amphibians 58, 68, **72–73**
  eggs 80, 81
  Eryops 74
  jaws 82
  larvae 81
  lissamphibians 76
Amphicyon **410**
amynodont mammals 432
anapsid reptiles **82**
Anatosaurus 242
Anchiceratops 250
Anchiornis **115**, **338–339**, *339*,
  363, *363*
Anchisaurus **204–205**, *204*
Andrewsarchus 404, *405*
Andrias scheuchzeri 76
angiosperm plants **24–27**
ankylosaur dinosaurs **226–227**,
  228, 230
  Antarctic 350
  armour 272
  beaks 280
  tails 301
Anning, Mary 100, 103
Antarctic dinosaurs **350–351**
Antarctopelta **350**
Apatosaurus 208, *209*, **214–**
  215, 346
  size 266
apes **454–455**
arachnids 32
Arandaspis **51**
araucaria trees 194
Archaefructus **24**, *25*, 26
Archaeomeryx **416**
Archaeopsittacus 376
Archaeopteryx 113, 184, 185,
  362, 364, *365*, **366–367**,
  367
  fossils 328
Archelon 93

Archicebus **450–451**, *451*
archosaurs **126–127**
Archosaurus 127
Arctocyon 419
Ardipithecus 458, **460–461**,
  461
Ardipithecus,
  A. kadabba **460**
  A. ramidus **460**, *461*
Argentavis magnificens **378–**
  379, *379*
Argentinosaurus **159**, **206**,
  349
  size 266
armoured dinosaurs 226,
  228, *229*, 230, 232, 233,
  272–273
  Antarctic 350
  Gobi Desert 335
  North America 345
  tails 301
art, human evolution **492–493**
Arthropleura **33**, *33*
arthropods,
  first **32–33**
  trilobites 34
artiodactyl mammals 421,
  422–423, 443
Asian dinosaurs **332–333**, *332*
Atlascopcosaurus 341
atmosphere,
  early Earth 12, 13
  oxygen 68
Australia,
  dinosaurs **340–343**, *341*, 350
  marsupial mammals 394,
   395, **396–397**
australopithecines 455, 462
  brains **482–483**
Australopithecus 458, *475*
  A. afarensis **464–465**, *465*,
   475, *482*
  A. africanus **462–463**, *462*
  A. anemensis **460**

Avimimus **180**, *181*
  China 337
  Gobi Desert 335

B

backboned animals 48, 66
bacteria 13, 18
Bactrosaurus 242
balance, dinosaurs 300, 301
baleen whales 444
Baluchitherium 434
Barapasaurus **333**
Barosaurus *195*, 346
  stomach stones *289*
Baryonyx **144–145**, *145*, 160
  dinosaur names 354, 356, *356*
Basilosaurus **444–445**, *445*
bats **426–427**
beaks, dinosaur **280–281**
beetles 36
Beipiaosaurus inexpectus
  192–193, *192*
Bevhalstia 27
bipedal dinosaurs 294, *295*
bipedal/quadrupedal dinosaurs
  295
birds,
  Archaeopteryx 113, 184,
    185, 328, 362, 364, *365*,
    366–367, 367
  archosaurs 126
  body temperature 304, 305
  diapsid reptiles 82
  dinosaurs 166, 167, 180,
    184, 185
  elephant 372, *373*
  evolution **362–369**
  flightless **372–373**
  fossils **364–365**
  land **376–377**
  terror **370–371**
  toes 296
  water **374–375**

Birkenia 15
birth,
  ichthyosaurs 102
  mammals 384
bivalves 42
blue shark *54*
blue-green algae 13, 18, 19
boas 94
body temperature,
  birds 304, 305
  dinosaurs 290, **304–305**
  mammals 386
  reptiles 304, 305
  Stegosaurus 222
Bonaparte, José 352
'Bone Wars' *353*
bony fish **58–59**
brachiopods **40–41**, *41*
Brachiosaurus 208, **210–211**,
  211
  brain 286
  legs *294*
  life span 326
  nose 282
  size 266
  speed 306
  stomach stones 288
Brachylophosaurus **244–245**,
  245
  reconstruction 358–359
brains,
  ape 454
  australopithecine **482–483**
  Australopithecus afarensis
    482
  carnivorous mammal 405
  cephalopod 43
  dinosaur 285, **286–287**
  first reptiles 78
  hominid **482–483**
  Homo erectus **483**
  H. ergaster **483**
  H. habilis 466, **482–483**, *482*
  H. heidelbergensis 470

brains (*cont.*)
  H. sapiens 474, *483*
  human **483**
  Leaellynasaura 316
  Neanderthal 472
  primate **482–483**
Branchiostoma **48**
breathing,
  Acanthostega 71
  tetrapods **68–69**
breeding display,
  Anchiornis feathers 338
  dinosaurs 138, 180, 290
bristles, *Pegomastax* 236, *237*
brittlestars 38, *38*, 39
Brontomerus **214–215**, *215*
Brontosaurus 214
brontotheres **421**
Brontotherium **421**, 436
Broom, Robert 463
bryophytes 19
Buckland, William 128
Burgess Shale, Canada 32, 48
burrows, mammals 382, *383*

C

Caenagnathasia 169
Caenopus **432**
caimans 89
Camarasaurus **212–213**, *214*,
  346
  brain *287*
  migration 314
Cambrian Period *15*
  brachiopods 40
  echinoderms 38
  jawless fish 50
  molluscs 42
  trilobites *35*
camels 416
camouflage in dinosaurs 180,
  181, 271
Camptosaurus 329

caniform mammals 404
Caninia **31**
Cantius **448**
Carboniferous Period *15*
  amphibians 72
  arthropods 33
  corals 31
  first reptiles 78
  gymnosperm plants 22
  insects 36, *37*
  reptiles 82, 84
  sharks 55
Carcharodon megalodon
  56–57, *57*
Carcharodontosaurus **154–**
  155, *155*, 160
Carnivora 404
carnivorous mammals 402,
  403, **404–405**, 406
carnosaur dinosaurs
  (Carnosauria) 154, 282
Carnotaurus **148–149**, *149*
  276, 352
Carolini, Rubén 158
cartilage,
  Leedsichthys 62
  sharks 54, 56
  fish 54
Castoroides 415
cats 404, **406–407**, 408
Caudipteryx **166–167**, *167*,
  337
cave paintings **492–493**, *492*
cells, first life 13
Cenozoic Era **14**, *14–15*
Centrosaurus 250
  discovery 352
  migration 315
cephalopods 42, **43**, 44
ceratopsian (horned) dinosaurs
  248, **250–251**, *251*, 252,
  254, 256, 257, 258, 260
  beaks 280, *280*
  horns 274

Ceratosaurus 346
Ceresiosaurus **98**
cetacean mammals 443
Cetiosaurus **208**, 330
Cetotherium 444
chain coral 31
chalicothere mammals **421**
Chalicotherium **421**
Charnia **29**, *29*
Chasmosaurus 250, *251*
Cheirolepis **58**
chelonians **92–93**
chevrotains 416
chimpanzees,
  language *485*
  Sahelanthropus 456
China,
  Anchiornis **338–339**, *339*
  dinosaurs 332, **336–339**, *336*
  fossil hunters 352
chlorophyll 18
chordates, early 48
cladistics 181
Cladoselache **54**
clams 42
classification 181
claws,
  Baryonyx 356
  dinosaur footprints 311
  dinosaurs **296**, *296*, **298–299**
Climatius 53
club mosses 194
cobras 94
cockles 42
cockroaches 36
coelocanths 58, *59*
Coelophysis **136–137**, *137*,
  345
cold blood **304–305**
colonies, dinosaur 320
colours,
  Anchiornis feathers 338, *339*
  dinosaurs **270–271**
compound eyes, trilobites 34

Compsognathus **168**, *168*
  bird evolution 362, 366
  coprolites 308
  fossils 328, 329
  life span 26
  tail *300*, 301
condylarth mammals **418–419**
cones 22, *23*
Confusciornis **368–369**, *369*
conifers 22, 23, *23*, 194, *195*,
  329
Conocoryphe **35**, *35*
continental drift 125
convergent evolution 102
Cooksonia **20**, *21*, 22
Cope, Edward Drinker 212,
  352, *353*
coprolites **308–309**, *309*, 382
  dinosaur **308**, *309*
  prehistoric timescale *17*
corals *41*
  first **30–31**, *30*, *31*
Corythosaurus 242, *243*, 303
crabs 32
creodont mammals **402–403**,
  404
Cretaceous Period 14, *15*
  ammonites 44
  amphibians 72
  angiosperms 26, 27
  Antarctic dinosaurs 350
  Australian dinosaurs 342
  birds 368, 374
  chelonians 93
  Chinese dinosaurs *337*
  crocodiles 90
  dinosaur evolution 188
  dinosaur migration *314*
  dinosaurs 124, 125, 164,
    166, 174, 176, 186, 188,
    192, 194, 206, 214, 230,
    240, 246, 248, 299
  flying reptiles 116, 118, 120
  ichthyosaurs 102

Cretaceous Period (*cont.*)
  mammals 390
  plesiosaurs 100
  snakes 94
crickets 36
crinoids *15*, 38
Cro-Magnon People *475*, **476**
  cave paintings **492**
  tools **487**
crocodiles 88, 89, 90, 126, *127*, 170
  cold blood *305*
  diapsid reptiles 82
  life span *327*
  posture 295
crocodilians **88–89**
Crocodylomorpha **88**
crustaceans 32
Cryolophosaurus **351**, *351*
cuttlefish 42
Cuvier, Baron Georges 400
cyanobacteria 13, 18
cycads 22, *22*, 23, 194, *329*
cynodonts 84

D

Daeodon **424**, *425*
Dart, Raymond 462, 463
Darwin, Charles 114, 400, 452
Darwinius **452–453**, *453*
Darwinopterus **114–115**, *115*
Daspletosaurus,
  growth **324**, 325
  teeth 279·
Deinocheirus 187
Deinonychus 170, 175, **174–175**, *174*
  claws 299, *299*
  legs 294
Deinosuchus **89**
deinotheres 429
Denisovan people **480–481**, *480*

Devonian Period *15*
  Acanthostega 71
  insects 36
  jawless fish 51
  placoderms 60
  sharks 55
  vascular plants 20
Diamantinasaurus matildae **342–343**, *342*
diapsid reptiles **82**
  mosasaurs 104
Dichobune 422
Dicraeosaurus 330
Dictyonema 42
dicynodont reptiles 84, *85*
Didanodons 356
Diictodon *84*
Dilong *271*
Dilophosaurus **138–139**, *139*
  head crests 276
Dimetrodon **84**, **86–87**, *87*
Dimorphodon **112**, *113*
Dinichthys *60*
Dinictis 407
Dinilysia **94**
Dinofelis *406*, 407
Dinohyus 424, *425*
Dinornis 372
Dinosaur National Monument, USA 345, **346–347**, *346*
Dinosauria 128
dinosaurs,
  Africa **330–331**, *331*
  Age of **124–125**
  ancestors **130–131**
  Anchiornis **338–339**, *339*
  Antarctic **350–351**
  armour **272–273**
  Asia **332–333**, *332*
  Australia **340–343**, *341*
  beaks **280–281**
  birds 166, 167, 180, 184, 185, 362

dinosaurs (*cont.*)
  body temperature 290, **304–305**
  brains 285, **286–287**
  China **336–339**, *336*
  claws **298–299**
  colours **270–271**
  coprolites **308–309**, *309*
  diapsid reptiles 82
  earliest **132–133**
  eggs 320, **322–323**, *323*, 329, 335
  estimating sizeof **266–267**
  Europe **328–329**, *328*
  eyes **284–285**
  feathers **180–181**
  feet **296–297**
  footprints **310–311**
  fossils 16, 17, *16–17*
  Gobi Desert 332, **334–335**, *335*
  growth **324–325**, 326
  head crests **276–277**
  herds **312–313**
  hibernation **316–317**
  hip bones **292–293**
  horns **274–275**
  life span **326–327**
  migration **314–315**, *315*
  names **354–357**
  nests **320–321**, 322
  North America **344–347**, *344*
  noses **282–283**
  ostrich **186–187**
  pack hunters **170–171**, 174
  posture 295
  raptors **172–173**, 174, 176, 182
  reconstruction **358–359**, *358*
  sails **290–291**
  smallest **168–169**
  sounds **318–319**
  South America **348–349**, *349*
  speed **306–307**

dinosaurs (*cont.*)
 stomach stones **288–289**
 tails **300–301**
 teeth **278–279**
 therizinosaurs **188–189**
Diplocaulus 15, **72**, *73*
Diplodocus 208, **216–217**, *217*
 claws 298
 dinosaur names 357
 D. hallorum **206**, *206*
 D. longus 206
 herds 312
 migration 314
 North America *344*, 346
 stomach stones 288
 tail 300
Diprotodon **396**, *397*
displays,
 Anchiornis feathers 338
 dinosaur 138, 180
dissorophids *77*
dogs 404, **410–411**
draco lizard **108**
dragonflies 36
Dravidosaurus **333**
dromaeosaur dinosaurs 172,
 173, 174, 176, 182, 184,
 185, 362
 legs 294
Dromaeosaurus **173**
Dromiceiomimus 186
Dryopithecus *454*, **455**
Dubois, Egène 468
duckbilled dinosaurs (*see also*
 hadrosaur dinosaurs) *14*,
 242–243, 244
 beaks 280
 dinosaur names 356
 feet 297
 Gobi Desert 335
 head crests 302–303
 North America 345
 reconstruction 358
 sounds 318

dinosaurs (*cont.*)
 tails 301
 teeth 279
 speed 306
Dunkle, David 60
Dunkleosteus 55, **60–61**, *61*

E

Earth's formation **12**
echinoderms **38**
echolocation 426, *426*
Edaphosaurus **84**
Ediacara fossil beds, Australia
 28
Edmontonia **230**, *231*
Edmontosaurus **242**, **243**, 294
 sounds 319
 speed 306
 teeth *279*
eggs,
 Darwinopterus 115
 dinosaur 164, 169, 178, 253,
  320, **322–323**, *323*, 329,
  335
 mammal 384
 Psittacosaurus 249
 reptile 78, **80–81**, *81*
 snake *80*, *81*
Elasmosaurus **100**, *101*
Elasmotherium *413*, **432**
elephant birds 372, *373*
elephants **428–429**
embryos,
 dinosaur eggs *323*
 reptile eggs 81, *81*
Entelodon **424**
entelodont mammals **424–425**
Eocene Epoch,
 birds 370, 376
 frogs and salamanders 77
 mammals 404, 421, 424,
  432, 438
 primates 450

Eodromaeus **134–135**, *135*
Eohippus **439**
Eomaia 388
Eoraptor **132**, 134, 135, 348
Eozostrodon 384, **386**
Epigaulus **414**, *415*
epochs **14**
Equus **441**
eras **14**
erosion *17*, *18*
Eryops **74–75**
Eudimorphodon **112**
Euhelopus 219
Euoplocephalus **226**, *227*,
 345, *358*
Euparkeria **130**, *130*
European dinosaurs **328–329**,
 328
euryapsid reptiles **82**
Eusthenopteron **66**, *67*
Eustreptospondylus **140–141**,
 141
eusuchians **89**
eutherian mammals 388,
 389
eutriconodont mammals 391
evolutionary convergence **396**,
 398
exoskeletons 33
extinction,
 mass 41
 coral 31
 moas 372
 nothosaurs 99
 rhinoceroses 433
 trilobites 35
eyes,
 agnathan 51
 cephalopod 43
 dinosaur 264, **284–285**
 Eryops 75
 Leaellynasaura 316
 reptile **285**
 trilobite 34

500

F

Fabrosaurus **196–197**
Falcarius **190–191**, *191*
feather stars 38
feathers,
  Anchiornis 338, *339*
  Archaeopteryx 366
  Beipiaosaurus 192, *192*
  birds and dinosaurs 362,
    363
  Chinese dinosaurs 337, *337*
  Confuciornis 368, *369*
  dinosaur body temperature
    305
  dinosaur colours 270, *271*
  dinosaurs with *126*, 142,
    150, *165*, 166, *173*, *174*,
    176, **180–181**, *181*, 182,
    183, 184
  therizinosaur dinosaurs 188
feet, dinosaur **296–297**
feliform mammals 404
felines 406, 407, 408
female dinosaurs **302–303**,
  303
ferns 23, 194, *329*
filter feeding,
  brachiopods 40
  Leedsichthys 62
fins,
  Leedsichthys 62
  lobe-finned fish 66, *67*
  ray-finned fish 58
  sharks 54
fire 469, *469*, 488
'First Family' **464**
first life **12–13**
fish **46–63**
  bony **58–59**
  cartilaginous 54
  early jawed **52–53**
  jawless **50–51**
  lobe-finned 58, *58*, 66
  ray-finned **58**

flight,
  and gliding 108
  Archaeopteryx 366
  Confusciornis 368
  Microraptor 182
flightless birds **372–373**
flowering plants **24–27**, 194
flowers 24, *25*, *26*
'flying lizard' **108**, 110
flying reptiles 112, 116, 117
footprints,
  Amphicyon 410
  Australian dinosaurs **341**
  dinosaur **310–311**
  dinosaur herds 312, 313,
    313
  dinosaur migrations 314
  fossil 17
fossils,
  angiosperm 24
  Antarctic dinosaur 350
  bird **364–365**
  coprolite **308–309**, *309*
  dinosaur 128
  dinosaur footprint 310,
    311
  Dinosaur National
    Monument, USA 345,
    346–347, *346*
  fake 336
  first life 12
  formation of **16–17**, *16–17*
  fossil hunters **352–353**
  mammal 382
  mummified 358
  protist 28
  reconstructing dinosaurs
    358
  frogs **76–77**, *77*
    breathing in 68
  frogspawn 80, *80*
Fruitadens **238–239**, *239*
Fruitafossor **392–393**, *393*
fungus and lichens *18*

fur (hair),
  Homo habilis 466
  mammoth *382*, *383*, **386**,
    430
  primates 452

G

Gallimimus **186**, 296, *334*,
  335
Gallinuloides 376
Gastornis **370**, *371*
gastroliths **288–289**, *288*
gastropods 42
Geocoma **39**
gharials 89
Gigantopithecus **455**
Gigantoraptor **178–179**, *178*
Giganotosaurus **158–159**, 349
  G. carolinii **158–159**, *159*,
    160
gills,
  Acanthostega 71
  amphibians 81
  arches and jaws **52**
  breathing 68, 69, 70
Ginkgo biloba 23
ginkgo trees *22*, 23, 194, *195*,
  329
Giraffatitan 210
  Africa 330, 331
  discovery 352
  size 266, *266*
gliding reptiles **108–111**
Glossopteris 23
glyptodont mammals 399
Gobi Desert dinosaurs 332,
  334–335, *335*
Gondwanaland 125, *125*, 198
graptolites *15*, 42, **43**, *42*
grasshoppers 36
grasslands,
  horse evolution 439, 441
  mammal evolution 412

great white shark 56
griffinflies 36, *37*
growth in dinosaurs **324–325**, 326
Guidraco **118–119**, *118*
Gyposaurus 331

H

hadrosaurs (*see also* duckbilled dinosaurs) **242–247**
  beaks 280
  head crests 276, 302–303
  legs 294
  naming 356
  nests *321*
  noses 282
  reconstruction 358
  sounds 318, *318*, 319
  tails 301
  teeth 279
Hadrosaurus **242**
hagfish 51, *51*
hair (fur),
  Homo habilis 466
  mammoths *382*, *383*, 430
  primates 452
Halstead, Beverly 27
Halysites **31**
hands, *Homo habilis* 467
hares 414
Hatzegopteryx **120**
Hawkins, Waterhouse 128
head crests 138, **276–277**, 282, 302, 303, *303*, 318, *318*
hearts, dinosaurs *304*
Helicocystis **39**
Hemicyclaspis *50*, **51**
Hennig, Edwin 352
Henodus **96**
herbivores,
  dinosaur **194–195**
  mammal **412–413**

herds, dinosaur 252, **312–313**, *313*, 314
Herrerasaurus 132, *133*, 348, *354*
Hesperocyon **410**, *411*
heterodontosaur dinosaurs 238
Heterodontosaurus **234–235**, *234*, 236, 293, 297
hibernation, dinosaurs **316–317**
Hipparion **441**
hippopotomuses 422
hips,
  dinosaur **292–293**, 302, 306
  lobe-finned fish 66
hobbit people **478–479**
Homalocephale **263**
hominids 460, 462, 466, *475*
  brains **482–483**
hominins 463, *466*
  early 460
  hunting **488–489**
  language 484, *485*
  tools **486–487**
Homo erectus **468–469**, *469*, 470, 474, *475*
  brain **483**
  fire use 488
  hunting **488**
  language **484**
  tools *486*, **487**
H. ergaster 466, 468, 474
  brain **483**
  language **484**
H. floresiensis **478–479**, *478*, 481
H. habilis **466–467**, *466*, *467*, 474
  brain **482–483**, *482*
  hunting **488**
  tools **486**, *486*
H. heidelbergensis **470–471**, *471*, 474, *475*
  ceremonies **490**, *490*

hunting **488**
  language **485**
H. neanderthalensis **472–473**, *473*, 475
H. rhodesiensis 470, 474
H. sapiens **474–475**, *475*
  ancestors 470
  brain *483*
  hunting **489**
  tools *487*
H. s. sapiens 474, **476–477**, 480
  language **485**
hoofed mammals **418–419**, 420, 421, 422–423, 436, 441, 443
hooves, dinosaur 296, 298, 311
horned dinosaurs *see* ceratopsian dinosaurs
Horner, John 'Jack' 322
horns, dinosaur **274–275**
horses *14*, 398, 421, **438–441**, *438*
horsetails 23, 194, *329*
humans,
  ancestors 458, 460, 464, 468, 470
  brains **483**
  ice age 430
  language **484–485**, *485*
  modern 474, 475, **476–477**, 480
  Sahelanthropus 456
  tools **487**
hunting,
  hominin **488–489**
  Homo erectus **488**
  H. habilis **488**
  H. heidelbergensis **488**
  H. sapiens **489**
  human **488–489**
  Neanderthal **488**, *489*
Huxley, Thomas Hardy 362

Hyaenodon **402–403**, *403*
Hybodus *55*
Hylonomus **78**, *78*
Hypselosaurus 329
Hypsilophodon 329
Hyracodon **432**
Hyracotherium *14*, **438–439**, *438*

I

Icaronycteris **426–427**, *426*
Icarosaurus **108**
ice ages *433*
  Neanderthals 472
Ichthyornis **374**
ichthyosaurs 82, **102–103**
Ichthyosaurus **102**, *103*
Ichthyostega **68**
Iguanodon 128, **240–241**, *241*
  beak 280
  discovery 328
  feet 297
  footprints 311
  herds 312
  migration 314
  speed 306
  teeth 278
Indricotherium 434
insectivores 386
insectivorous mammals 386, 448
insects 32, **36–37**
invertebrates *41*
  first **28–29**
  trilobites 34
Isotelus **35**

J

Janensch, Werner 352
Janenschia 294, *330*
Java Man *475*

jawed fish, early **52–53**, *53*
jawless fish **50–51**, *50*
jaws,
  amphibian 82
  Guidraco 118
  jawed fish **52**
  Mosasaurus 104
  plesiosaur 100, 101
  ray-finned fish 58
  reptile 78, 82
  Sarcosuchus 90
jellyfish 28
Juramaia sinensis **388–389**, *399*
Jurassic Period 14, *15*
  Antarctic dinosaurs 350, 351
  Archaeopteryx 366
  Chinese dinosaurs 337
  conifers 23, *23*
  Crocodylomorpha 88
  dinosaurs 124, 125, 142, 146, 168, 184, 194, *195*, 196, 199, 204, 206, 208, 212, 216, 218, 222, 224, 228, 230, 234, 236, 238
  echinoderms 38
  European dinosaurs *329*
  flying reptiles 112, 114, 116
  ichthyosaurs 102
  Leedsichthys 62
  lissamphibians 76
  mammals 386, 388, 392
  South American dinosaurs 349

K

Kentrosaurus **220**, *221*
  Africa 330
  discovery 352
keratin,
  dinosaur claws 298
  dinosaur horns 274

Kol 357
Kolihapeltis *34*
Komodo dragon 104
Koolasuchus **72**
Kritosaurus 242, 319
Kuehneosaurus **108**, *108*

L

Lagosuchus **130**
Lambe, Lawrence 352, 356
Lambeosaurus *318*
  dinosaur names 356
  head crests 302–303, *303*
  North America 345
lampreys 51
lampshells **40**
land birds **376–377**
language,
  Homo erectus **484**
  H. ergaster **484**
  H. heidelbergensis 470, **485**
  H. sapiens sapiens **485**
  human evolution **484–485**
  Neanderthal **485**
Largerperton **130**
Larson, Gary 225
larvae, amphibian 81
Lascaux cave paintings, France *492*
Latirhinus **246–247**, *247*
Laurasia 125, *125*
Leaellynasaura,
  Australia 341
  eyes of 285
  hibernation of **316**, *317*
Leakey, Louis 466, *466*
Leakey, Mary 466, *466*
leaves,
  angiosperm 24
  conifer *23*
  gymnosperm *22*
Leeds, Alfred 62
Leedsichthys **62–63**, *62*

legs,
 Acanthostega 71
 dinosaur **294–295**, 306
Leidy, Joseph 352
Lepidodendron 15
Leptictidium 371, *387*
Lesothosaurus **196–197**, *197*
Levallois flakes 487
lichens *18*, *19*, *19*
life, first **12–13**
limbs,
 first reptile 78
 Mosasaurus 105
 plesiosaur 100
limpets 42
Lingula **41**, *41*
Linnaeus, Carl 450
Liopleurodon **100**
lissamphibians 76
liverworts 19, 20
lizards,
 diapsid reptiles 82
 gliding 108, 110
 monitor 104
 posture 295
 snakes and 94
lobe-finned fish 58, *58*
 lungs 68, *70*
 tetrapods 66
lobsters 32
Loganograptus 42
'Lucy' **464–465**
Lufengosaurus **199**, 337
lungfish 58, 68, *68*
lungs,
 Acanthostega 71
 amphibian 81
 fish 68, *69*, *70*
 lobe-finned fish 66

M

machairodont mammals 408
Macrauchenia 399

magnolia 24
Maiasaura,
 coprolites 308
 young *321*, **322**
maidenhair trees *22*, **23**
Makela, Robert 322
male dinosaurs **302–303**, *303*
Mamenchisaurus 208, **218–219**, *219*
 China 337
 nose 282
mammal evolution,
 artiodactyls 421, **422–423**
 Australia 394, 395, **396–397**
 bats **426–427**
 body temperature 304
 brontotheres **421**
 carnivores 402, 403, **404–405**
 chalicotheres **421**
 condylarths **418–419**
 creodonts **402–403**, 404
 early mammals 384, **386–387**
 elephants **428–429**
 entelodonts **424–425**
 eutherian 388, 389
 fossils **382–383**
 herbivores **412–413**
 hoofed mammals **418–419**, 420, 421, **422–423**, 436, 441, 443
 horses **438–441**, *438*
 marsupials 384, **394–395**
 Paraceratherium 434
 perissodactyls **420–421**, 436
 placental mammals 384, 386
 primates **448–451**
 rhinoceroses **432–433**
 rodents **414–415**
 ruminants **416–417**
 synapsid reptiles 82, *83*, 84
 toes 296
 whales **442–445**
 young **384–385**

mammal-like reptiles 82, 84, *85*
mammoths *382*, 428, 429
 fossils *383*
 frozen **383**
 prehistoric timescale *14*
 woolly **430–431**
Mammuthus primigenius 430
maniraptoran dinosaurs 180, 362
Mantell, Gideon **128**
Mapusaurus **156–157**, *157*
Marasuchus **130**
Marrella **32**
Marsh, Othniel Charles 208, 214, 352, *353*, 357
marsupial mammals 384, **394–395**
 Australia 394, 395, **396–397**
 South America 394, 395, **398–399**
Mason, Roger 29
mass extinction, Permian Period 41
Massospondylus **202–203**, *203*
 Africa 331
 stomach stones 288
Mawsonites 28
mayflies 36
meat-eating dinosaurs,
 claws 298
 coprolites 308
 footprints 311, 312
 Saurithschia 292
 speed 306
 tails 301
Megacerops **436–437**, *436*
Megalodon **56–57**, *56*
Megalosaurus **128**, *129*, 140
Meganeuropsis **36**, *37*
Megatherium 398, **400–401**, *401*

Megazostrodon 384, **386**
Mei **168**, *168*, 363
Melanorosaurus **198**
Merychippus **440**, *440*
mesoeucrocodylians **88**
Mesohippus **439**, 440
mesonychid mammals 443
Mesonyx 404
Mesopithecus **449**
Mesozoic Era **14**
   ammonites 44
   dinosaurs 124, 125
   gymnosperms 23
Messel fossils, Germany 77,
   94, 364, *387*, 452
Metamynodon **432**
Metriorhynchus **88**
miacid mammals 404
Microchiroptera *426*
Microraptor **182–183**, *183*,
   337, *337*
migration,
   dinosaurs **314–315**, *315*
   human ancestors 476, *476*
milk 384, 394
millipedes 32
Minmi 354
Miocene Epoch,
   Australian mammals 396
   birds 374, 378
   chelonians 93
   mammals 402, 412, 415,
   417, 422, 424
   primates 455
   salamanders 76
   snakes 94
Miotapirus **421**
moas 372
modern humans **476–477**,
   480
   language *485*
   tools **487**
Moeritherium **428**, *429*
molluscs **42–43**, 44

monitor lizards 94, 104
monkey puzzle trees *23*, 194
monkeys 449, 450
Monograptus *42*
monotremes **384**
Morganucodon 384, **386**
mosasaurs **104–105**
Mosasaurus **104**, *105*
mosses 19, 20
mountain formation 12
mummified fossils 358
Murphy, Nate 359
Mussaurus **169**
mussels 42
Muttaburrasaurus,
   Australia 340, *340*
   migration 314
   speed 306
myriapods 32

N

naming dinosaurs **354–357**
nautiloids *43*
Nautilus **44**
Neanderthals 470, **472–473**,
   472, *475*, 476, 480
   ceremonies **490**
   hunting **488**, *489*
   language **485**
   tools **487**
necks,
   plesiosaur 100, 101
   tetrapod 67
Neocathartes 377
Neogene Period,
   mammal evolution 432
   marsupial mammals 394,
   395
   prehistoric timescale *14*
nests,
   bird 362
   dinosaur 253, **320–321**, 322,
   362

neural spines 86
newts 68
Nigersaurus 330
nodosaurs **230–233**
   armour 272
   horns 275
Nodosaurus 230
North America,
   dinosaurs **344–347**, *344*
   fossil hunters 352
noses, dinosaurs **282–283**
nostrils,
   jawed fish 52
   nothosaur *99*
Notharctus **448**
nothosaurs 96, **98–99**, *99*
Nothosaurus **98**, *99*
notochord 48

O

oceans, early Earth 12
octopuses 42, 43
odonatan insects 36
Ogygoptynx **376**
Oldowan tools 467
Olduvai Gorge, Tanzania 486
Oligocene Epoch,
   Australian mammals 396
   birds 370, 376
   mammal evolution 404, 407,
   432
   primate evolution 454
Omeisaurus 219
Opisthocoelicaudia 335, 354
optic lobes, dinosaurs 285
orbits, dinosaurs 285
Ordovician Period *15*
ornithischian dinosaurs 197
Ornitholestes **162–163**, *163*,
   301
ornithomimosaur dinosaurs
   186, 354
Ornithomimus 186, *187*

ornithopod dinosaurs 197, 240
  beaks 280
  feet 297
  migration 314
ornithosuchians 126
Ornithosuchus **126**, *126*, **127**
ornithischian dinosaurs **293**, *293*
Orodromeus **320**
Ororaphidia **36**
Orrorin **458–459**, *459*
Orthoceratites *43*
Orthograptus *42*
Osborn, Henry Fairfield 428
Osteodontornis **374**, *374*
ostrich dinosaurs **186–187**
  beaks 280, 281
  dinosaur names 354
  feet 296
  speed 306
ostrich feet *297*
Ostrom, John 177
Othniela 357
Ouranosaurus **290**, *290*
  Africa 330
  colours 270
'Out of Africa' **476**
Oviraptor 178, **164–165**, *165*,
  253
  beaks 281
  Gobi Desert 335
  nests **320**
Owen, Richard 128, 203, 208,
  228
Oxalaia 160
Oxyaena 404
oxygen 18, 68
oysters 42

P

pachycephalosaurs **262–263**,
  263, 264
Pachycephalosaurus **262–263**,
  262

Pachyrhinosaurus 314, *314*
pack hunting,
  dinosaurs **170–171**, 174
  dogs 410, *411*
Pakicetus *442*, **443**, 444
Palaeocene Epoch,
  birds 376
  mammals 402, 412, 421,
  438
Palaeochiropteryx 427
Palaeomastodon 429
palaeontologists 20
Palaeopython **94**
paleoepidemiology 156
Paleogene Period *14*
  birds 364, 374
  mammals 418, 421, 432
  marsupial mammals 394,
  395
  snakes 94
  tropical rainforests 24
Paleothyris 78
Paleozoic Era **14**
  brachiopods 40
Panderichthys 66
Pangaea 125, *125*
Panoplosaurus 275
Paraceratherium 420, **434–**
  435, *435*
Paramys 414
Parasaurolophus 242
  head crests 276, *277*, 303
  prehistoric timescale *14*
parental care, dinosaurs *321*,
  322
Parks, William 357
Parksosaurus 357
Parvicursor 169
Patagosaurus 349
Pegomastax **236–237**, *237*
'Peking Man' 468, **469**, *475*
pelycosaurs 84, *87*
Pentaceratops 250
Pentacrinites **39**

periods and timescales **14**
perissodactyl mammals **420–**
  421, 436
Permian Period *15*
  amphibians 72, 74
  archosaurs 127
  Crocodylomorpha 88
  insects 36
  lissamphibians 76
  mass extinction 41
  synapsid reptiles *83*, 84, 86
Peteinosaurus **112**
Phenacodus **418**
Phiomia **428**
Phorusrhacus 370
photosynthesis 18
Phyllograptus *42*
Piatnitzkysaurus 348, **349**
Pikaia **48–49**, *49*
Pinacosaurus **226–227**, 335
pinniped mammals 404, 405
Pisanosaurus **133**
Pithecanthus erectus 468
placental mammals 384, 386
  South America **398–399**
placoderms **60**
placodonts **96–97**
Placodus **96**, *96*
plant-eating dinosaurs,
  claws 298
  coprolites 308
  footprints 311
  herds 312
  Ornithschia 293
  speed 306
  tails 300
Planté, Gaston 371
plants,
  first **18–19**
  flowering **24–27**
  gymnosperm **22–23**
  oxygen 68
  vascular **20–21**
plateosaurid dinosaurs 198

Plateosaurus 198, **200–201**, *201*
  fossils 329
  stomach stones 288
Platypittamys *414*
Plectronoceras **42**
Pleistocene Epoch,
  human evolution 488
  Neanderthals 472
Plesiadapis **448**, *449*, 450
Plesianthropus transvaalensis 463
plesiosaurs 82, 99, **100–101**, *101*
Plesiosaurus **100**
Pliocene Epoch 429
Pliohippus **441**
pliosaurs 101
poisonous snakes 94
Polacanthus **230–231**
pollen 24
polyps, coral 30, *30*
Prenocephale 263, **264–265**, *265*
  Gobi Desert 335
Presbyornis **374**, 375
primates,
  apes **454–455**
  brains **482–483**
  Darwinius **452–453**
  language in 484
  mammal evolution **448–451**
Primelephas *429*
Proboscidea **428–429**
Procampsognathus **133**
Proceptodon 396
Proconsul **454–455**
Proganochelys **92**, *92*
prosauropod dinosaurs 194, **198–199**, 202
  Africa 331
  China 337
  stomach stones of 288
Prosqualodon **445**

protists **28**
Protoceratops 164, **252–253**, *253*
  beaks *281*
  nests 320
protosuchians **88**
Protosuchus **88**, *89*
protozoans **28**
Protungulatum **418**
Psephoderma **96**
pseudosuchians 126
pseudotooth birds 375
Psittacosaurus **248–249**, *248*
  beaks *280*, 281
  China 337
  eggs 322
  stomach stones of 288
Pteranodon **116–117**, *117*
pterodactyls 114, **116**, 118
Pterodactylus **116**
pterosaurs 108, **112–117**, 118, 126
  diapsid reptiles 82
  early 112
  giant **120–121**
Pyrotherium 398
pythons 94

Q

quadrupedal dinosaurs 294, *294*
Quaternary Period *14*
Quetzalcoatlus **120**, 121, *121*

R

rabbits 414
Ramapithecus 455
Rancho La Brea tar pits, USA 382
raptor dinosaurs 166, **172– 173**, 174, 176, 182, 184
ray-finned fish **58**

rays 54
Rebbachisaurus **208**
reconstructing dinosaurs **358– 359**, *358*
Red Deer Cave people **480– 481**
reefs, coral 30, *41*
Repenomamus **390–391**, *391*
  R. giganticus **390**
  R. robusticus **390**
reptiles,
  amphibians, development from 72
  aquatic/marine 96, 98, *99*, 100, *103*, 104
  archosaurs 126
  body temperature in 304, 305
  brains 286
  claws 298
  eggs **80–81**, *81*
  eyes **285**
  first **78–79**
  flying 112, 116, 117
  gliding **108–111**
  life span 326, 327
  migration 314
  pack hunting **170–171**
  posture 295
  reconstructing dinosaurs 358
  skull openings in 82
  sounds 318
  toes 296
Rhadinichthys **58**
rhamphorhynchoids **112–113**, 114
Rhamphorhyncus *15*, **112**, 116
rhaphidiopteran insects 36
rhinoceroses *420*
  mammal evolution **432–433**, 434
  woolly *433*
Rhodesian Man *475*
Rhoetosaurus **340–341**

Rhynie chert fossils, Scotland 36
Rhyniognatha **36**
Riojasaurus **198**, *199*
  stomach stones 288
rodents **414–415**
roots,
  angiosperm 24
  vascular plants 20
rugose corals 31
ruminants **416–417**

S

sabre-tooth cats 406, *406*, 407, 408
Sacabambaspis **51**
Sahelanthropus **456–457**, *457*, 458
sails, dinosaur **290–291**
salamanders **76–77**
Saltasaurus,
  armour **272–273**, *272*
  South America 332, *333*, 348, *348*
Sarcosuchus 89, **90–91**, *91*
saurischian dinosaurs **292–293**, *292*
Saurolophus 242
Sauropelta 230, **232–233**, *232*
sauropod dinosaurs 199, 204, **206–209**, *209*, 212, *213*, 214, 216, 219
  Africa 331
  Asia 332, 333
  Australia 342
  estimating size 266
  feet 296
  footprints 311
  Gobi Desert 335
  herbivores 194
  legs 294
  life span 326

sauropod dinosaurs (*cont.*)
  migration 314
  North America 346
  noses 282
  Saurischia 293
  South America 348, 349
  speed 306
  stomach stones 288, 289, *289*
  tails 300, 301, *301*
Saurornithoides 363
Scelidosaurus **228–229**, *229*
Scheuchzer, Johannes 76
Sciurimimus **142–143**, *143*
scleractinian corals 31
sea anemones *41*
sea cucumbers 38
sea lilies 38, 39
sea pens 29, *29*
sea urchins **38–39**, *41*
seas, early Earth 12
seaweeds 19
seed-ferns 22, 194
seeds,
  angiosperm 24, *25*
  gymnosperm 22
segnosaur dinosaurs **188**
Seismosaurus **206**
'Selam' **464**
Sellosaurus **198**
sense of smell,
  dinosaurs 282
  dogs 410
  mammals 403
senses,
  carnivorous mammals 405
  primates 448
Sereno, Paul 352
sharks **54–55**, *54*
  great white 56
  Megalodon 56
  'spiny sharks' *53*
Shastasaurus **102**

shells,
  ammonite 44, *44*
  brachiopod 40
  nautiloid *43*
  reptile egg 80, 81, *81*
  turtle and tortoise 92, 93
Shunosaurus **301**
Silurian Period,
  bony fish 58
  corals 31
  jawed fish 52
  placoderms 60
  prehistoric timescale *15*
  sharks 54
Sinanthropus pekinensis 468
Sinocalliopteryx 369
Sinoconodon **386**
Sinosauropteryx **180**
  China 337
  colours 270
Sivapithecus **455**
skates 54
skin and breathing 68
skulls,
  amphibian and reptile **82–83**
  Sarcosuchus 90
  synapsid reptile 84
slugs 42, 43
Smilodectes **448**
Smilodon **408–409**, *408*
snails 42, 43
snakefly 36
snakes **94–95**, *94*
  diapsid reptiles 82
  eggs *80*, *81*
Solnhofen, Germany 113, 328, 364
sounds, dinosaur **318–319**
South America,
  dinosaurs **348–349**, *349*
  fossil hunters 352
  mammals 394, 395, **398–399**, 400
spiders 32

Spinops **254–255**, *255*
  S. sternbergorum 255
spinosaurs 160
Spinosaurus 152, **160–161**,
  160, **290**
  Africa 330
  colours 270
'spiny sharks' *53*
spores 20, *21*
Sprigg, Reg 28
Spriggina **28**
squids 42, 43
squirrels 414
starfish **38–39**, *39*
Staurikosaurus **132**
Stegoceras **263**
stegosaur dinosaurs **220–225**,
  228
  Africa 330
  beaks 280
  colours 270
  stomach stones 288
Stegosaurus 220, **222–223**,
  223
  brain 286
  North America *344*, 346
stems 20, *21*
Stephanoceras 15, **44**
Stephanosaurus 356
Sternberg, Charles H 254
Stethacanthus **54**, 55
stomach stones **288–289**
stomata 20
stromatolites 13, *13*
Struthiomimus **186**, 306
Styracosaurus 250, *251*
  horns 274, *275*
Suchomimus 160
Supersaurus **206**
swimming, dinosaurs 301
synapsid reptiles **82**, *83*,
  84–85, *87*
Synthetoceras 411, *423*
Syringopora **31**

T

tabulate corals 31
tadpoles 81
tails, dinosaurs **300–301**
Tanius 276
tar pit fossils 382
Tarbosaurus 265
  legs *295*
Taung child 463
teeth,
  Ajkaceratops 257
  Anchisaurus 204
  ankylosaur 226
  Brachiosaurus 211
  Camarasaurus 213
  ceratopsian dinosaur 250
  Darwinopterus 114
  Dimetrodon 86
  dinosaur **278–279**, 281
  Diplodocus 217
  dogs 410
  early primates 451
  entelodont mammals 424
  Fabrosaurus 196
  Falcarius 190
  Fruitadens 238
  Guidraco 118, *118*
  Heterodontosaurus 234–
    235
  Homo sapiens 474
  horses 439, 441
  jawed fish **52**
  La Brea tar pit fossil 408
  Lesothosaurus 196
  mammals 382, 384, 386,
    392
  Massospondylus 203
  Megalodon 56
  Mosasaurus 104
  Nigersaurus 330
  nothosaurs 98
  Pegomastax 236
  placodonts 96, *96*

teeth (*cont.*)
  Plateosaurus 200
  plesiosaurs 100, 101
  Psittacosaurus 249
  rhamphorhynchoids 112
  Sarcosuchus 90
  Scelidosaurus 228
  sharks *54*
  synapsid reptiles 84, 85
  therizinosaur dinosaurs
    190
  Triceratops 260
  Tuojiangosaurus 225
  whales 444
teleost fish **58**
temnospondyls *77*
temperature control,
  birds 304, 305
  dinosaurs 290, **304–305**
  mammals 386
  reptiles 304, 305
  Stegosaurus 222
Tenontosaurus 170
Terrestrisuchus **88**
terror birds **370–371**
tetrapods **66–67**
  Acanthostega 71
  amphibians 72
  eggs 81
  Eryops 74
  synapsid reptiles 84
  'thagomizer' 225
Thaumastotherium 434
thecodonts 130
therapsids 84
therizinosaur dinosaurs **188–**
  191, *191*, 192
  claws 298
  Gobi Desert 335
Therizinosaurus **188**, *189*
theropod dinosaurs 136, 138,
  148, 162, 164, 188, 190,
  192, 297
Thescelosaurus 304

Thoatherium 398
thumbs, primate 448
Thylacinus **396**, 397
Thylacoleo *395*, **396**
Thylacosmilus 398
Titanis **370**
Titanoboa *94*
titanosaurs 342
Titanosaurus,
　Asia **332**, *333*
　South America 348
toes,
　Acanthostega 71
　dinosaur footprints 311
　dinosaur 296, *296*
tools,
　Cro-Magnon **487**
　Homo erectus *486*, **487**
　H. floresiensis 478, *478*,
　　479
　H. habilis 467, **486**, *486*
　H. heidelbergensis 470
　H. sapiens *487*
　human **487**
　Neanderthal 472, **487**
toothed whales 445
Tornieri 331
Torosaurus **250**
torpor 316
tortoises 82, **92–93**
　life span 327
Toxodon *385*
trace fossils **17**
　dinosaur footprints 310,
　　311
trackways, fossil 310
tree ferns *195*, *329*
Triadobatrachus **76**, *77*
Triassic Period **14**, *15*
　chelonians 92
　corals 31
　Crocodylomorpha 88
　dinosaurs 124, 125, 132,
　　133, 134, 194

Triassic Period (*cont.*)
　flying reptiles 112
　gliding reptiles 108
　ichthyosaurs 102
　lissamphibians 76
　nothosaurs 99
　plesiosaurs 100
　placodonts 96
Triceratops 250, *251*, **260–**
　261, *261*, 293
　beaks 280
　colours 270
　herds 312
　horns 274
　North America *344*
Trigonias **432**
trilobites *15*, **34–35**, *34*, *35*
Trinucleus *34*
Troodon *171*, 180, 363
　brain 286, *287*
　claws 298
　discovery 352
　eyes 285, *285*
troodontid dinosaurs 338, 362,
　363
tropical rainforests 24
Tsintaosaurus 276–277
Tuojiangosaurus **224–225**,
　225, 337
turtles **92–93**
　anapsid reptiles 82
　life span of 327
Tyrannosaurus 170
　claws 298
　coprolites 308
　feet *296*
　footprints 311
　growth 324, **325**, *325*, 326
　North America *344*
　nose 282, *283*
　speed 306, *307*
　teeth of *278*
　T rex **152–153**, *153*, *284*
Tyrrell, Joseph 352

U

Uintatherium 412
Ultrasaurus **206**
Utahraptor ostrommaysorum
　176–177, *177*

V

varanid lizards 94
Varanosaurus *83*
vascular plants, first **20–21**
Velociraptor **172**, *173*, *174*,
　253
　Gobi Desert 335
vertebrates, flying 112
vipers 94
volcanoes, early earth 12
von Stromer, Ernst 160
Vulcanodon 285, 331
vultures *377*, 378

W

Walker, Alick 140
Walker, Bill 356
walking, human ancestors
　460, 463, 464
Wannanosaurus *263*
warm blood,
　dinosaurs **304–305**
　mammals 386
　synapsid reptiles 85
water birds **374–375**
water lilies *26*
weapons, dinosaur *301*
Westlothiana lizziae 78
whales **442–445**
whiskers, synapsid reptiles 85
Williams, Jesse 138
wings,
　early insect 36
　Microraptor 182
　pterosaur 120
　Xiaotingia 184, *185*

woolly mammoth **430–431**, *431*
woolly rhinoceros *433*
worms 28

X
Xenoceratops **258–259**, *259*
Xianglong **110–111**, *111*
Xiaoting, Zheng *185*
Xiaotingia **184–185**, *185*

Y
Yalkaparidon 397
Yutyrannus **150–151**, *151*

Z
Zhong-jiang, Yang 352

Acknowledgements

The publishers would like to thank the Peter Bull Art Studio and Stuart Jackson-Carter for their illustrations. All other artworks are from the Miles Kelly Artwork Bank

Cover artwork by Stuart Jackson-Carter

The publishers would like to thank the following sources for the use of their photographs:

Alamy 27 Custom Life Science Images; 73 Sergey Krasovskiy/Stocktrek Images; 193 National Geographic Image Collection; 197 MasPix; 232–232 Stocktrek Images, Inc.; 355 Ronald Karpilo; 419 Stocktrek Images, Inc.; 452–453 Martin Shields

Corbis 43 Walter Myers/Stocktrek Images; 135 Mike Hettwer/handout/dpa; 149 Craig Brown/Stocktrek Images; 224–225 Roman Garcia Mora/Stocktrek Images; 269 Louie Psihoyos; 292 Eric Preau/Sygma; 319 Roman Garcia Mora/Stocktrek Images; 322 James L. Amos; 333 Sergey Krasovskiy/Stocktrek Images; 334 DK Limited; 377 Walter Myers/Stocktrek Images; 406–407 Daniel Eskridge/Stocktrek Images; 462 Regis Bossu/Sygma; 493 Philippe Wojazer/Reuters

Fotolia.com 122–123 DX

Glow Images 205, 467 Superstock

National Geographic Creative 339 Xing Lida; 347 Lowell Georgi; 387 Jonathon Blair; 395 Adrie and Alfons Kennis

Rex Features 245 REX/KPA/Zuma

Shutterstock.com 10–11 BMJ; 12–13 Rob Bayer; 19 BergelmLicht; 22t Madlen; 22b Petr Salinger; 26 Tungphoto; 31 Paul Vinten; 38 MarcelClemens; 39 Amanda Nicholls; 41 Suphatthra China; 46–47 Michael Rosskothen; 64–65 Michael Rosskothen; 80t Nicky Rhodes; 87 leonello calvetti; 103, 106–107, 112–113 Michael Rosskothen; 120–121 Computer Earth; 126 troyka; 127 Trevor Kelly; 136–137 leonello calvetti; 138–139 Jean-Michel Girard; 159 Linda Bucklin; 160–161 Kostyantyn Ivanyshen; 162–163; 169b; 172–173, 174–175, 177, 202–203 Linda Bucklin; 209 Catmando; 212–213 Michael Rosskothen; 216–217 Catmando; 220–221 Bob; 227 Ralf Juergen KraftOrsillo; 243 Linda Bucklin; 261, 262 leonello calvetti; 267 Linda Bucklin; 275 Ozja; 277 Jean-Michel Girard; 278 ags1973; 284 DM7; 294 Linda Bucklin; 299 Michael Rosskothen; 305 John Kasawa; 307 leonello calvetti; 325 DM7; 327 Naypong; 343, 345 Michael Rosskothen; 351 Bob Orsillo; 360–361 Andreas Meyer; 367, 380–381 Catmando; 383 Rich Koele; 399, 413, 425 Ralf Juergen Kraft; 431 Ozja; 435, 437 Catmando; 446–447 Procy

Science Photo Library 57, 63, 90–91, 93, 95, 97, 98–99 Jaime Chirinos; 114–115 Mark P. Witton; 157, 179 Jaime Chirinos; 189 Jose Antonia Penas; 207, 253 Mark Hallett PaleoArt; 287 Laurie O'Keefe; 304 Jim Page/North Carolina Museum of Natural Sciences; 315 Natural History Museum, London; 371, 373, 375, 379, 385 Jaime Chirinos; 393 Jose Antonio Penas; 397 Mauricio Anton; 411 Mark Hallett PaleoArt; 415, 417, 444–445 Natural History Museum, London; 457 Christian Jegou Publiphoto Diffusion; 465 Mauricio Anton; 471 Raul Martin/MSF; 473 Mauricio Anton; 474–475 Natural History Museum, London; 477 Claus Lunau; 479 Mauricio Anton; 481 Ria Novosti; 489 Christian Jegou Publiphoto Diffusion; 491 Kennis and Kennis/MSF

All other photographs are from:
Corel, digitalSTOCK, digitalvision, iStockphoto.com, John Foxx, PhotoAlto, PhotoEssentials, PhotoPro, Stockbyte

Every effort has been made to acknowledge the source and copyright holder of each picture. Miles Kelly Publishing apologises for any unintentional errors or omissions.